The New Covenant

THE NEW COVENANT

Jewish Writers and the American Idea

Sam B. Girgus

The University of North Carolina Press

Chapel Hill and London

© 1984 The University of North Carolina Press
All rights reserved
Manufactured in the United States of America
Library of Congress Cataloging in Publication Data

Girgus, Sam B., 1941–
    The new covenant.

    Bibliography: p.
    Includes index.
    1. American fiction—Jewish authors—History and
criticism. 2. American fiction—20th century—
History and criticism. 3. Jews in literature.
4. Jews—United States. 5. United States—
Civilization. I. Title.
PA374.J48G57 1984   813'.5'098924   83-12458
ISBN 0-8078-1577-2

To my mother,
my wife, Scottie, and
our daughters, Katya, Meighan, and Jennifer

Contents

IV. The Book of America

Acknowledgments

I once again would like to express special appreciation and thanks to Sacvan Bercovitch. His insights into and understanding of the American experience helped me to formulate and develop the thesis and argument of this book. While his ideas and work have been a great influence on my own writings, his continued friendship and encouragement have been of equal personal importance to me. I especially thank him for taking the time to read the manuscript and comment upon it. I also would like to thank Jules Chametzky who graciously read the manuscript and shared his wealth of scholarship and critical sensitivity with me in the form of invaluable editorial suggestions. George Arms, Joel Jones, Peter White, and Lee Bartlett all read the manuscript and provided me with insights and ideas that proved indispensable. I cannot thank them enough for their efforts. Throughout the years Ham Hill's continuing conversation and counsel on scholarly and academic matters along with the pleasure of his friendship have been of enormous personal and professional benefit. The advice of Robert Sklar and Henry Nash Smith regarding this book as well as their generous support and interest are also greatly appreciated.

At the risk of appearing sentimental and redundant I would like to note my appreciation of and affection for that immediate audience of colleagues and friends whose interest, indulgence, and patience contributed to the completion of the book: the Anayas, Elizabeth Arms, the Barbours, Mary Bartlett, the Baughmans, Marshall Berman, Charles Biebel, the Blairs, Gus Blaisdell, Angela Boone, Edith Buchanan, Lawrence Buell, Jane Caputi, John Cawelti, Helen Damico, David Dunaway, the Eaveses, the Flemings, Cheryl Fresch, the Gallachers, Chris Garcia, Arlette Hill, Mike Hogan, Tamara Holzhapfel, Leon Howard, Mac Hull, the Brian Joneses, Linda Kjeldgaard, Leonard Kriegel, Peter Lupsha, Charlene Mc-Dermott, Nancy Magnuson, Margaret Meaders, Bob Michael, Pat Nelson, Vera Norwood, the O'Neils, Jack Salzman, Joe Scaletti, Lillian Schlissel, Dieter Schulz, the Thorsons, Dick Tomasson, Alan Trachtenberg, Marta Weigle, Mary Bess Whidden, and Mary Ann White. I also would like to acknowledge the students who read portions of the manuscript in various forms and who engaged in innumerable dialogues with me over its central ideas: Ed Barragiola, Santiko Budi, Carrie Cleavinger, Kazik Dziamka, Annie Eysturoy, Kyle Fiore, Erica Gantry, Robert Gold, Darlene Goodman, Elizabeth Ground, Faye Hadley, George Hartley, Jerry Kammer, Susan Kilgore, William James Kohr, Gordene Mackenzie, Kate Parker, Chuck Preston, Mary Jane Sanchez, Wayne Shrubsall, Darwin Wheat, and Linda Wood.

Parts of this book were presented in places of special importance to me. The first was at Temple Beth Shalom of Santa Fe and I would like to thank Ellen Biderman and Rabbi Larry Hellman for their generosity and sensitivity. The second was at the Chavura Hamidbar of Albuquerque. A book such as this is something of a personal quest, and I would like to thank some of the persons from the Chavura Hamidbar who were especially important in helping me make that quest: the Bennahums, the Gissers, the Liebermans, the Pugaches, the Rosenbergs, the Rosensteins, and the Robert Whites. Special thanks also go to Robert Miller.

Portions of this book were published in somewhat different form in "A Poetics of the American Idea: The Jewish Writer and America," *Prospects 8* (1984), and in *The American Self: Myth, Ideology, and Popular Culture*, edited by Sam B. Girgus, © 1981 by the University of New Mexico Press.

I greatly appreciate the enthusiasm and assistance of Iris Tillman Hill and Sandra Eisdorfer of the University of North Carolina Press. For typing the manuscript during its many stages and phases, I am indebted to the following: Debi Kahn, Stacie Pope, Terry Smith, Marcella Spriggs, and Maria Warren.

A Rockefeller Humanities Fellowship in 1980 provided me with the time and resources to complete the mansucript.

Finally, of course, I would like to thank my family: Mrs. Aida Scot-Smith, Audrey and Harris Shapiro, the Winters, Stuart and Ida Sosniak, and Joan Girgus. My mother and daughters have been great sources of support. The most important help and encouragement has come from my wife. She provided suggestions on critical matters of both style and substance. For example, it was in response to her enthusiasm that I decided to reread Doctorow, whose works became a key part of my thesis. She also often served as first reader and editor. It would be hard to exaggerate the importance of her help. On this, as in so many other matters, she made the difference.

Abbreviations

PART I

A Poetics of the American Idea

Chapter 1

A New Hero of Thought
in a New Narrative

The history of the Jews in America is to a considerable extent the history of an idea. It is the story of how Jewish history was transformed by the idea of America and how, in turn, Jewish writers, intellectuals, artists, and public figures helped to sustain and modernize this idea.[1] While the American idea altered the modern Jewish experience, Jewish thinkers often led in the effort to make the idea of America relevant to the needs of an urban, industrial, and even post-industrial age. The work of such writers and thinkers served to keep the American idea meaningful in a time of competing authoritarian and totalitarian ideologies. By the American idea I mean the set of values, beliefs, and traditions of freedom, democracy, equality, and republicanism that are known as the American Way and that give America a unique identity in history. For the Jews this idea included the concept of emancipation. It often has been noted that only in America did emancipation precede Jewish life. In the context of the American idea, emancipation meant that Jews could expect to be treated as individuals on a basis of equality with all other individuals. This new freedom inspired a devotion to the American Way that paralleled and for many even strengthened the devotion to God and to people. An important measure of the power of the American Way upon Jewish writers and thinkers can be found in the numbers of leading Jewish radicals who adopted the American idea while continuing to believe in one form or another of socialism. From Abraham Cahan, whose brand of imported radicalism represented the thinking and heritage of his own generation of immigrants, to Irving Howe, whose democratic socialism now sustains the "respectable" American left, the American Way provides a basis from which to espouse radical causes and programs. After escaping from the Czarist police and arriving in America, it took Cahan almost no time to reconsider and reorganize his basic political principles in order to account for the American system of politics. For other Jews as well, a rigid form of radicalism simply could not compete with the attraction of the ideology of America. They either qualified their radicalism or abandoned it totally for the American idea. Thus, in his comprehensive and sympathetic study, *Jews and the Left*, Arthur Liebman maintains that the "radical subculture was only one of several subcultures that existed within the American Jewish community" and further argues that "it is important to stress the fact that, even in the heyday of Jewish socialism in Czarist Russia or in the United States, most Jews are not active or committed Leftists."[2]

However, one important scholar of American Judaism and American culture argues what seems to be the reverse of my own thesis about the significance of the American idea to the mainstream Jewish experience in America. In *Judaism and the American Idea*, Milton R. Konvitz maintains that the principles that comprise the American idea, as expressed in the works of such people as Theodore Parker, Ralph Waldo Emerson, and Walt Whitman, derive actually from Hebrew scriptures and Talmudic teachings. In a sense, however, Konvitz's point sustains the importance of the ideology of America to many Jewish thinkers and writers. His argument represents a modern version of how one group of Jewish leaders saw in the American Way the development of Jewish values and beliefs that proved the consistency and compatibility between both traditions. For some of these Jewish leaders the American Way was almost a mirror image of the most important teachings of Jewish culture and tradition. These Jews, who often represented the long years of German Jewish influence in America, anticipated Konvitz by maintaining that American Jews can be most Jewish by being totally devoted to the ideals of the American Way since Jewish concepts of human dignity and freedom provide the foundation for the American idea in the first place. Through a useful kind of circularity, this line of argument demolishes the wall dividing Jewish from American identities and heals conflicting loyalties by making Judaism and Americanism mutually reenforcing ideologies.

Variations of this argument were made by Oscar Straus, ambassador to Turkey and secretary of commerce and labor under Theodore Roosevelt, who emphasized the Hebrew origins of the political beliefs of the Puritans; Louis Marshall of the American Jewish Committee, who saw the protection of civil liberties for all citizens as the best defense of the rights of the Jews; and Horace Kallen, who promulgated a philosophy of cultural pluralism that was designed to maintain and strengthen both ethnic and national identities. However, Supreme Court Justice Louis Brandeis presented the most elaborate and influential body of thought in defense of the theory that Judaism, Zionism, and Americanism were all part of the same system of concerns and ideas. In addition, Brandeis also proffered a complete social, political, and legal philosophy that constituted a vital modernization of the American Way. Brandeis's philosophy established an important and complex set of bridges connecting traditional democratic beliefs with modern realities and Jewish radical views of social justice with the pragmatic American approach to politics.

The idea of America was also important to many Jewish writers and thinkers with roots in the East European immigration experience. As Mark Shechner indicates, historians and students of Jewish writing and life in America often cite "two historical conditions" to explain the connection between that immigration experience and "the sociology of the mass entry of Jews into American letters." The first is the historic commitment of the Jews to learning and writing. Shechner says, "Whatever else the Jews did, be it in Judea or Canaan or Egypt or Spain or Poland, they were devoted to the reading and writing of books." Shechner links this intellectual devotion to the proposition, as delineated by Irving Howe and others, "that the great immigration was itself the expression of a cultural revolution in full career throughout the Jewish world. From the eighteenth century onward, successive waves of Hasidic enthusiasm, Enlightenment liberalism, Zionism, trade unionism, and socialism had swept through the rural villages (*shtetlach*) and urban ghettoes of Eastern Europe, undermining the traditional life of stoic pietism and stirring the Jews to restless self-scrutiny and revolt."[3] In theory, therefore, the Jewish love of learning and the word in combination with the devastation of modernity upon traditional Jewish culture worked to create the atmosphere, sensibility, and consciousness that produced the Jewish literary movement in America.

However, as the accounts of Cahan, Mary Antin, Anzia Yezierska, and so many others indicate, one of the most compelling forces sweeping through the ghettos and shtetlach Shechner mentions was the idea of

America itself as a counter to the economic, political, religious, and cultural repression of Europe. This may help to explain how so many Jewish intellectuals and writers, the so-called New York intellectuals who emerged from the immigrant experience, became committed, almost to the point of obsession, to the responsibility of interpreting America to herself. This group includes people of widely diverse political opinions and backgrounds. Some among them are leftist and radical literary figures, but most are traditional liberals or disaffected former radicals who write for what Edmund Wilson, according to Alfred Kazin, termed the "Partisansky Review." This group includes Lionel Trilling, Alfred Kazin, Paul Goodman, Harold Rosenberg, Isaac Rosenfeld, Robert Warshow, Clement Greenberg, Leslie Fiedler, Daniel Aaron, and Leonard Kriegel. However, the intellectuals and writers who now most strongly identify with the American idea are part of the neoconservative movement. The leading figures in this group are Daniel Bell, Nathan Glazer, and Irving Kristol. They often write for *Commentary*, the publication of the American Jewish Committee. In fact, Norman Podhoretz, the editor of *Commentary*, relates his sense of himself as a Jew to the American idea. He writes, "I was speaking that day as an American in defense of America, in defense of the liberal democratic system under which the country lived, and in defense of its right and its duty to ensure the survival of that system against all who wished to discredit or destroy it. The fact that I as an individual, and the ethnic group of which I was a member, had experienced the blessings of the liberal democratic system in such abundance certainly inclined me to speak in its defense."[4]

The American idea is so basic to Jewish identity and to the modern Jewish mind that a novel by one of our most talented new Jewish writers focuses precisely on the relationship of the American idea to the Jewish experience and to the kind of Jewish intellectual I have just discussed. Johanna Kaplan takes the title of her novel from lines in John Donne's nineteenth elegy—"O my America! my new-found-land"—in which America stands as a magnificent conceit and is used to express the depth of a lover's desire to explore and to know his mistress. The mistress is so mysterious and awesome and the thought of making love to her raises hopes of so much pleasure that the experience can be compared only with something as exotic as the idea of America. The passion created by the desire becomes the center of the lover's existence and way of being in the world. This is also how the hero of Kaplan's novel relates to his America. Thus, the obituary in the *New York Times* for the hero Ezra Slavin quotes him as saying, " 'I have had a lifelong affair with the idea of America.' " " 'And,' " he continues, " 'when people find that difficult to believe, I remind them of the flintier vision which is bound to result when love is unrequited.' "[5]

In some ways Slavin resembles Norman Mailer. The bravado of Slavin's personal life and the multiplicity of his wives and loves, including one wife who seems to embody and epitomize the heart of gentile America, compare with aspects of Mailer's own biography. In *The Armies of the Night*, Mailer describes how each of his wives symbolizes a particular culture—Jewish, Latin, and English—and that "now he was married to an American girl." Like the fictional character in Kaplan's book, Mailer also relates his love for the idea of America to love for a woman. "Mailer," he writes, "finally came to decide that his love for his wife while not at all equal or congruent to his love for America was damnably parallel." Thus, Mailer sees his fourth wife as so representative of the magic of America that it was not "inconceivable" that some diminution for him of her charm would cause him to "finally lose some part of his love affair with America."[6] Also comparable to such intellectuals as Paul Goodman and Alfred Kazin, Slavin builds his career and reputation upon his ability to function as a student of the American idea.[7] A visiting professor of American Studies at a prestigious Massachusetts college, he literally makes his living by exploring the American idea for meanings and possibilities that can be conveyed to his students. Like Professor Konvitz, he relies heavily upon Theodore Parker's interpretation and understanding of the American idea. Slavin emphasizes Parker's commitment as a major nineteenth-century transcendentalist to radical individualism and to overcoming the limitations of history in order to claim the freedom to determine one's own future. The quote from Alexis de Tocqueville at the beginning of the novel indicates Kaplan's awareness of both the dangers and the opportunities involved in this commitment to the self. The freedom of the American idea nurtures new life at the risk of destroying much of the good in the old. However, as Werner Sollors notes in the *Harvard Encyclopedia of American Ethnic Groups*, for the new immigrant and the second-generation American the opportunity to create a new identity out of an earlier European existence often proved irresistible.[8] Slavin embodies this hope for new life. Kaplan artfully shows how the American idea puts such an individual in the situation of a gambler who feels compelled to stake his very existence on the prayer for regeneration. She writes of Slavin, "Hell-bent on winning a private, impossible sweepstake, a prize you could never touch, he had put all his money on an idea of America he had just gone ahead and made up. And so what if it had come out of libraries instead of race tracks. It was what he had lived for: a horse with such long odds it would never come in."[9] Of course, Slavin gambles on the American idea in the knowledge that the point is not to win but to continue the game and venture, to go forth like Gatsby on a quixotic journey after an impossible dream.

In the light of Kaplan's novel it is significant how Mailer maintains by implication through his reference to "sons of immigrants" that the Jewish writer took over the responsibility of interpreting America from the most American—meaning gentile and WASP—writers. It is also important that Mailer weds his theory of the second-generation writer to his fascination for the meaning of America in human history. Mailer writes:

> The people who were most American by birth, and who had the most to do with managing America, gave themselves a literature which had the least to say about the real phenomena of American life, most particularly the accelerated rate, the awful rate, of growth and anomaly through all of society. That sort of literature and that kind of attempt to explain America was left to the sons of immigrants who, if they were vigorous enough, and fortunate enough to be educated, now had the opportunity to see that America was a phenomenon never before described, indeed never before visible in the record of history. There was something going on in American life which was either grand or horrible or both, but it was going on—at a dizzy rate—and the future glory or doom of the world was not necessarily divorced from it.[10]

Accordingly, Mailer's imagination sustains one myth, the belief in the uniqueness of America, by investing into it a second myth of the Jewish writer and thinker who feels compelled to both describe and influence the "something going on in American life which was either grand or horrible or both."

However, a caveat needs to be introduced here. It should be noted, as the eminent Jewish linguist Joshua Fishman once reminded me, that this tradition of Jewish thinkers and the American idea can be exaggerated to stand for the entire story of the Jews in America. There have been and there continue to be Jews in America who look elsewhere than to the American idea for their identity and their sense of being in the world. The failed attempt by Chief Rabbi Jacob Joseph of Vilna to unite the Jewry of New York's Lower East Side in the late 1880s and 1890s provides one important example of such a religious leader. Today, Jews who concentrate on maintaining the religious and cultural traditions are the focus of the fiction of a writer such as Cynthia Ozick. For Ozick, as A. Alvarez says, "redemption is racial and religious: it lies in Jewish conscience, Jewish history, Jewish magic, and the Hebrew language." Still other Jewish writers and thinkers in America in both the past and the present should not be included in the "New Covenant" tradition because of commitments to the kind of radicalism that Liebman describes or to a form of artistic modernism that develops into its own ideology, as in the writings of Nathanael West and, perhaps, Jerzy Kosinski. Moreover, for Jacob Neusner, an important scholar of Judaism in America, the American Jew remains a "stranger at home." Neusner argues that being a Jew in America, especially in the context of "the Holocaust" and Zionism, involves a complex situation that forces one "to retreat from confrontation with one's own reality and to seek mediating structures in the experiences of others."[11] However, I do believe that the thinkers who are concerned about the American idea do represent the mainstream and most influential aspect of Jewish life and thought in America.

Johanna Kaplan's *O My America!* and Mailer's many works and literary and cultural views demonstrate how the American idea manifests itself in the form of myth as well as ideology. Here I mean myth and ideology as Roland Barthes uses those terms, at least insofar as he sees mythology as involving a science of signs and forms that turns into ideology when applied to historical uses and concerns.[12] Or, as Sacvan Bercovitch says, ideology in Barthes's sense "speaks of the day-to-day *uses* of myth."[13] As an expression of the American idea both myth and ideology also can be seen in works of literature and prose to function in a manner that is relevant to Hayden White's theory of "metahistory." White maintains the existence of a "poetic" basis for interpretations of history. He assumes a poetics of history. It involves "precognitive" and "precritical" linguistic acts that determine the style, substance, and argumentative mode of elaborate structures of historical analysis.[14] This "essentially poetic act" derives, according to White, from a "deep level of consciousness on which a historical thinker chooses conceptual strategies by which to explain or represent his data."[15]

A poetics of the American idea also exists. It can be discerned in the myth and ideology of America that provide the linguistic foundation for the American idea. As linguistic acts, the rhetorical and narrative structures of the myth and ideology of America constitute this poetics of the American Way and experience. Thus, both the rhetorical and narrative structures of the myth of America have been the subject of extensive study by scholars of American culture. Moreover, as Mailer indicates, modern Jewish writers and thinkers have played a crucial role in the development and organization of these linguistic structures. Of all their areas of contribution to the shaping and direction of modern American culture and character perhaps none equals the impact of their linguistic leadership in modernizing the rhetorical and narrative strategies for expressing the idea of America through myth and ideology. The linguistic influence of Jewish writers and thinkers upon the American mind has grown steadily since the 1880s when the massive wave of immigration from Eastern Europe began. In the period following World War II, Jewish writers achieved what Irving Malin and Irwin Stark describe as a "breakthrough." As Malin and Stark state, "For the first time in history a large and impressively gifted group of serious American-Jewish writers has broken through the psychic barriers of the past to become an important, possibly a major reformative influence in American life and letters."[16] The impact of Jewish writers and thinkers upon the poetics of the American idea through their development of the rhetorical and narrative structures of the myth and ideology of America demonstrates this "reformative influence."

Bercovitch traces the rhetorical structure of the myth of America back to the Puritan jeremiad. He follows Perry Miller in seeing the jeremiad as a political sermon that was initiated by the Puritans and became a public ritual of renewal.[17] He believes that understanding the rhetoric of the jeremiad form can provide a key to unlocking the American mind. For Bercovitch as for White, language enables us not only to understand a culture but also to perceive how a culture understands itself. He writes:

> Rhetoric functions within a culture. It reflects and affects a set of particular psychic, social and historical needs. This is conspicuously true of the American jeremiad, a mode of public exhortation that

originated in the European pulpit, was transformed in both form and content by the New England Puritans, persisted through the eighteenth century, and helped sustain a national dream through two hundred years of turbulence and change. The American jeremiad was a ritual designed to join social criticism to spiritual renewal, public to private identity, the shifting "signs of the times" to certain traditional metaphors, themes and symbols. To argue (as I do) that the jeremiad has played a major role in fashioning the myth of America is to define it at once in literary and in historical terms. Myth may clothe history as fiction, but it persuades in proportion to its capacity to help men act in history. Ultimately, its effectiveness derives from its functional relationship to facts.[18]

The psychology of the jeremiad involves continual grief in the community over the moral failure to live up to the heavenly mission. The jeremiad, however, allows the community to renew itself by proclaiming again and again its allegiance and devotion to its mission. Bercovitch believes that this ritualistic rhetoric of mission and conscience provided the cohesion for the formation of the "ideological consensus" that comprises the American Way. The jeremiad and the ideology of consensus give America the sense of being one culture and one people with a shared history and a common destiny. As Bercovitch says:

The ritual of the jeremiad bespeaks an ideological consensus—in moral, religious, economic, social, and intellectual matters— unmatched in any other modern culture. And the power of consensus is nowhere more evident than in the symbolic meaning that the jeremiads infused into the term America. . . . Of all symbols of identity, only *America* has united nationality and universality, civic and spiritual selfhood, secular and redemptive history, the country's past and paradise to be, in a single synthetic ideal. The symbol of America is the triumphant issue of early New England rhetoric and a long-ripened ritual of socialization.[19]

In this view, therefore, the Puritans had the most persuasive and lasting impact upon the myth of America. John Winthrop's vision in 1630 aboard the *Arbella* "that we shall be as a Citty upon a Hill, the eies of all people are uppon us" initiated a rhetorical tradition whose influences can be found throughout American literature and thought.[20] Images and symbols of a "chosen people" in a New Zion and a new Promised Land have helped to define our national character in terms of a national mission ever since. Thus, as Allen Guttmann indicates, the millions of Jews who followed the original Puritans to America tended to considerably "complicate the metaphor that made America the Promised Land."[21]

In modern American intellectual and literary history, a tradition has emerged of Jewish writers, intellectuals, and public figures who assume the burden of the jeremiad. The rhetoric of the jeremiad, with its concomitant psychology of moral anxiety and its ideology of consensus, has become a basic means by which these thinkers can relate to the American idea. In the manner of Jeremiah, who describes the making of "a new covenant with the house of Israel, and with the house of Judah" (31:31–32), these Jewish thinkers in America often write with the vision and sensibility of prophets and judges who stand between the American Way and the people. In this sense, the Jews, who had been a model for the Puritans, become the "New Puritans," and Jewish writers and thinkers function in the role of "New Jeremiahs" preaching to the people to understand the meaning of America. For these writers and thinkers, the New Covenant does not imply blind allegiance to national and cultural interests. It means, instead, a call in the rhetorical tradition of Jeremiah for both introspection and cultural renewal in the light of an ideology that sees America as a new way of life.

This New Covenant appears like a badge on the works and endeavors of many of America's most important Jewish writers, artists, and thinkers. However, the nature of the commitment and the complexity of ideas represented by the badge vary as much as the great diversity of works produced during the past one hundred years by these individual Jews. Although the New Covenant manifests itself most clearly in written works, it can be heard as well in the music of two of our century's most "American" composers—Aaron Copland of Brooklyn and George Gershwin of New York's Lower East Side. The music of both men seems to possess America and re-create American themes and values in the form of a new language that now is part of American consciousness and culture. Both men represent the marriage of a unique cultural milieu and tradition in America with the American Way. From a literary perspective, the music of Copland and Gershwin can be considered as background for the compulsive effort of so many Jewish writers and intellectuals to wrestle with the charms and dangers of the American idea.

Puritan leaders such as Samuel Danforth articulated the rhetoric of the jeremiad in election-day sermons while others such as Mary Rowlandson developed the sermon narrative as the means for dramatizing the Puritan conscience. Similarly, Jewish writers in their role as New Jeremiahs also developed a number of modes to express and elaborate upon the basic rhetorical structure of the jeremiad. For Jewish writers, the novel has been one of the most important vehicles for dramatizing the state of mind that the jeremiad represents. At their best, such as in the work of Kaplan and Mailer, these writers integrate both the rhetorical and narrative strategies of rendering the myth and ideology of America. Thus, they modernize the traditional, sermon-narrative form of the Puritan experience. Starting with this Puritan literary form, the narrative structure of the myth of America has received considerable critical attention from a distinguished line of American scholars such as Henry Nash Smith, Richard Slotkin, John Cawelti, Leo Marx, Alan Trachtenberg, R. W. B. Lewis, Leslie Fiedler, John William Ward, Annette Kolodny, Judith Fryer, Ann Douglas, John Kasson, and Will Wright.[22] In general, they define myth as a narrative structure that symbolically presents and dramatizes the values, ideals, paradoxes, conflicts, and tensions of a given culture. In addition, they tend to see the myth of America as centering on the theme of individual regeneration and cultural renewal. American Jewish writers have been in the forefront of not only sustaining in their stories the rhetoric of the jeremiad but also in transforming the mythic sermon-narrative to a modern setting that expresses the condition and dilemma of the modern American.

In the works of those novelists who attempt to combine the sermonic, rhetorical, and narrative structures of the myth and ideology of America, and in the prose pieces of Jewish critics and intellectuals, the idea of America becomes a complicated matter. However, three basic ways of dealing with the rhetorical and sermonic structure of the myth appear in these works of fiction and nonfiction. The first involves a basic espousal of the myth as an ideal and vision of America. The second way of expressing the myth is in terms of an antimyth, which constitutes an attack on the culture because of the failure to live up to the myth. In this form, the reality of failure serves as a means to strive for the ideal. Thus, alienation from the myth becomes an expression of a greater affirmation of it. The third way of dealing with the myth, however, involves a deeper form of alienation through ideological disavowal and psychological rejection of the myth of America. Sometimes these different attitudes toward the myth and different ways of expressing it operate together in the same work. In other writers, however, we get clear-cut models of these different forms of the myth of America. For example, in her autobiographical writings, Mary Antin offers one of the strongest expressions of the myth of America as an ideal and vision. She speaks of her "healing ointment—my faith in America" and writes, "No! it is not I that belong to the past, but the past that belongs to me. America is the youngest of the nations, and inherits all that went before in history. And I am the youngest of America's children, and into my hands is given all her priceless heritage, to the last white star espied through the telescope, to the last great thought of the philosopher. Mine is the whole majestic past, and mine is the shining future."[23]

However, such enthusiastic idealism invites a counterstatement. The idealism of the myth creates its own negation or antimyth in the interests of achieving a truer form of the mythic vision. As in the long tradition of the American version of the jeremiad including Paine, Thoreau, Emerson, Whitman, Howells, the Jameses, Fitzgerald, and others, myth and anti-myth operate together in the works of Jewish writers and thinkers in the New Covenant tradition. In our own time, one of the most provocative examples of this use of the antimyth can be found in an often-quoted section from Mailer's *The Armies of the Night*:

> Let the bugle blow. The death of America rides in on the smog. America—the land where a new kind of man was born from the idea that God was present in every man not only as compassion but as power, and so the country belonged to the people; for the will of the people—if the locks of their life could be given the art to turn— was then the will of God. . . . Brood on that country who expresses our will. She is America, once a beauty of magnificence unparal- leled, now a beauty with leprous skin. She is heavy with child—no one knows if legitimate—and languishes in a dungeon whose walls are never seen. Now the first contractions of her fearsome labor be- gin—it will go on: no doctor exists to tell the hour. It is only known that false labor is not likely on her now, no, she will prob- ably give birth, and to what?—the most fearsome totalitarianism the world has ever known? or can she, poor giant, tormented lovely girl, deliver a babe of a new world brave and tender, artful and wild? Rush to the locks. God writhes in his bonds. Rush to the

locks. Deliver us from our curse. For we must end on the road to that mystery where courage, death, and the dream of love give promise of sleep.[24]

Mailer's attack of course constitutes an affirmation of the dream and ideal. In fact, as someone who so strongly espoused radical and alternative causes, his ultimate faith in and hope for the dream provide an important example of the power of the myth of America. His own version of the myth indicates how difficult it has been throughout our history to find viable and meaningful alternatives to the myth.

The third way of dealing with the myth by insisting on separating one's self totally from it has proven difficult not only for Jews but for other Americans as well. The fate of those who operate outside of the myth is interesting. Such writers are in the tradition of what Bercovitch calls the antijeremiad in which the disappearance of the myth becomes equivalent to turning off the sun in the cosmos. "When they abandoned their faith in America," Bercovitch writes, "they had no other recourse. . . . In this country, both the jeremiad and the anti-jeremiad foreclosed alternatives: the one by absorbing the hopes of mankind into the meaning of America, the other by reading into America the futility and fraud of hope itself."[25] Michael Gold, who wrote *Jews without Money*, serves as an example of a Jewish writer in the antijeremiad tradition. Gold developed an ardent passion for communism as a substitute for the myth and ideology of America.[26] Modern heirs to his vision of a political alternative outside of the American Way were represented copiously in the new left. However, the writers from Gold's era who rejected the myth represent an important irony. Some of these writers found a perfect way to express their sense of futility and exhaustion by helping to create the new "plastic" culture of Hollywood. The attraction of Hollywood to some Jewish writers such as Samuel Ornitz, Ben Hecht, and Budd Schulberg, and their proclivity to project in their work popular-culture images and stereotypes of Jews and Jewish values and beliefs, serve as an indication of their cultural isolation and alienation.

In contrast to the writers of the antijeremiad, those in the tradition of the New Covenant have seen their identity partly in terms of their under-standing of the American Way. The New Covenant writers faced a basic challenge in attempting to relate the rhetorical and narrative structures of the myth and ideology of America to the context and conditions of modern America. According to at least one school of thought, such an effort involves a contradiction within the very nature of mythology. Thus, Richard Slotkin maintains that throughout American history there has persisted an attempt "to fabricate" an American mythology based upon an "essentially artificial and typically American" idea of the meaning of myth. "True myths," he argues, "are generated on a sub-literary level by the historical experience of a people and thus constitute part of that inner reality which the work of the artist draws on, illuminates and explains." Slotkin further extends his criticism of the artificial mythmakers to scholars. "Even scholarly critics who address themselves to the problem of the 'myth of America' have a marked tendency to engage in the manufacture of the myth they pretend to analyze in an attempt to reshape the character of their people or to justify some preconceived or inherited notion of American uniqueness. Such critics are themselves a part of this national phenomenon of myth-consciousness, this continual preoccupation with the necessity of defining or creating a national identity, a character for us to live in the world."[27]

Nevertheless, Slotkin goes on to accept Philip Wheelwright's theory of myth based on "stages of development in the evolution of myth-artifacts"—the primary, romantic, and consummatory. It is in the third stage that Jewish writers of the past one hundred years fall. Slotkin maintains that the "consummatory myth-maker" operates in a mode distinctly different from that of his predecessors. Slotkin writes, "First, he is aware of and capable of articulating the need for myth *as myth*—that is, as a construction of symbols and values, derived from real and imaginary experience and ordered by the imagination according to the deepest needs of the psyche. In addition, he has the benefit of historical knowledge and can look back over a span of time in which myths have developed and decayed, have shaped and been shaped by human and national history. Given this double awareness, the consummatory myth-maker has a degree of critical distance from his material and his works which does not exist for the mystic of the primary myth or the conventional imitator of romantic myth." The Jewish writers in this study, therefore, are performing a function consistent with the nature of myth "in highly sophisticated cultures, such as that of modern Europe and the West."[28] Moreover, in working with the unique "construction of symbols and values" known as the myth of America, they are also operating in an ongoing historical tradition and cultural process that sees the meaning of America in terms of continual redemption, renewal, and revolution. In his analysis of this cultural tradition, Bercovitch summarizes it succinctly in his description of one of Emerson's essays as "a summons to continuing revolution that joins New England's errand, the Great Awakening, the War of Independence, and the Civil War, through the typology of America's mission."[29] Jewish writers in America extended this process by dealing with the myth of America during a time of shattering change and turmoil characterized by such factors as urbanization, industrialization, and immigration itself. In doing so they had to parallel a process involving the commercialization and popularization of the myth of the frontier that Slotkin and others see as so crucial. They thereby were reinventing American identity in a manner that gave major significance to the concomitant reinvention of Jewish identity in America.

Within the context of the rhetoric and ideology of America as the symbol of redemption, renewal, and revolution, the most influential Jewish writers of the past century constructed a narrative structure for the myth of America composed of symbols and metaphors relevant to the conditions of the modern American experience. The elements in this narrative structure are worth examining especially insofar as they contrast with the traditional frontier version of the myth as derived primarily from the archetypal figures of Daniel Boone and James Fenimore Cooper's Natty Bumppo. The most outstanding element of change may be the most obvious. The hero of the piece is often Jewish and as such stands for an aspect of the modern condition, modern consciousness, or the modern sensibility. Or, in cases where the hero is not Jewish, as in many of the works of Mailer and Heller, the presence and sensibility of the author imbue the language and atmosphere of the work with an urban tone and intellectual tension that are characteristic of the Jewish novel in this country and century. As in so many other matters, Abraham Cahan was a pioneer in the invention of a new American hero. In his first novel, *Yekl: A Tale of the New York Ghetto*, the hero simply represents the new immigrant. However, in his later novel, *The Rise of David Levinsky*, Cahan develops a far more complex figure that anticipates many of the literary and cultural themes of the following decades. As Kermit Vanderbilt indicates, William Dean Howells was the first to recognize the importance to American literature and American culture of Cahan's work as an example of the new school of realism. Cahan was in effect beginning a tradition of the Jewish novel that came to dominate a large part of the American literary scene.[30]

Another major element in the new narrative involves the importance of the urban landscape. In a recent study, Murray Baumgarten considers the urban experience and the transnational linguistic influence of Yiddish as the key elements in modern Jewish consciousness.[31] In America, the city is depicted in ambivalent terms that bring together opposing images and values. The city in the myth is an urban wilderness of violence, danger, and corruption, but it also can be a place of opportunity for the aggressive, ambitious, and intelligent. The classic picture of the city as a jungle environment can perhaps be found in Henry Roth's *Call It Sleep* in which the young David Schearl suffers all the pains and agonies of growing up on the New York streets. Even in that novel, however, Roth presents a portrait of the city as a place that ultimately could allow and even nurture the formation of a Whitmanesque American character. Such conflicting images about the city appear throughout New Covenant literature in Cahan's and Yezierska's visions of the city, in Mailer's numerous essays, stories, and novels of urban conflict, and in Bellow's novels about the individual in the city from Augie March to Artur Sammler and Von Humboldt Fleisher.

The radical change in the landscape of this modern myth of America from the myth of the frontier leads to another important change. We go from a nineteenth-century idea of lateral mobility across frontiers to a new emphasis on upward mobility so that success and all the problems and ambiguities related to it become a major theme in the new narrative. Appearing first and in some ways in its most influential expression in *The Rise of David Levinsky*, the theme of success remains a pervasive idea until the most recent works of Norman Podhoretz, Philip Roth, and Joseph Heller. A parallel and related theme is the concern for moral elevation in a competitive and brutal world. It dominates David Schearl's quest for both freedom and some kind of moral certainty and plagues David Levinsky who feels guilty throughout the novel because of his rejection of his past. The moral theme represents an important current in Mailer, Malamud, Roth, Heller, and Bellow. Often this problem of moral elevation in a morally ambiguous and complicated age is compounded by another theme of assimilation or the confrontation with America—a theme that Allen Guttmann sees as basic for understanding the Jewish experience in

America. In this theme, the hero questions his identity and the purpose of his life in a confrontation with the moral environment of a predominantly gentile America with which he deals on a daily basis. One expects this theme to be critical in early writings, but in fact it has achieved considerable intensity in some of the most recent Jewish literature such as Roth's *Portnoy's Complaint* and Heller's *Good as Gold*. Moreover, this confrontation leads to another basic theme of alienation and the confrontation with the self in which the hero such as Herzog, Bruce Gold, Levin in Malamud's *A New Life*, and David Kepesh in Roth's *The Professor of Desire* must deal with existential questions of anxiety, doubt, and identity in the attempt to find a place and a home. The *shikse*, or gentile love-goddess theme, is often central to the development and resolution of all these themes. In the love-goddess theme, we find in Jewish writers the continuation on a psychological and metaphorical level of the symbol of America as a woman. Even in David Schearl, we see this theme in his subconscious associations with the Statue of Liberty. Leslie Fiedler identifies and deprecates a counterpart to this theme of the shikse in the form of the Jewish writer "as the exponent of the instinctual life, as the lover." Although this idea is antithetical to the Jewish tradition, "it is in the role of passionate lover," Fiedler writes, "that the American-Jewish novelist sees himself at the moment of his entry into American literature; and the community with which he seeks to unite himself he sees as the *shikse*."[32]

However, even more significant than sexual aggressiveness are intellectual aggressiveness and the life of the mind as important characteristics of this new narrative form. This proclivity toward intellectual debate and discussion in the Jewish writer prompted Mary McCarthy to make a controversial statement about the importance of ideas in novels by Jews. "In the U.S.A.," she says, "a special license has always been granted to the Jewish novel, which is free to juggle ideas in full view of the public; Bellow, Malamud, Philip Roth still avail themselves of the right, which is never conceded to us goys."[33] Another critic believes that Jewish American novels function primarily as education novels.[34] Accordingly, at the core of this narrative form a heroic consciousness exists that is deeply concerned with ideas. Moreover, this new heroic consciousness generally does more in the narrative than simply personify or embody the values and life-styles of the modern intellectual. The new hero tends, instead, to represent a special kind of hero of the mind. The intellectual consciousness at the heart of the narrative becomes what Mark A. Weinstein calls a "hero of thought." As such, the hero self-consciously sees himself as a historical consciousness. He performs the role of a historical focal point who can, as Weinstein says, "recreate the past."[35] Moreover, the sense of the past not only illuminates the present in the narrative but it also enables the hero to project into the future. He functions, in other words, as a prophetic consciousness by anticipating the implications for his culture and society of contemporary values and behavior. In a variation from this pattern, the center of the novel may be an antiheroic or negative character who serves as a vehicle for the author's own strategy of attack on the failures and shortcomings of his culture. In either case, the moral thrust of the narrative fulfills the demands of the jeremiad and casts the writer in the role of a New Jeremiah.

Joseph Heller's *Good as Gold* represents one important version of the narrative we have been discussing. Like Johanna Kaplan's *O My America!*, Heller's novel self-consciously elaborates upon the theme of the Jewish intellectual or hero of thought who teaches and writes about the Jewish-American experience. Moreover, *Good as Gold* itself constitutes an inward turn by being a jeremiad against a prospective New Jeremiah. As a phony intellectual and academic opportunist who betrays those closest to him and cynically defies most of the values of meaningful human relationships, Bruce Gold epitomizes many of the things we all detest. Although Heller's earlier masterpiece, *Catch-22*, is a war novel that obviously does not fit the pattern of the urban novel under discussion, it does demonstrate the intensity of the author's concern for dramatizing ideas through a hero of thought. As Brian Way notes, the novel really concerns modern thought itself so that "Catch-22 is a pattern of non-reason, a habit of mind, a perversion of logic" that represents a modern bureaucratic way of thinking.[36] In an "impolite interview," Heller himself emphasizes the importance of ideas and thought in his novel. Calling the novel "almost an encyclopedia of the current mental atmosphere," Heller goes on to say that it "is certainly a novel of *comment*; there are comments about the loyalty oath, about the free enterprise system, about civil rights, about bureaucracy, about patriotism—but these are the ingredients out of which to create a fictional narrative."[37]

Of all contemporary Jewish authors, perhaps Saul Bellow most consistently and vigorously develops the character of the hero of thought. In his famous speech of acceptance for the National Book Award for *Herzog*, Bellow blamed the absence of thought on the part of contemporary writers for the inadequate state of current fiction. "There is nothing left for us novelists to do but think," he said. "For unless we think, unless we make a clearer estimate of our condition, we will continue to write kid stuff, to fail in our function; we will lack serious interests and become truly irrelevant."[38] Thus, Bellow's heroes reflect this mandate to think. Moses Herzog seems to embody both the condition and much of the learning associated with literary and philosophical modernism. Artur Sammler certainly qualifies as a sensitive intellectual while Charles Citrine in *Humboldt's Gift* is a historian and the author of *Some Americans: The Sense of Being in the U.S.A.* In addition, while his perspective, as Ruth Wisse indicates, includes a considerable amount of irony, Bellow's point of view cannot be separated from his moral vision.[39] As Michelle Carbone Loris says, "For Saul Bellow the essential quest is spiritual: it is a search for humanness in a world that daily assaults and denies such a search. This struggle to be human is the author's one story and the various versions of that same story simply indicate the individual progress each protagonist—Joseph, Asa, Wilhelm, Herzog, Sammler—makes on that journey. To find the genuinely human is the hero's task." Accordingly, for Bellow historic consciousness and moral awareness merge.[40]

Furthermore, Bellow's belief as a Jew and a writer in the continued relevance of the American idea provides a major support and example of the New Covenant. Bellow dramatizes his position on the meaning of America through the character of Albert Corde, the hero of *The Dean's December*, who explains the motivation behind his political pieces by saying, "Again, the *high* intention—to prevent the American idea from being pounded into dust altogether. And here is our American idea: liberty, equality, justice, democracy, abundance."[41] In a speech Bellow gave upon receiving the Anti-Defamation League's America's Democratic Legacy Award, he connects this passion for the American idea to his identity as a Jew. He regards, he says, his Jewish and American origins with "piety," using that word in Santayana's sense of " 'reverence for the sources of one's being.' " He says, "One could have better sources, undoubtedly. I could make a list of those more desirable sources, but they are not mine, and I cannot revere them. The only life I can love, or hate, is the life that I—that we—have found here, this American life of the Twentieth Century, the life of Americans who are also Jews. Which of these sources, the American or the Jewish, should elicit the greater piety? Are the two exclusive? Must a choice be made?" In this speech, Bellow indicates that he identifies with America as a Jew who sees the success of the American idea as a guarantee for Jewish and human freedom. To make his point, he significantly refers to two leading Jewish political philosophers who are devoted students of the American experience. Bellow perceives in the lives and works of Morris R. Cohen and Sidney Hook a living tradition and learned precedent that justify and validate his own position. "When I read last summer in the *American Scholar* an article by Professor Sidney Hook on the great teacher and philosopher Morris R. Cohen, I was stirred by Cohen's belief that 'the future of liberal civilization was bound up with America's survival and its ability to make use of the heritage of human rights formulated by Jefferson and Lincoln,'" Bellow says. "Professor Cohen was no sentimentalist. He was a tough-minded man, not a patriotic rhetorician." Sharing Cohen's feeling of reverence for America, Bellow cannot seriously believe that America would go the way of other countries that either expelled or destroyed their Jews. By arguing that America is not like "other Christian countries," he suggests that the harmony between American and Jewish interests and values helps to prove the special importance of America to the world for preserving human freedom and liberal values. The conclusion of Bellow's speech sounds like a testimony of faith in the ability of America to fulfill its moral destiny. In addition, the conclusion also clearly imposes upon the Jewish American writer the moral and political obligation to eschew both a false nihilism and excessive patriotism in favor of at least recognizing the potential of the American ideology for the future of mankind. Bellow says:

> It is sufficient to say in the most matter of fact way what is or
> should be obvious to everyone. In spite of the vastness and oppres-
> siveness of corporate and governmental powers the principle of the
> moral equality of all human beings has not been rejected in the
> United States. Not yet, at any rate. Sigmund Freud, I remember
> reading, once observed that America was an interesting experiment,
> but that he did not believe that it would succeed. Well, maybe not.
> But it would be base to abandon it. To do so would destroy our rev-
> erence for the sources of our being. We would inflict on ourselves

a mutilation from which we might never recover. And if Cohen is right, and the future of liberal civilization is bound up with America's survival, the damage would be universal and irreparable.[42]

Bellow's continued belief in the American experiment reflects at least in part something of his discomfort with the extremism in both politics and art of the radical left during the sixties and early seventies. However, it also indicates a sense of commitment to values and traditions he relates to his roots as both a Jew and an American. Clearly, this commitment of a major Jewish writer to the rhetoric and narrative of the American myth makes Bellow a leader in the tradition of the New Covenant. The tradition extends at least from Cahan to Malamud. It includes such writers as Henry Roth, Anzia Yezierska, and Philip Roth, each of whom deals with questions of Jewish isolation and alienation. The tradition of the New Covenant culminates in the works of two writers, E. L. Doctorow and Norman Mailer. Both Mailer and Doctorow experiment in different ways to attempt to unite literature to history and contemporary culture. They each make their works out of the substance and materials of American culture and history, thereby achieving a new intensity in the relationship between the Jewish writer and the American idea.

Chapter 2

In Search of the Real America
Bernard Malamud

By maintaining their commitment to the American idea, Jewish writers follow in the path of earlier American "Jeremiahs." As Sacvan Bercovitch says, "What distinguishes the American writer—and the American Jeremiah from the late seventeenth century on—is his *refusal* to abandon the national covenant."[1] The commitment of Jewish writers and thinkers to the national covenant grew out of and reflected the interest of the larger Jewish culture in achieving a secure place within the national consensus. Some established leaders of the dominant Protestant culture like Howells, Mark Twain, and Hutchins Hapgood encouraged Jewish participation in the cultural process of renewing the myth and ideology of America. For example, Hapgood believed that Jews in America could teach the rest of the culture a great deal about achieving a harmony between religious and material concerns. In his classic study of the Jewish ghetto, he wrote, "What we need at the present time more than anything else is a spiritual unity such as, perhaps, will only be the distant result of our present special activities. We need something similar to the spirit underlying the national and religious unity of the orthodox Jewish culture."[2] However, other leading figures in America saw in the Jews as a people an unwanted challenge to their own class and cultural hegemony. In this sense, the anti-Semitism of such figures as Henry Adams and Frederick Jackson Turner provides a negative form of documentation of Jewish interest in the myth and symbol of America. Thus, Henry Adams wrote about himself: "His world was dead. Not a Polish Jew fresh from Warsaw or Cracow—not a furtive Yacoob or Ysaac still reeking of the Ghetto, snarling a weird Yiddish to the officers of the customs—but had a keener instinct, an intenser energy, and a freer hand than he—American of Americans with Heaven knew how many Puritans and Patriots behind him, and an education that had cost a civil war."[3] As E. Digby Baltzell indicates, Adams, in his reaction to the Jews, not only "increasingly blamed the Jews for all he disliked about his age" but revealed something deep within himself. "The Adams family," Baltzell says, "had always taken a leading part in the destiny of America, and Henry's anti-Semitism was indeed a kind of self-hate born of his abhorrence of the path now taken by 'His America.' In fact, the more one contemplates the mind of Henry Adams, the more one sees it as a symbol *par excellence* of the powerless brahmin who is finally forced to embrace the idea of caste after losing faith in aristocracy."[4]

Frederick Jackson Turner had somewhat similar feelings and problems. Daniel Aaron quotes Turner's description in 1887 of his discomfort upon being lost in the Jewish ghetto of Boston. "'I was in Jewry,'" he wrote, "'the street consecrated to "old clothers," pawnbrokers, and similar followers of Abraham.'" He describes the streets as "'filled with big Jew men—long bearded and carrying a staff as you see in a picture,—and with Jew youths and maidens—some of the latter pretty—as you sometimes see a lilly in the green muddy slime.'" He notes further with relief that he finally was able to extricate himself "'after much elbowing'" from "'this mass of oriental noise and squalor.'" More than three decades later the descendants of many of those Jews were crowding into Harvard, and Turner expressed his concern about the ultimate issue of reconciling "'New English ideals of liberalism'" with the fear of the growing influence and power of the immigrants. He confessed that "'I don't like the prospects of Harvard a New Jerusalem and Boston already a new Cork. Bad old world and the times out of joint.'"[5]

Turner's point of view may be based in part upon his understanding of the frontier as the source of America's strength. He developed and took for granted the thesis that the greatest qualities of American character derived from the frontier experience. In his famous address before the American Historical Association in Chicago in 1893, Turner further suggested that with the frontier closed American culture itself would be forced to endure a distressing change. Clearly, the immigrants arriving in America indicated the wave of the future that seemed to Turner to counter the heart of what he considered to be most American. Ironically, the very qualities of national character that Turner calls the "traits of the frontier" could be cited with validity to describe the character of new immigrants. Thus, Turner attributes to the frontier character "that coarseness and strength combined with acuteness and acquisitiveness; that practical, inventive turn of mind, quick to find expedients; that masterful grasp of material things, lacking in the artistic but powerful to effect great ends; that restless, nervous energy; that dominant individualism, working for good and for evil, and withal that buoyancy and exuberance which comes with freedom." To modern immigrants America still seemed to offer what Turner thought was possible only from the conditions of an open frontier —"a new field of opportunity, a gate of escape from the bondage of the past; and freshness, and confidence, and scorn of older society, impatience of its restraints and its ideas, and indifference to its lessons."[6] In a way, these immigrants did more than challenge Turner's sense of America. Even more galling for a historian, in effect they proved his thesis to be part of a larger myth rather than an analytical fact.

Accordingly, the myth of America could not be relegated exclusively to the myth of regeneration on the frontier for it to be relevant to the experience of the new immigrants. In the modern immigrant experience, the frontier was closed, but the belief in America as "promised land" and as an ideal remained. At the same time, the myth of the frontier and the West with its suggestion of freedom and renewal could titillate and captivate the imagination of Jews as much as gentiles. For example, Alfred Kazin reports his lasting disappointment with his father for failing to remain in the West where he could have settled permanently on a homestead. Kazin writes, "*Omaha* was the most beautiful word I had ever heard, *homestead* almost as beautiful; but I could never forgive him for not having accepted that homestead."[7] However, while many Jews dreamed about finding their freedom and acceptance in the West, the actual experience often proved quite different from their expectations. For such Jews the encounter with the West inspired a reaction that included irony and sometimes suspicion and fear.

One of the most interesting autobiographical accounts of the West as a place for rebirth as an American can be found in Marcus Ravage's *An American in the Making*. In the book, Ravage seems to become a confirmed adherent to the myth of the regeneration and rebirth of the individual in the West. However, beneath the surface of his affirmation one senses layers of doubt and insecurity about the permanence and reality of his transmogrification into a "real American." Ravage's account describes the typical immigrant's journey from Rumania to New York. After years of labor, education, and struggle, he decides to go to college in what he and his friends consider to be a portion of the wild West—the University of Missouri. "I was going," he writes, "to the land of the 'real Americans.'" He spent a bitterly long and frustrating first year feeling like an alien and outsider among his college mates. With some justification he decides that "unpalatable as the truth was, there was no evading the patent fact that if I was not taken in among the Missourians the fault was with me and not with them." By the end of the autobiography, Ravage has become convinced that "the loneliness I had endured, the snubbing, the ridicule, the inner struggles—all the dreariness and the sadness of my life in exile" had been worthwhile when compared with the "idealized vision of the clean manhood, the large human dignity, the wholesome, bracing atmosphere" that had opened itself to him in the West. He comes to feel that his manhood and freedom depend upon his completion of the break with the East that would enable him to continue the process of Americanization in the West. His new sense of alienation from his past becomes distressingly apparent during a return visit to New York when he feels uncomfortable among his old friends. Changed by his vision of the real America, he hears old radical arguments in New York that now seem based on a misunderstanding of the true nature of the American system. "I listened to it all with an alien ear," he writes. "Soon I caught myself defending the enemy out there. What did these folks know of Americans, anyhow?" Finally, he makes an emotional appeal to his best friend to follow him to Missouri to find her salvation as an American. "'Save yourself, my dear,'" he says. "'Run as fast as you can. You will find a bigger and freer world than this. Promise me that you will follow me to the West this fall. You will thank me for it. Those big, genuine people out in Missouri are the salt of the earth. Whatever they may think about the problem of universal brotherhood, they have already solved it for their next-door neighbors. There is no need of the social revolution in Missouri; they have a generous slice of the kingdom of heaven.'"[8]

While Ravage admits to the likelihood of exaggeration on his part, his statement and feeling about the West indicate a deeper level of insecurity and defensiveness. He seems to be caught in a classic bind between wanting to escape a minority culture in order to achieve dominant-culture acceptance while also feeling the equally powerful need to defend and justify his own culture. The ambiguity and conflict in Ravage's position lead him in his autobiography to see in the West, and in Missouri especially, qualities that not only were superhuman but super-American as well.

In other works by Jews about the encounter with the West, the same set of conflicts and ambiguities occur and lead to a process of irony and demythologization. Thus, David Levinsky, like Ravage, equates "the real America" with the West. "The road," Cahan writes, "was a great school of business and life to me. . . . I saw much of the United States. Every time I returned home I felt as though, in comparison with the places I had just visited, New York was not an American city at all, and as though my last trip had greatly added to the 'real American' quality in me." In contrast to Ravage, however, Cahan views this feeling with irony because he understands about the guilt and insecurity involved in this process of self-transformation. This real America turns out to be one of manners and gestures that will never give Levinsky any sense of peace or place. Rather than a new sense of self, Levinsky only finds himself caught in a drive toward conformity. He grows embarrassed by "my Talmudic gesticulations, a habit that worried me like a physical defect. It was so distressingly un-American."[9] For other Jewish writers as well, the myth of the West became filled with irony. Perhaps it achieves its most bitter treatment in Nathanael West's *A Day of the Locust* in which the West in the form of California becomes the exact opposite of the place for renewal. California is the end of the road where Americans go to die. It is a burial ground rather than a garden.

However, a more explicit treatment of the theme of the encounter of the city Jew with the myth of the West can be found in Bernard Malamud's *A New Life*. As the title suggests, the novel is literally about the myth. The hero, Sy Levin, a former alcoholic who has already been a failure in what could not be described even charitably as an academic career, moves from New York to a small college in the Pacific Northwest in a modern version of the traditional frontier pursuit of "a new life." "One always hopes," he says, "that a new place will inspire change—in one's life."[10] Moreover, he has bought the myth that such a change can occur most readily in the West, which, theoretically, has been the scene of regeneration for millions of Americans. "My God, the West, Levin thought," writes Malamud. "He imagined the pioneers in covered wagons entering this valley for the first time, and found it a moving thought. Although he had lived little in nature Levin had always loved it, and the sense of having done the right thing in leaving New York was renewed in him. He shuddered at his good fortune" (*NL*, 8). His gratitude for being part of this experience in the West is both naive and honest. "He was himself a stranger in the West but that didn't matter," Levin intimates to his students. "By some miracle of movement and change, standing before them as their English instructor by virtue of his appointment, Levin welcomed them from wherever they came: the Northwest states, California, and a few from beyond the Rockies, a thrilling representation to a man who had in all his life never been west of Jersey City" (*NL*, 85). His naiveté allows him to believe that he approaches a successful metamorphosis. With his students in mind, he thinks, "In his heart he thanked them, sensing he had created their welcome of him. They represented the America he had so often heard of, the fabulous friendly West" (*NL*, 85).

Of course, Levin must come to realize that there is no "new life" in a myth that takes him outside of his essential self. He is the classic *schlemiel*-victim figure in Jewish writing and humor who cannot escape his past. Malamud writes, "His escape to the West had thus far come to nothing, space corrupted by time, the past-contaminated self. . . . A white-eyed hound bayed at him from the window—his classic fear, failure after grimy years to master himself. He lay in silence, solitude and darkness. More than once he experienced crawling self-hatred. It left him frightened because he thought he had outdistanced it by three thousand miles. The future as new life was no longer predictable. That caused the floor to move under his bed" (*NL*, 155).

Malamud intends in the novel for Levin to succeed through failure by seeing through himself and the society around him. In the reverse of the usual interpretation of David Levinsky's career, Sy Levin fails in the professional world in order to rise in the moral sphere. By finally accepting this failure he transcends and overcomes the false world and values of the new world in which he wanted so desperately to succeed. It is this aspect of the novel that so annoys Leslie Fiedler. In a typically brilliant and devastating article about the novel, Fiedler complains that the book fails to fulfill its potential of "becoming the first real Jewish anti-Western." Fiedler maintains that Malamud either "out of lack of nerve or excess of ambition" attempts to turn Levin into "a heroic defender of the Liberal Tradition, which is to say an insufferable prig like Stephen Dedalus rather than an unloved, loveable victim like Leopold Bloom."[11]

It seems to me, however, that Levin's strength ultimately derives not from false heroics or brave deeds that are inconsistent with his character but from the very elements that comprise and govern his sense of self. In other words, a major force behind his qualities as a schlemiel-victim is the intensity of his beliefs and his unswerving sincerity. He is a victim and a schlemiel because he cares. In this sense, he accepts responsibility for his character. Those around him, like the Missourians who so intrigued Ravage, would be more than happy to have him act like one of them. Levin's charm, however, is a product of his inability to go along in spite of his desire to be part of the group. He finds that he cannot do the easy thing. In one of his conversations with a colleague, Levin reveals these aspects of himself.

> "The way the world is now," Levin said, "I sometimes feel I'm engaged in a great irrelevancy, teaching people how to write who don't know what to write. I can give them subjects but not subject matter. I worry I'm not teaching how to keep civilization from destroying itself." The instructor laughed embarrassedly. "Imagine that, Bucket, I know it sounds ridiculous, pretentious. I'm not particularly gifted—ordinary if the truth be told—with a not very talented intellect, and how much good would I do, if any? Still, I have the strongest urge to say they must understand what humanism means or they won't know when freedom no longer exists. And that they must either be the best—masters or ideas and of themselves— or choose the best to lead them; in either case democracy wins. I have the strongest compulsion to be involved with such thoughts in the classroom, if you know what I mean." (*NL*, 109)

In one sense, this speech sounds like Malamud's voice in almost a Howellsian form of address to the audience announcing moral priorities and principles. However, it clearly also is designed for comic effect portraying for sophisticated readers Sy Levin as a kind of Miss Lonelyhearts of the humanities and academic freedom. At the same time, the speech opens an important window to Levin's consciousness and adds depth to his qualities as a character. The result is not an epic clash between Sy Levin, the

Matthew Arnold of Cascadia, and the forces of darkness and evil in the form of the corrupt and cowardly department administration. Rather, we get a realistic encounter between a born loser and defender of lost causes who fumbles his way to a self-determined defeat that leaves him carrying the moral baggage for others. Certainly, any sense of victory or triumph for Levin occurs with enough ambiguity, irony, and loss to maintain consistency with the central qualities of his character. Although he proves capable of getting the woman to leave with him, his initial status as a surrogate lover for her and her dubious distinctions and qualities tend to mitigate the value of his triumph. Furthermore, any moral victory he achieves goes unrecognized while his slight impact on improving the department meets with deep silence from his colleagues. He leaves as a failure again but seems able to face his new problems and his "new life."

However, while Sy Levin functions as a realistic modern hero in the manner of the victim and the schlemiel figure, the novel itself belongs in the tradition of the American jeremiad. Through the character of a lonely "pariah" figure, who is not that much unlike classic American loners and nonconformists, Malamud attacks and criticizes his society and culture for failing to live up to its ideal vision of itself. Moreover, he does this by debunking one myth of America—the myth of regeneration in the West—while revivifying a modern version of America as an ideal consistent with the rhetoric of the jeremiad. Clearly, Malamud sees Levin as a fragile guardian of the values and ideals of the myth of America just as Yakov Bok in *The Fixer* must tragically assume the burden of being Jewish in a way that makes him appear to be both the archetypal victim and the hero. In addition, in *A New Life*, Malamud leaves intact the narrative structure of the myth of America as it has emerged out of the Jewish urban experience. The one important variation in this book is the Northwest setting, but Malamud in effect simply has moved the city novel in the form of Sy Levin's consciousness into the country. The shikse in the novel ties many of these themes together by indicating that she had literally "called" Levin in the mythic sense to perform his mission in the Northwest because of his Jewish looks. Because of her role in the selection process for the job, she was instrumental in hiring Levin. She says, "'Your picture reminded me of a Jewish boy I knew in college who was very kind to me during a trying time in my life.'" "'So I was chosen,' Levin said" (*NL*, 331).

In the light of the rhetorical aspects of this novel, it is significant that the hero of Malamud's recent novel *Dubin's Lives* has studied and written biographies about some of America's most important nineteenth-century Jeremiahs—Lincoln, Thoreau, Whitman, Twain. It is also interesting that *The Tenants*, another Malamud novel written after *A New Life*, concerns a conflict between a Jewish writer and a black writer. In their competition and hostility they live what they write so that fantasy, fiction, and reality all intermingle. The novel suggests that the outcome of their struggle will help determine who will write the future story of America. "'No Jew can treat me like a man—male or female,'" the black writer says to the Jew. "'You think you are the Chosen People. Well, you are wrong on that. *We* are the Chosen People from as of now on. You gonna find that out soon enough, you gonna lose your fuckn pride.'"[12] The novel ends with no false resolution of the conflict or bright promise for the future. It does, however, perform the vital function of dramatizing the central challenge facing the myth of America today. Can the myth work as a means of consensus and unity for blacks and other minorities?

In 1883, a Jewish poet, Emma Lazarus, who saw herself as a disciple of Ralph Waldo Emerson, metaphorically extended the myth of America to new immigrants through her poem "The New Colossus," which transformed the meaning of the Statue of Liberty into a symbol of asylum. More recently some black leaders also saw the destiny of blacks in terms of joining the myth of American destiny and national consensus. As Bercovitch has noted, Martin Luther King, Jr., attacked segregation "as a violation of the American dream."[13] Similar rhetoric has been adopted by leaders of other ethnic and minority groups such as Cesar Chavez, the Mexican American leader.

At the same time, the question of the viability of the myth in our own day remains. Strident voices often call for a kind of separatism reminiscent of the antijeremiad tradition. Among other things, such radicals fear destruction through absorption into the national consensus. Moreover, some of our best students of American pluralism and consensus question whether any meaningful consensus can exist today. Thus, John Higham believes that contemporary concerns with power and status among ethnic groups have superseded the earlier quest for "an inclusive community" that makes pluralism possible. "Apparently," Higham writes, "a decent multiethnic society must rest on a unifying ideology, faith, or myth. One of our tasks today is to learn how to revitalize a common faith amid multiplying claims for status and power."[14]

The response of Jews to this challenge is interesting. For one thing, for some Jews the myth of America itself may serve as a conservative influence. The so-called new conservatism of some Jewish intellectuals perhaps can be explained as a natural outgrowth of those values associated with their original allegiance to the myth of America.[15] Unfortunately, such conservative positions may cast some Jews in the role once played by Adams and Turner. A failure to incorporate new people and groups into the myth and national consensus can lead to a kind of caste system and cultural isolationism that at one time assured the political impotence and the downfall of established Protestants who were so afraid that the New Jerusalem of America would become a home for too many Jews. It would be a mistake for the Jews to imitate the "real Americans" in this regard. As Thomas Sowell says, "In a sense, Jews are the classic American success story—from rags to riches against all opposition. Moreover, like other groups that have found in the United States opportunities denied them in their homelands, Jews have been proud and patriotic Americans. Yet the history of Jews is longer and larger than the history of the United States. At other times and other places, Jews have risen to heights of prosperity and influence, only to have it all destroyed in unpredictable outbursts of anti-Semitic fury. Jews could not readily become complacent members of the establishment, however much they might possess all of its visible signs."[16] Rather than complacency or fear, the times obviously demand the kind of cultural and political invention that has characterized the contribution of modern Jews to American life and the American ideology.

PART II

Ideology and Culture

Chapter 3

The American Way
From the Colonial Era to
Louis Brandeis, Sidney Hillman, and
the Liberal Consensus

Among the crew that sailed to the New World with Columbus in 1492 were many Marranos, Spaniards of Jewish descent who were forced to convert to Christianity. It is possible that one of these converts named Luis de Torres was a translator in the initial landing party. Many other Jews were involved in financing and developing Columbus's mission to the New World. Ironically, in the summer of the same year that America was discovered, Ferdinand and Isabella expelled some 100,000 to 150,000 Jews. These Jews began one of the most momentous migrations in the Diaspora since some of their descendants ultimately found their way to New Amsterdam in 1654 where they became the first Jewish settlers in America. The Jews who remained behind in Spain following the expulsion in 1492 existed as Marranos (a term that could mean "swine" when used by the enemies of such converts) under the continual threat of the Inquisition initiated by Ferdinand and Isabella in 1480. The Inquisition lasted officially for three and a half centuries. For those Jews who left in 1492, the first stop was Portugal. They were expelled a year later and forced to move on to other countries, including Holland. Some of those who settled in Holland eventually went to what was then the Dutch colony of Brazil. When Portugal arrogated the colony, the Jews left for New Amsterdam. Thus, the first Jewish immigrants to America were twenty-four Sephardic Jews (Spanish Jews as opposed to Ashkenazim, or German Jews) who arrived from Recife, Brazil.

The meaning of this migration toward freedom, which began in 1492, would have shocked not only the Christians but the Marranos who had supported Columbus. As Salo Baron writes, "Indeed, the men behind Columbus would have been deeply disconcerted had they foreseen that the new countries were to become havens of refuge for the persecuted of their own and their successors' tyrannical regimes."[1]

The Jews who arrived in New Amsterdam immediately encountered the opposition of Governor Peter Stuyvesant. However, through their refusal to abide Stuyvesant's intolerance, these Jews in effect established a paradigm for what would become the basic Jewish American experience. The new immigrants appealed for and received help from the Jewish members of the board of the Dutch West India Company. The success of their efforts was the first intimation of how America would be different for the Jews. There would be many cases of individual discrimination and prejudice.[2] The kind of arrogance and intolerance evidenced by Stuyvesant would not be uncommon. In addition, there would be attempts during the early years of colonial history to restrict Jewish liberties. But in fact there would never be any official national discrimination or policy against the Jews in America. As many scholars have indicated, in America Jews began with emancipation.[3] Especially when compared with their status elsewhere throughout the Diaspora, the Jews in America were treated primarily as individuals on an equal basis with other religious groups. As Milton Konvitz writes, "The Jews who came to the United States found this country to be indeed a New World. For the first time in their lives they did not need to apologize for their religious difference. . . . In America, although Jews were subject to some civil and political disabilities in the colonies, and even at times in some of the states, as citizens of the United States they enjoyed full equality with other citizens."[4]

Accordingly, the tradition of the New Covenant between the Jewish writer and thinker and the American idea did not grow out of a political or cultural vacuum. It was based on a history of acceptance in America and an appreciation by Jews for the idea of America as a new ideological reality in the world. The New Covenant emerged out of the dialectic formed between the American ideology and the Jewish experience of it. The reality of the ideology paved the way, so to speak, for the writers and thinkers who later took for granted their role as prophets of America. Thus, it is important to understand the nature and meaning of the relationship of Jews to the ideology of America. The connection between Jews and the American Way was constructed by many Jews who not only adopted the American Way and were adopted by it but who also worked to change and modernize it. Different students of contemporary political theory from Raymond Williams to Ben Halpern have developed theories of the definition and role of modern ideology.[5] However, the American Way, as Sacvan Bercovitch indicates, seems truly unique among modern ideologies because it associates a total system of political beliefs, behavior, and institutions with a national entity that in turn claims universal appeal to all men. Thus, in his study of American ideology, Yehoshua Arieli writes, "In the United States, national consciousness was shaped by social and political values which claimed universal validity and which were nevertheless the American way of life."[6] Arieli elaborates on how its identification with a national culture and character gives the American Way as an ideological "ism" a unique quality over other modern ideologies. He writes, "Like socialists and communists, Americans believed that their social system was universally applicable to all mankind. This position was unique in the contemporary world. Socialism, communism, and humanitarian liberalism never identified themselves with the interest of any particular nation; their sphere of action transcended national boundaries and interests, although communism under certain conditions furthered nationalistic movements as a means toward an end." Arieli also maintains that the elements of the American Way do speak to the interests of modern men. He writes, "Democracy and liberty, 'the American way of life,' 'the system of individualism,' or 'the free enterprise system' conveyed a message of universal truth, based upon a total world view."[7] Thus, the American Way offered what so many Jews wanted so desperately—a national identity and home combined with an ideology that could make them part of the world community and human history. The fact that many of the values and beliefs of the American Way derived from or were intimately related to Hebrew teachings and Jewish life made the attraction of America even greater to many Jews.

A landmark in the history of the Jewish experience in the American ideology can be found in the famous correspondence between President George Washington and Moses Seixas of the Newport congregation in Rhode Island during August 1790. With the new nation formed and the Constitution finally ratified, the Jews of Newport, like those Jews in other cities such as Savannah, obviously felt the need for a clarification of their status. Seixas's strategy in approaching Washington on the issue of Jewish rights in America is interesting. Obviously aware of the fragility through-out history of the Jewish situation in other countries, Seixas attempts to deal with this insecurity by combining the confidence of an American with the eloquence and tact of a diplomat representing a nation within a nation. Seixas writes, "Deprived as we have hitherto been of the invalu-able rights of free citizens, we now . . . behold a Government . . . which to bigotry gives no sanction, to persecution no assistance—but generously affording to All liberty of conscience, and immunities of citizenship—deeming every one, of whatever nation, tongue, or language equal parts of the great governmental machine. . . . For all the blessings of civil and religious liberty which we enjoy under an equal and benign administra-tion we desire to send up our thanks."[8] Thus, by assuming the equality of Jews, Seixas pretends a confidence about Jewish life in America which dissimulates the very uncertainty that inspired the letter in the first place.

Furthermore, the statement from Seixas is of importance because of the response it elicited from Washington. Not only did Washington acquiesce to the assertions of equality, but he adopted Seixas's very language in a manner that indicates their compatibility. Washington wrote that "the government of the United States, which gives to bigotry no sanction, to persecution no assistance, requires only that they who live under its pro-tection should demean themselves as good citizens, in giving it on all occasions their effectual support." He happily assured the Jews that in America "every one shall sit in safety under his own vine and fig-tree, and there shall be none to make him afraid." However, as a Deist, Washington took one additional step beyond affirming the ideas of Jewish equality and liberty espoused by Seixas. As Morris Schappes notes, Washington repre-sents a new attitude toward the concept of the toleration of religious minorities. In a sense, he advances the idea of toleration by denying the need for it as something almost medieval. For Washington, toleration implies inferiority and condescension rather than equality and recogni-tion. He writes, "All possess alike liberty of conscience and immunities of citizenship. It is now no more that toleration is spoken of, as if it was by the indulgence of one class of people, that another enjoyed the exercise of their inherent natural rights."[9] Washington's idea of toleration comes close to representing a revolution in the treatment of and attitude toward Jews. As Lawrence H. Fuchs says, "Here was a new concept of rights—

not privileges—and of citizenship which was defined solely by obedience to a non-coercive set of rules established to permit and encourage the free exercise of religion, speech, and enterprise."[10] Washington's espousal of this new way of dealing with Jews demonstrates how much better and freer life could be for Jews in America than in Europe. This policy turned America into a beacon for many of the Jews of Europe, while for those Jews who stayed in Europe the freedom of America became an example toward which to strive in their own countries. As Richard B. Morris writes, "America's toleration toward Jews and other religious minorities, and the steps taken to guarantee their civil and political rights, served as a spur to the movement on the European continent for the emancipation of the Jews, so long victims of discriminatory laws. In their petition to the French National Assembly of January 1790, the Jews of France pointed to America, citing that Revolutionary land for having 'rejected the word toleration from its code,' for, they cogently reasoned, 'to tolerate is, in fact, to suffer that which you could, if you wished, prevent and prohibit.'"[11]

As father of his country and as a combination of a Moses and Joshua leading a new chosen people, Washington's attitude toward the Jews constitutes a welcome to them to follow the ideology of the American Way. Through Washington, the Jews in effect proved the universality and applicability of the American Way to all people. As a way of life synthesizing values, belief, and institutions, the American ideology provided the necessary counterpart and support for the myth of America as a promised land. The belief in America as an ideology in itself, as an "ism," sustained the myth. For two centuries it offered the Jews of Europe a political alternative to the ideologies and revolutions in their native lands. An example of such a Jew is Leopold Kompert, who had grown discouraged about the possibility of being emancipated in mid-nineteenth-century Europe. Feeling betrayed as a Jew and as a free man by the nations of Europe, Kompert in an article published on May 6, 1848, called for his fellow Jews to move "on to America." "No help has come to us!," he writes. "The sun of freedom has risen for the Fatherland; for us it is merely a bloody northern light." As a result he proposes a mass migration to America. After noting the irony of fleeing to a new world discovered under the Spanish flag of a nation "bespattered with the blood of thousands of our brethren," he says, "our yearning now goes out to that same America, thither you should depart."[12]

Kompert's passion for freedom and America is an important part of the developing relationship between the Jews and the American Way. It dramatizes the Jewish sense of personal and cultural investment in the success of the American ideology. Throughout much of the nineteenth century, the steady immersion of a relatively small but quickly growing Jewish population (from 6,000 in 1826 to about 150,000 in 1860) was achieved with little real drama or controversy.[13] The one major exception involved the famous incident during the Civil War of General Ulysses S. Grant's notorious General Order No. 11 of December 1862 requiring all "Jews, as a class" to leave the area of Tennessee within twenty-four hours. The incident grew out of a scandal concerning cotton speculation and trading. Grant was disturbed because the corruption not only pervaded parts of the military and federal bureaucracy but also touched his own family. For the Jews in America, the episode is significant because of their refusal to be turned into scapegoats. Telegrams were immediately sent to President Lincoln. Meetings were held with Jewish leaders, members of Congress, and Lincoln, who canceled Grant's order. In his discussion of this event, Milton Konvitz notes of the Jews of Kentucky that in making their protests to Lincoln, "there was nothing cringing in their words, no plea for mere toleration or compassion; the Jews took their stand on their legal, civil rights, on their rights as American citizens."[14] The vigor of their response indicates how much the Jews had grown in terms of confidence and power, even since the days of Seixas's correspondence with Washington. But it also needs to be remembered that the Grant incident does not foreshadow a turning point or new beginning in Jewish history in America. Rather, it was the culmination of a growing tradition and relationship between Jews and America. It is important because it so well dramatizes what were in fact the norms of the Jewish situation in this country. The confidence of Jews in America allowed them to concentrate through much of the nineteenth century on achieving a place within the American economy and American society. Partly because of the heavy influx of German Jews, the mid-nineteenth century in America marks the beginning of the establishment of those Jewish commercial and financial dynasties such as the Seligmans, Loebs, Schiffs, Strauses, Lehmans, and Guggenheims. In fact, the same Grant who issued his notorious order also asked Joseph Seligman to become his secretary of the treasury.[15]

However, in the last two decades of the century, the growing power and prominence of these Jews and the arrival of the great masses of Jews from

Eastern Europe altered the dynamics of the Jewish experience in America. Along with the changes in the contours and compositions of the Jewish community in America, there developed a concomitant rise in what John Higham calls ideological and social anti-Semitism. Ideological anti-Semitism as practiced and preached by Populists, patricians, and the urban poor constituted an attack on the place of the Jews in American life and in the American Way.[16] Such anti-Semitism identified the Jews as a threat to American institutions and values. Because deeper social, economic, and cultural crises behind ideological anti-Semitism posed a real threat to Jewish life, it became imperative in this atmosphere for Jews to rearticulate both the meaning of the ideology of America and the inherent right of Jews to be a part of it. It was important to state that in the very terms and traditions of the American ideology, equality and freedom for Jews were essential to the success of the American experiment in democracy. One of those most ready to publicize and explain the special relationship between Jews and American history was Oscar S. Straus. The author of a book entitled *The Origin of the Republican Form of Government in the United States* (1885), Straus saw his own family's rise to success and wealth as proof of his thesis about the importance of the relationship between Jewish and American cultures to American liberty. His politically liberal father, Lazarus, had emigrated from Otterburg, Bavaria, in 1852 because of the oppression and discrimination of life in Germany. Soon after, the rest of the family arrived in America including the mother, Sara, a daughter, Hermine, and the sons, Isidor, Nathan, and the youngest, Oscar. After initial successes in Georgia, the family moved north to New York to business triumphs that resulted in ownership of R. H. Macy and Company and partnership in Abraham and Straus. While brothers Isidor and Nathan continued the family tradition of business leadership and innovation, Oscar became interested in law, scholarship and, ultimately, in public service and politics. His career culminated in his ambassadorship to Turkey and his services as secretary of commerce and labor under Theodore Roosevelt. Straus, however, saw more in such success than a testimony to the generosity of the American Way. He was too knowledgeable about Judaism and Jewish history to believe that his religious and cultural heritage was in a subservient relationship to another culture. American culture, he maintained, derived as much from the culture and traditions of the Jews as they received from the advantages of the American Way.[17]

Straus believed that both the Puritans and the Founding Fathers of the Republic relied upon Jewish sources for their intellectual and spiritual inspiration. For Straus, the Jews provided not only the theocratic model for the Puritans but the model for the American Republic as well. Jews, he felt, set the example for the democratic state. In "The Hebrew Commonwealth, The First Federal Republic," he wrote: "Thus we see at this early period of mankind—1,500 years and more before the Christian era, before Rome had obtained a foothold in history, 500 years before Homer sang, and 1,000 years before Plato had dreamed of his ideal republic, when all Western Europe was an untrodden wilderness—the children of Israel on the banks of the Jordan, who had just emerged from centuries of bondage, not only recognized the guiding principles of civil and religious liberty that 'all men are created equal,' that God and the law are the only kings, but also established a free commonwealth, a pure democratic-republic under a written constitution, 'a government of the people, by the people, and for the people.'"[18] He proved that Jewish culture and thought were central to the founding and life of the Republic by quoting the leading ministers of colonial and revolutionary times. He referred to the works of men like Ezra Stiles of Yale and Jonathan Mayhew of Harvard. Thus, in "The Influence of the Hebrew Commonwealth upon the Origin of Republican Government in the United States," he noted that "a volume would not contain all the politico-theological discourses delivered during the decade prior to the restoration of peace, wherein the Hebrew Commonwealth was held up as a model, and its history as a guide for the American people in their mighty struggle for the blessings of civil and religious liberty."[19] Therefore, to make his list of authorities both manageable and credible he insisted upon quoting only the "discourses" of "ministers who were eminent not only in the pulpit, but were equally distinguished as scholars, as patriots, and as legislators." While the heavy reliance of these men upon Jewish writings and symbols seemed to Straus to indicate the importance of Judaism to the American Way, he was equally impressed to find that congregations and popular audiences apparently responded to the stream of biblical references. He wrote, "These constant references, parallels, and analogies to the children of Israel in their struggle for political liberty would not have been made again and again if they did not meet with a responsive echo in the minds and sentiments of the large audiences to whom they were addressed throughout the thirteen colonies."[20] In addition to Stiles and Mayhew, he also referred to such figures as Samuel Langdon of Harvard, the Reverend George Duffield of the Third Presbyterian Church in Philadelphia, and the Reverend Simon Howard of the West Church of Boston. Straus, however, could not resist frequently going outside of the clergy to find American leaders who were influenced by Jewish sources in their thinking. Thus, it was of special importance to Straus that he discovered in Benjamin Franklin, John Adams, and Thomas Jefferson almost a visible sign of appreciation for the Hebrew experience as a foundation for the Republic. Straus wrote that it was "not at all surprising that the committee, which was appointed on the same day the Declaration of Independence was adopted, consisting of Dr. Franklin, Mr. Adams, and Mr. Jefferson, to prepare a device for a seal for the United States, should, as they did, have proposed as such device, Pharaoh sitting in an open chariot, a crown on his head and a sword in his hand, passing through the dividing waters of the Red Sea in pursuit of the Israelites; with rays from a pillar of fire beaming on Moses, who is represented as standing on the shore extending his hand over the sea, causes it to overwhelm Pharaoh; and underneath, the motto: 'Rebellion to tyrants is obedience to God.' "[21]

As Straus's activities and prominence in national politics increased, his sense of the importance of Jewish history and tradition to the American Way continued. In an address delivered in 1911, the year before he ran as a Progressive for governor of New York, Straus strongly reiterated his theme of the connection between Jewish and American traditions. Speaking before a meeting of the American Hebrew Congregations he said, "The spirit of Judaism became the mother spirit of Puritanism in Old England; and the history of Israel and its democratic model under the Judges inspired and guided the Pilgrims and Puritans in their wandering hither and in laying the foundation of their commonwealths in New England. The piety and learning of the Jews bridged the chasm of the middle ages; and the torch they bore amidst trials and sufferings lighted the pathway from the ancient to the modern world." In this talk Straus also emphasizes a theme that was important to Reform Jews. He argues that America operates for the Jews as a homeland and can satisfy the need for a return to Zion. America, for Straus, becomes a new Zion just as it was for the Puritans. He says, "While Zionism is a pious hope and a vision out of despair in countries where the victims of oppression are still counted by

millions, the republicanism of the United States is the nearest approach to
the ideals of the prophets of Israel that ever has been incorporated in the
form of a State. . . . Ours is peculiarly a promised land wherein the spirit
of the teachings of the ancient prophets inspired the work of the fathers of
our country."[22]

Straus's political philosophy as well as his sense of identity depended to
a considerable degree upon his fusion of the two cultures and traditions
that nurtured him. He was not an "uptown" Jew interested in exchanging
his Jewish identity and responsibilities for the comfort of assimilation.
Naomi Cohen suggests that "rather than choose between Americanism
and Judaism, or even feel required to compartmentalize the two as separate entities, he worked out a different solution to the problem of identity
which confronted all emancipated Jews. He fused his Jewish ideals with
his interpretation of Americanism." Cohen argues that "Straus bridged his
Judaism and Americanism by finding foundations common to both lega-
cies. In his mind loyalty to the two traditions raised no question of incom-
patibility. Indeed, rightly or wrongly, he saw them linked historically. His
numerous writings and speeches on the role of the Jew in the exploration
and colonization of the New World, and on early Jewish history as the
source of inspiration for American settlers, had aimed to show the historical connection between Jews and America. Straus also saw an almost religious tie between Judaism and America, for the United States was 'a
promised land wherein the spirit of the ancient prophets inspired the
work of the fathers of our country.'"[23]

Unfortunately, Straus's abstract model of the harmonious unity between his two cultures and tradition had little flexibility. His detached
understanding of the historical relationship between Americanism and Judaism served to sustain his political ideology which remained basically
conservative in spite of his commitments to Roosevelt and progressivism.
His interpretation of history and the political system was designed to
preserve the traditions he so loved as he understood them. Ultimately, his
model failed because it did not clarify the problems of the present and did
not anticipate the future. It only brilliantly reaffirmed a past without making it relevant to the economic, cultural, and political upheavals that characterized the first two decades of this century and have continued to
dominate our own times. His model of history, politics, and class effectively dismissed the ideas that challenged him without proffering work-

able alternatives. Thus, in a speech in Georgia in 1908 entitled "Our Commercial Age," he said: "Yes, we welcome the immigrant to our country, the self-respecting and honest-minded alien, no matter from what country he comes, who is willing to share with us not only the blessings but also the duties and responsibilities of our great country; but they, as well as all our people, must understand that in this land of liberty, equality, and justice there is no room for socialism, communism, collectivism, or any other form of 'ism' than Americanism, which rests upon the Ten Commandments, the Declaration of Independence, and the Constitution of the United States."[24] In a speech four years later he said, "Radicalism in the United States gets little support from our people, because with awakened intelligence they learn to know that the rights of each consonant with the liberty of all lay at the basis of our system of democracy."[25] Straus probably did not recognize the paternalism and condescension in his own words. A man of great intelligence and cultivation, he felt so secure in his marriage of Judaism and Americanism that he failed to fully understand that the strength of both traditions rested in part on their ability to change and grow. Thus, he was unable to alter his own classic concepts to make them compatible with modern realities. "Since his own personal achievements had taught him the path to success," writes Naomi Cohen, "Straus remained unconvinced of the need to go much beyond the classical ideal of free and equal competition. His reform activities, which were for the most part conservative, stressed the ideal of individual liberty and the need to restore a social framework wherein such liberty could function unfettered."[26] The historic basis of his perspective from within his own class and ideology hindered Straus from imagining changes in what he called the "American Spirit." It would take another Jewish American thinker of this period to conceptualize and construct the bridges between cultures and periods that so interested Straus. Like Straus, Louis D. Brandeis believed in the importance to human history of the union between Judaism and Americanism. In contrast to Straus, however, Brandeis saw that such marriages should produce new ideas and institutions in order to enable future generations to assume control over their own destiny.

In terms of this study, there are three key parts to the thought of Louis Dembitz Brandeis, each of which merged in the mature years of Brandeis's life to form one basic and consistent philosophy. First, as a Progressive and reformist, Brandeis attempted to modernize the American ideology by adapting traditional values and ideals to contemporary economic and industrial conditions and cultural mores. Second, his concern for the daily working lives and circumstances of the common man formed a bridge over which socialistic and radically oriented European Jews could travel in order to moderate and Americanize their European-based ideologies. Brandeis's reformist philosophy and liberal ideology and his intimate involvement with labor and popular causes presented a real alternative to radical dogmas learned in Europe. Finally, Brandeis saw a connection between Judaism and Americanism that was not only natural but essential to the vitality and health of both cultures. Brandeis proffered a total world view that helped Jews and Americans as a whole deal with and understand the complexities of the rapidly changing world around them.

Brandeis's interest in America as an ideology was influenced at least in part by his fascination for the New England Way. In an early biography of Brandeis, his friend Jacob de Haas, who had helped Brandeis find his way to Zionism, wrote that Brandeis had "adopted wholly the Puritanism of early New England." De Haas was thinking primarily of Brandeis's "Spartan simplicity of habit" rather than his way of thinking or "philosophy."[27] However, a recent biographer more perceptively analyzes the depth of Brandeis's commitment to the Puritan way of life and thought. "In Brandeis's developing identity, his relation to the traditions of New England played a pivotal role," writes Allon Gal. "Brandeis deeply admired native New Englanders and their heritage of individualism, hard work, excellence, reform, and tempered realism. He wrote to his sister: 'the sense of being always under the necessity of preparedness to justify myself—is doubtless as wholesome as Puritan ancestry.'"[28] Described once by a law partner as "'more Brahmin than the Brahmins,'" Brandeis, according to Melvin Urofsky, "was intellectually and emotionally a New Englander of the finest variety."[29]

Ironically, Brandeis did not discover the New England that he loved so much until his nineteenth year when he entered Harvard Law School. Born in Louisville in 1856 and influenced primarily by the uncle after whom he was named, Brandeis's parents had emigrated to America after the failures of the 1848 revolution in Bohemia. His family later sent him to a *Realschule* in Dresden for advanced work, but he decided against further education in Europe in order to begin the study of law. He entered

Harvard without any real strong connections or ties to the region. However, the combination of the university's intellectual life, the atmosphere of Boston, and an expanding community of friends all changed his life. "As a student," writes Gal, "Brandeis came to love deeply New England's landscapes. And Boston's cultural and intellectual life totally absorbed him. It is in the context of his feelings about the region that his reverence for Emerson is understandable. 'I have been indulging in Emerson,' he wrote, 'and can conscientiously say that my admiration for him is on the increase. I have read a few sentences of his which are alone enough to make a man immortal.'"[30] As Gal reports, Brandeis's friend and first law partner, Samuel D. Warren, told him, "'In many ways you are a better example of New England virtues than the natives.'"[31] Nevertheless, it was partly out of this attraction to the region that Brandeis encouraged the development of new laws and institutions designed to maintain basic American values of individualism, liberty, and democracy that he believed to have derived from the New England Way. He maintained that "the conditions in the early days of the colonies and states of New England" were such that "American democracy reached there its fullest expression; for the Puritans were trained in implicit obedience to stern duty by constant study of the Prophets."[32] Believing firmly in the modern relevance of these values, Brandeis moved in his middle years to help create a new social philosophy designed to make it possible for all individuals to achieve what he considered to be the "True Americanism" of "the American ideals," which consisted of "the development of the individual for his own and the common good; the development of the individual through liberty; and the attainment of the common good through democracy and social justice."[33]

Motivated by the desire to democratize the New England Way for all Americans, Brandeis by 1896 was known as "The People's Attorney."[34] At that point in his career, he had been practicing law in Boston for almost twenty years. He built his firm into an extremely influential and lucrative enterprise partly by developing lasting relationships with Boston's mercantile and commercial interests such as the Filenes and the Hechts. Many of the clients also overlapped with his growing interest in the Jewish community. By the 1890s, however, a combination of many factors—local politics, rising social discrimination and prejudice, the inflexibility of privileged leaders, and the failure of national leadership and conventional politics—inspired Brandeis to become increasingly active in Progressive and reform causes. Thus, up until his controversial nomination by Woodrow Wilson in 1916 to the Supreme Court, Brandeis led an enormous range of legal and civic battles through the courts, public hearings, and the press. In *Mueller* vs. *Oregon* in 1908, Brandeis argued and won a case for the legality of limiting working hours for women. This case earned him fame as an advocate of the modern "living law" philosophy of jurisprudence that emphasizes the connection between law and social and cultural realities.[35] He mediated the 1910 cloakmakers strike in New York by devising the landmark solution of "the preferential union shop" in which union men received preference for employment. He fought for insurance and banking reforms and the rights of labor against monopolies and trusts. To many such as the historian Charles A. Beard, Brandeis became an important leader for reform and change. Beard asked, "Is the America of tomorrow to be the society of 'the new freedom' so effectively portrayed by Mr. Brandeis and the President who appointed him? Or will the march of integration in finance and industry override the small enterprises which they sought to preserve against extinction?"[36]

Brandeis, therefore, became an important symbol in the Progressive and reform battles during the first two decades of the century. The aura created by his record of successful activities and causes made him onerous to conservatives such as Henry Cabot Lodge.[37] Enemies like Lodge, however, helped turn Brandeis into a hero to the Jews of America. By 1909 the Jewish press such as the *Jewish Advocate* of Boston clearly identified Brandeis as a Jewish leader.[38] To the Jewish reader of both the Jewish and the English press, Brandeis's interest in reform, unionism, and regulation presented alternatives to European ideologies of the times. In a lengthy address, "Life Insurance: The Abuses and the Remedies," presented in 1905 in Boston, he said:

> Our Government does not yet grapple successfully with the duties
> which it has assumed, and should not extend its operations at least
> until it does. But whatever and however strong our conviction
> against the extension of governmental functions may be, we shall in-
> evitably be swept farther toward socialism unless we can curb the ex-
> cesses of our financial magnates. The talk of the agitator alone does
> not advance socialism a step; but the formation of great trusts—the
> huge railroad consolidations—the insurance "racers" with the atten-

dant rapacity or the dishonesty of their potent managers, and their frequent corruption of councils and legislatures is hastening us almost irresistibly into socialistic measures. The great captains of industry and of finance, who profess the greatest horror of the extension of governmental functions, are the chief makers of socialism. Socialistic thinkers smile approvingly at the operations of Morgan, Perkins and Rockefeller, and of the Hydes, McCalls and McCurdys. They see approaching the glad day when monopoly shall have brought all industry and finance under a single head, so that with the cutting of a single neck, as Nero vainly wished for his Christian subjects, destruction of the enemy may be accomplished. Our great trust-building, trust-abusing capitalists have in their selfish short-sightedness become the makers of socialism, proclaiming by their acts, like the nobles of France, "After us, the Deluge!"[39]

This sort of negative argument, designed to arouse fears by waving the dreaded flag of socialism, does not fairly characterize Brandeis's usual approach to public issues and debate. However, it is instructive because it indicates that he saw socialism as a danger to the American Way. For him socialism did not represent a means for extending freedom into the modern age. So, when Brandeis used the term Americanism, he was well aware of the attention other "isms" were receiving in the world. He was afraid that antidemocratic forces within liberal capitalism would invite the system's collapse and encourage a socialistic alternative. However, he also believed that the system as represented by the American ideology contained the seeds for its own renewal. He turned his attention to nurturing such a new life. In his actions and speeches, therefore, Brandeis tried to demonstrate how the American ideology was part of a usable past that could be helpful in solving contemporary social problems.

Accordingly, his social and economic writings from 1896 to 1916 seem to concentrate on two themes that he considered essential to the continued relevance of the American ideology. Brandeis understood that the ideology was based in part on the assumption of an economy of free and independent entrepreneurs operating in an open capitalistic system. He was concerned about how that model could apply to the economic conditions of his own times during which America became a nation of salaried workers. The dependence of these workers upon impersonal corporations ran counter to the liberal vision of a nation of independent property owners and producers. His concern about the economic dependence of these workers was related to his interests in the meaning of what he called "industrial democracy or liberty." He believed that the values and ideals of the American ideology demanded the expansion of the concepts of freedom and participation into the industrial and economic realm. He believed that workers should have a means for participating in the industrial and economic decision-making processes that affected their daily lives. He felt that the survival of democracy depended upon the ability of the culture to invent the kinds of institutions and processes that would make such industrial liberty possible. "'We need,'" he said, "'*social inventions*, each of many able men adding his work until the invention is perfected.'" Many of Brandeis's causes and activities were focused on economic independence and security within the context of industrial democracy, and he believed that the failure to address these twin themes would hasten the trend toward inequality. "'We are sure to have for the next generation an ever-increasing contest between those who have and those who have not,'" he said.[40]

Brandeis's discussion of the independence of the salaried worker constitutes a radical redefinition of the meaning of freedom in modern society. He attempted to go beyond the traditional understanding of freedom in the American ideology in order to account for the changes that had transpired in the worker's daily life. "American democracy," he said, in a speech in 1911, "rests upon the basis of the free citizen. . . . We give thus to the citizen the rights of a free man. . . . Politically, the American workingman is free—so far as law can make him so. But is he really free? Can any man be really free who is constantly in danger of becoming dependent for mere subsistence upon somebody and something else than his own exertion and conduct? Men are not free while financially dependent upon the will of other individuals."[41] Brandeis's idea of economic freedom as a counterpart to traditional political freedom would seem inadequate to socialists and dangerously opportunistic to conservatives. However, it suggests the kind of systemic reforms that became an increasing part of later liberal economic programs. At the same time, he was willing to avoid government intervention in the economy if security for the individual could be gained through other means. In a speech concerning the monopolistic proclivities of the New Haven Railroad, he warned that "the efficiency of regulation, even within its acknowledged sphere, is quite limited." With a concession to competition that would hearten modern opponents of big government, Brandeis warned, "To abandon competition in transportation and rely upon regulation as a safeguard against the evils of monopoly would be like surrendering liberty and regulating despotism."[42] Thus, his concepts of reform reflected his business background and his continuing commitments to free enterprise.

Nevertheless, in spite of such qualifications, his program for economic freedom still amounted to a major change in emphasis in the American Way that aroused the ire of corporations and monopolies. With an optimism that once characterized the manner in which liberals viewed economic and political problems, Brandeis advocated cooperation between different segments of the economy, which he felt would restore security and independence to the individual. He believed that new forms of industrial and unemployment insurance along with new pension programs would be of great significance in assuring such independence. He maintained that one of the greatest forces for such security would be the union movement.

As early as 1902, Brandeis strongly defended the unions as being "largely instrumental in securing reasonable hours of labor and proper conditions of work; in raising materially the scale of wages, and in protecting women and children from industrial oppression. The trade unions have done this, not for the workingmen alone but for all of us; since the conditions under which so large a part of our fellow citizens work and live will determine, in great measure, the future of our country for good or for evil."[43] He soon came to feel that the future of political democracy and the American way of life depended upon the unions' ability to lead the nation toward industrial democracy.[44] Seeing the unions at first almost exclusively in terms of their importance for achieving economic gains and better working conditions, he began to believe they held a key to the survival of democracy because they had the potential to encourage significant worker participation in the economic process. In remarks before the United States Commission on Industrial Relations, he said, "Before we can really solve the problem of industrial unrest, the worker must have a part in the responsibility and management of the business." The goal of the union as Brandeis saw it was to help each worker achieve a sense of personal responsibility for his or her own welfare along with a sense of commitment to fellow workers. Gains made at the expense of such personal responsibility proved ultimately counterproductive because they undermined the very independence and individual strength the unions were created to nurture. Given his emphasis on character, his remarks before the commission are idealistic and Whitmanesque in tone. He said:

> We must bear in mind all the time that however much we may desire material improvement and must desire it for the comfort of the individual, that the United States is a democracy, and that we must have, above all things, men. It is the development of manhood to which any industrial and social system should be directed. We Americans are committed not only to social justice in the sense of avoiding things which bring suffering and harm, like unjust distribution of wealth; but we are committed primarily to democracy. The social justice for which we are striving is an incident of our democracy, not the main end. It is rather the result of democracy— perhaps its finest expression—but it rests upon democracy, which implies the rule by the people. And therefore the end for which we must strive is the attainment of rule by the people, and that involves industrial democracy as well as political democracy.[45]

The philosophy expressed here by Brandeis in 1914 and 1915 before the commission indicates the development of his social consciousness. Still basically progressive and reform-oriented, his remarks demonstrate an ideological openness to ideas and people. The unions in Brandeis's view should do more than fight for money and improved conditions while allowing management to exercise control over operations. Unions should also encourage individual and cultural freedom. This further step in Brandeis's thinking represents the rounding out of his social philosophy; it places his economic and political beliefs within the context of a democratic theory of culture. This step also may reflect an additional change, for it was just prior to this time that Brandeis gained a new sense of Jewish identity. A new openness to his own people, especially in the face of the anti-Semitism of Yankee society, may have helped him to conceptualize the possibility of a truly open and democratic culture. In addition, his renewed interest in Judaism seemed to cause the three key elements in his thought—the modernization of America as an ideology, the drive for reform and industrial democracy as an alternative to more radical ideologies, and the connection between Judaism and Americanism—to come together.

Brandeis's participation in the 1910 cloakmaker's strike helped to change his life not only because of his union activity but also because it enabled him to observe Jewish garment workers. Allon Gal writes:

> Brandeis was deeply moved by his New York experience. Several years later he described how, while striving for "the American ideals of democracy and social justice" in connection with this strike, he came "into close and almost continuous relations with Jews en masse, with employees and employers and with many who were but recent immigrants." He added: "I was impressed, deeply impressed, that these Jews with whom I dealt showed in a striking degree the qualities which, to my mind, make for the best American citizenship, that within them there was a true democratic feeling and a deep appreciation of the elements of social justice. . . . Observation and study revealed to me that this was not an accident, that it was due to the fact that twentieth-century ideals of America had been the age-old ideals of the Jews."[46]

Jacob de Haas points out that 1910 marks the first time that Brandeis ever took a "public part in Jewish affairs . . . though he had contributed to local Boston Jewish charities for many years."[47] Four years later, in response to war conditions, he accepted the post of chairman of the Provisional Executive Committee for General Zionist Affairs. Brandeis said, "I feel my disqualification for this task. Throughout long years which represent my own life, I have been to a great extent separated from Jews. I am very ignorant in things Jewish. But recent experiences, public and professional, have taught me this: I find Jews possessed of those very qualities which we of the twentieth century seek to develop in our struggle for justice and democracy: a deep moral feeling which makes them capable of noble acts; a deep sense of the brotherhood of man; and a high intelligence, the fruit of three thousand years of civilization."[48] Similarly, in an address dealing with Palestine in 1929, he noted that "I have lived most of my life largely apart from the Jewish people."[49] In spite of such separation and ignorance, Brandeis developed over a brief period an intense loyalty to Judaism that included a social philosophy of Jewish and American interdependence.

However, it also needs to be considered that the gusto with which Brandeis threw himself into his "new" Jewish identity may indicate a subsurface ambivalence about Judaism characteristic of those in the Diaspora.

He was profoundly aware of the minority status of Jews within America. In "A Call to the Educated Jew," he noted that "now it is one of the necessary incidents of a distinctive and minority people that the act of any one is in some degree attributed to the whole group. A single though inconspicuous instance of dishonorable conduct on the part of a Jew in any trade or profession has far-reaching evil effects extending to the many innocent members of the race."[50] The comment reveals a deep-seated insecurity and the feeling that in fact no Jew can be inconspicuous. It represents an attitude of responsibility toward membership in a minority group that probably would be rejected as unfair by most minority members today. It assumes the possibility of a cultural stigma or disability on all members of the minority. The fear of such a disability operates below the surface of Brandeis's description of the Jewish character in Austria in an essay with the unfortunate title "The Jewish Problem." In the speech Brandeis attempts to show how Zionism created a new strength in Jews. But the result tends to confirm stereotypes and a negative self-image:

> [Zionism's] effect upon the Jewish students of Austrian universities was immediate and striking. Until then they had been despised and often ill-treated. They had wormed their way into appointments and into the free professions by dint of pliancy, much humility, mental acuteness, and clandestine protection. If struck or spat upon by "Aryan" students, they rarely ventured to return the blow or the insult. But Zionism gave them courage. They formed associations, and learned athletic drill and fencing. Insult was requited with insult, and presently the best fencers of the fighting German corps found that Zionist students could gash cheeks quite as effectually as any Teuton, and the Jews were in a fair way to become the best swordsmen of the university. Today the purple cap of the Zionist is as respected as that of any academical association.[51]

This apologetic attitude over what he assumes to be negative Jewish behavior and character traits has its counterpart in an overcompensating myth of the Jew that Brandeis also espoused. Both attitudes indicate a defensiveness and uncertainty about Jewishness in Brandeis. Thus, in another essay Brandeis celebrates what he avows to be special Jewish qualities. "Whence comes this combination of qualities of mind, body and character? These are qualities with which every one of us is familiar, singly and in combination; which you find in friends and relatives; and which others doubtless discover in you."[52]

These ambiguities and conflicts that Brandeis felt seemed to become resolved by his identification of Jewish culture with Americanism. For Brandeis, Judaism, Americanism, and Zionism all became part of one effort to achieve freedom and democracy. Each part supported and maintained the other. Thus, his Zionism enriched his Jewish identity in a way that made him a better American. In "True Americanism," he maintained that "America has believed that each race had something of peculiar value which it can contribute to the attainment of those high ideals for which it is striving. America has believed that we must not only give to the immigrant the best that we have, but must preserve for America the good that is in the immigrant and develop in him the best of which he is capable. America has believed that in differentiation, not uniformity, lies the path of progress."[53] This attitude reflected the ideas of cultural pluralism espoused by Horace Kallen whom Brandeis knew through work with the Menorah Society at Harvard.[54] It was consistent with such a cultural philosophy for Brandeis to say that his "approach to Zionism was through Americanism."[55] He saw it as his responsibility as an American to encourage Jews to again assume the duties of "a priestly people today as they were in the prophetic days."[56] "By battling for the Zionist cause," he said in 1915, "the American ideal of democracy, of social justice and of liberty will be given wider expression."[57]

However, Brandeis also saw a deeper connection between Zionism and Americanism than a self-fulfilling confirmation of cultural pluralism. This link joined the origins and roots of American democracy to earlier Jewish concepts and history. Brandeis was like Straus in arguing that the Jewish commitment to democratic principles anticipated the American experience by many centuries. "The ability of the Russian Jew to adjust himself to America's essentially democratic conditions is not to be explained by Jewish adaptability," Brandeis argued. "The explanation lies mainly in the fact that the twentieth-century ideals of America have been the ideals of the Jew for more than twenty centuries. We have inherited these ideals of democracy and of social justice as we have the qualities of mind, body and character to which I referred."[58] In Palestine and Zionism, Brandeis saw something of a grand cultural and historic synthesis in which prophetic Judaism and modern Americanism were merged in the new Jewish pioneers. History for him seemed to unfold itself in this case in repetitive patterns that testified to the enrichment of both Judaism and Americanism. For the brave pioneers of Palestine, Brandeis maintained, should revivify the spirit of democracy in both Jewish and Christian Americans. In other words, the modern Jews of Palestine, like the earlier Jews in biblical history, should inspire America to realize its own democratic goals and ideals. Accordingly, he referred to the settlers in Palestine as "Jewish Pilgrim Fathers."[59] The very term, which he repeats various times, indicates how in Brandeis's mind the two cultures and traditions merged. While still separate and unique cultural entities, they have historic connections and a common destiny that make them one.

The capacity of Brandeis to change and to grow enabled him to play a unique role in the history of the Jews in America. Solidly entrenched in traditional values, he also was responsive to the ethnicity of the new immigrants and was committed as a true democrat to the working class. His own ideology developed in a manner that was consistent with his principles and with the revolutionary changes occurring within both American and Jewish cultures. The very qualities of openness that made Brandeis so sensitive to his times caused concern among the "uptown Jews."[60] In time, however, Brandeis's stature enabled him to become "the respected elder statesman of all Jewish factions."[61] In both popular political notions and serious political thought, Brandeis embodied an ideology that touched all aspects of the American Jewish community. His insight into the unique relationship of the Jews to the ideology of America can be compared with the stance of Louis Marshall and the American Jewish Committee, which was formed in 1906 and saw itself as the guardian of American civil liberties. On the other hand, his social philosophy of reform and activism reaches into the heart of modern unionism, especially in the garment industry. Brandeis's broad influence indicates something of the complexity of the relationship between Jewish and American ideology and thought.

In some ways the compatibility between the ideology of American Jews and the American Way is most clearly evidenced by the history and philosophy of the American Jewish Committee. In her book about the American Jewish Committee, Naomi Cohen describes the unique connection between the committee and American institutions: "To fight bigotry and to defend human freedoms, to uphold rational order, due process of law, and individual merit were in the self-interest of the group. But they were also the national ideals stamped by the Enlightenment upon eighteenth-century America. . . . The American Jewish Committee not only derived strength from American ideals, it helped sustain them."[62] From its very beginnings, the committee did indeed establish a pattern of defending Jewish interests and liberties not by appealing to group interests but by arguing in terms of American ideals and institutions, thus confirming how Americanism and Judaism overlapped. For example, Louis Marshall, who became the second president of the committee, argued in a letter in 1907 against immigration restriction because it would be "contrary to the genius of our institutions." To President Coolidge in 1924 he attacked the Ku Klux Klan as an "un-American monstrosity." Similarly, he criticized an Iowa lawyer for his language about Jews and blacks as being contrary to "the best traditions of America."[63] Also, it should be noted that in the section of his papers dealing with discrimination and bigotry, there is an impressive collection of letters and other materials demonstrating the extent of Marshall's active involvement in fighting for the civil rights of blacks, Native Americans, and Japanese. As his biographer states, "Marshall's sometimes shaken, but always abiding, faith in the American people, his vigor in the defense of the constitutional liberties of all minorities, and his passionate patriotism affirmed his conviction that the health of America determined the fortunes of its Jewish citizens."[64] The strategy of defending Jewish interests by maintaining American values and institutions remained basic with the committee. The identification of Jewish values with a commitment to civil liberties and rights further strengthened the ties between Judaism and Americanism and became part of the growing urban liberal consensus.

While the American Jewish Committee strengthened the connections between Jews and the American Way that Brandeis helped to build, the union movement, with people like Sidney Hillman, converted ideas of industrial democracy into working institutions. One of the most important labor leaders in the movement, Hillman helped industrial democracy to become part of the American political mainstream. Concepts of industrial democracy and economic justice that were inherent in reform and left-oriented Jewish political thought became accepted by the established centers of political power in America. Hillman's ideas were realized in the union movement's influence on the growth of liberalism as the centerpiece of the political consensus that dominated American politics for several decades. Furthermore, this version of liberalism represents the evolution of the historic ideological consensus of the American Way along the lines anticipated by Brandeis's arguments for making Americanism as an ideology relevant to modern industrial and economic conditions. As Moses Rischin says, "It was Hillman's destiny to insinuate millions of Americans into the consciousness of the American middle class by demonstrating labor's ability to master the instrumentalities—financial, social, political, and technological—of our modern complex industrial society. First tested in the bailiwick of his own union and then injected into the mainstream of American life during the Roosevelt Revolution, so commonplace have these changes become, so 'middle class,' so 'American' that their value is no longer open to question."[65]

Born in 1887 in a village in Lithuania, Hillman came to America in 1907. A radical and revolutionary who had been arrested by the czarist police, Hillman arrived in New York still believing in socialism. He soon moved to Chicago where he eventually found a job with Hart, Schaffner and Marx as a clothing worker. This job put him in 1910 in the middle of what became a major strike in the history of the unionization of the garment industry. Because of his leadership and vigor during the strike, he was made a union officer in 1911. In 1914, he became the president of the new Amalgamated Clothing Workers of America. The story of his rise from immigrant and clothing worker to "labor statesman" parallels the change in his way of thinking from that of European radicalism to American liberal pragmatism. Soon after his arrival in this country, his European concepts were altered by American themes and ideas. Without the education and experience of Brandeis, he instinctively felt the contradiction in America between political freedom and economic suppression. He described this dichotomy in a manner that reflected the immediate influence of American sources and ideas upon him. Using Lincoln's description of a nation half slave and half free, he said that the individual today should not live "'free politically and slave industrially.'"[66] Hillman's biographer Matthew Josephson summarizes the union leader's transformation from immigrant and radical to "American." "It was strange," he writes, "how the former agitator for a popular revolution in Russia had, in a few short years in Chicago, become wholly *Americanized*, and in a most admirable way. The ideas, plans, ambitions that formed themselves in his mind were shaped by a close observation of purely American conditions, under the special environment of a typically mid-American industrial city. Here, among Wilsonian liberals and philanthropic capitalists, his concept of industrial democracy, his ideas of the trade-union movement, his opportunistic strategy were molded."[67]

The so-called Americanization of Hillman was possible because of the impact he and others were able to have on changing the ideology of the American Way. Hillman did indeed become less radical, but the ideology of America also changed and reflected the growing acceptance of the principles of industrial democracy. The successful pursuit of industrial democracy through unionism served to label him a "collaborator" among socialists.[68] However, such "collaboration" worked in various ways to change American society. Hillman conceived of the unions as a force to democratize American culture by changing the structure and nature of many basic social and economic institutions. "In a time of political reaction," writes Josephson, "the Amalgamated union almost alone continued to function as a 'school' for progressive labor action." Similarly, Moses Rischin writes, "Even from its earliest days, the Amalgamated was to become the prototype for the modern industrial union. The Amalgamated never was discouraged by barriers of culture and language as impediments to organization. Its newspapers were printed not only in English but in French, Italian, Yiddish, Polish, Lithuanian, and Bohemian. At the time when nativism and anti-immigration sentiment was at its height, Hillman replied to the detractors of his fellow immigrants that 'Americanism is not talking about it, but working out in its own sphere of action a system that will create less unrest.'"[69] Accordingly, Hillman led his union into such experimental areas as banking, housing, cooperative enterprises with business, insurance, education and recreation, urban renewal, national politics, and foreign affairs.

The social and political philosophy that Hillman's leadership put into action became known in the twenties as the "New Unionism." This movement not only led the fight for industrial democracy but it also seemed consistent in its principles and aims with the needs of the immigrants. The New Unionism, according to J. M. Budish and George Soule, provided the immigrants with new opportunities while effectively vitiating the attraction of radical alternatives. "They wanted the freedom of movement essential to the trader and business man, they wanted political liberty, and an opportunity for the development of individual business enterprise," write Soule and Budish. "They wanted educational opportunities for their children, and an absence of governmental interference with their religious and social customs. They wanted personal safety. In short, they sought the very institutions for which the American anti-Socialist values the United States."[70] Such a statement neither does justice to nor encompasses the complexity of motivations and actions of all Jewish immigrants. However, it does indicate how the ideology of the New Unionism came to coincide with the basic principles of the American Way.

As Brandeis had foreseen, the ideology of political liberty could include a program for industrial democracy. The resulting ideology found staunch opponents from both the left and the right. Such critics were united ultimately in the belief that the new version of the American ideology had become the dominant ideology of national consensus. The influence of Jews in supporting and then shaping the American ideology was significant. It achieved something like official recognition through the involvement of the Jews in the New Deal, especially as represented in the unique relationship between Hillman and Franklin Roosevelt. Early in Roosevelt's first administration, Hillman found himself, as Soule says, "inside the New Deal."[71] This sort of relationship made sense because, as Rischin says, by 1930 "Hillman and his associates had already outlined a program that foreshadowed the New Deal."[72] Thus, Hillman was commonly believed to be Roosevelt's chief labor adviser even though problems that were eventually surmounted developed between them during the war years.[73] As a way of demonstrating his trust in Hillman, Roosevelt in 1944 was reported to tell his senior advisers that before making any final decision on the selection of a vice-presidential candidate they were to "clear it with Sidney."[74] The phrase became a popular political expression of the time, for it dramatized a new sense of confidence and authority for Jews while it aroused the ire of those who resented the reputed growth of Jewish influence in the White House. For Jews, of course, Hillman held great symbolic importance. He was the radical immigrant who became the adviser and intimate friend of Roosevelt, the great patrician president. Together the two men seemed to symbolize the transformation and modernization of the American Way into an ideology embodying political and industrial democracy. Together they also stood for a modern version of the ideology of America that seemed ready to answer the other "isms" of the day. From the Jewish perspective, it was an answer that grew out of a long partnership between Jews and the American Way. At the same time, it must be said that perhaps a hunger on the part of some Jews for such a partnership served to make them less sensitive than they should have been to other issues, especially the moral tragedy of Roosevelt's failure to react to the Holocaust. On the other hand, Hillman's generation could point to the ultimate triumph over Hitler and the subsequent postwar creation of Israel as vindications of their faith in the idea of America.

Chapter 4

A Convert to America
Sex, Self, and Ideology
in Abraham Cahan

The world of European Jewry that sent forth waves of mass immigration to America has been described and dramatized in many tales and stories. This is the world of Heinrich Heine, Sholem Aleichem, and Isaac Bashevis Singer. It is a world of the ghetto and the schlemiel and of emancipation movements that had to look to the New World for examples of how to treat Jews with freedom and equality. With all its mystery, vitality, and richness, it is also a world of terror and ambiguity, of the loveless Jew, and of the wasted pariah who existed on the margins of society. Who better tells the story than the baptized Heine in "The Rabbi of Bacherach"? In this story Heine summarizes the history of the oppression of Jews in Europe: the Great Persecutions during the Crusades, the catastrophes at the time of the Great Plague, the rage of the rabble, the Flagellants, the blood libels, and the wafer desecration charges. Thus he weaves history into the story with a detailed account of a Passover service that devotedly renders the beauty of Jewish religious practice, customs, and belief. Throughout the story runs an ambivalence toward the culture of Germany and Europe. This ambivalence is seen in the image of "old, kind-hearted Father Rhine" who "cannot bear to see his children weep."[1] For the culture of the Rhine is also terrifying as it stands ready at any moment to change its mood and devastate its Jews. The unfinished novella by Heine trails off almost as though history must fill the silence and complete the story with our knowledge of the fate of European Jewry in our century. Heine's tale implies a catastrophe that only modern history could create.

To some Jewish historians, however, the disabilities of medieval and preemancipation Jewry were exaggerated by reform-oriented scholars and writers. Such reformers, it is argued, saw the preemancipation era in Europe in completely negative terms because they desired the Jews to modernize and sacrifice their ethnic and national identity for an exclusively religious affiliation that would allow them to be total citizens of the modern nation state. Thus, Salo W. Baron wrote in 1925, "Ardent advocates of liberalism and democracy, visioning a reformed society guided by beneficent rationalism, believing religiously that the world in general and the Jews particularly could be improved by an extension of rights, it is easy to see how they found it useful to take as black a view as possible of the pre-Revolutionary treatment of the Jews."[2] In a sense, according to Baron, such reformers were apologizing for Jewish "peculiarities" by seeing them as scars of oppression that should be healed through emancipation so that Jews could become like everyone else. In so doing, Baron felt, reformers also were ready to cast aside significant aspects of modern Diaspora Jewish character and culture. Baron's interest in correcting this historical view of the ghetto was based in part upon his uncertainty about the quality and the depth of emancipation for Jews in Europe. As it turned out, Jews who staked their security and identity upon their full emancipation in Europe built their futures upon quicksand. In Baron's later estimation, they mistook the visible signs of emancipation for solid and deep-based support from within European culture. The roots into Europe that seemingly nurtured their freedom were extirpated in modern times. Following the Holocaust and the war, Baron wrote that a major test for the reality of emancipation for Jews is the viability and endurance of the social and cultural structures upon which that emancipation is based. "On my part, I have long come to the conclusion," he writes, "that one cannot hope to understand the development of legal and political emancipation without a careful review of the basic social forces which brought them about. That is why one must deal at the same time with the impact of both the economic and cultural emancipation which had preceded the legal emancipation by several generations." In America Baron felt emancipation was built upon custom, belief, and opinion. His analysis of "long-range socioeconomic and cultural factors" as opposed to dramatic historic events indicated a long tradition of emancipation for Jews in America that provides a contrast with the more superficial emancipation movements in European countries.[3]

Emancipation in America in the context of continuing efforts to develop political, economic, and cultural democracy proved irresistible to many Jews, including, as I have already noted, many radical socialists who often were critical of American culture and politics while adhering to the principles of the American idea. The accommodation of these socialists to America anticipates the later movement of intellectuals who became what Alfred Kazin terms with apparent sarcasm *"converts* to America." These intellectuals, he says, grew inclined to view "America as an ideology."[4] This shift toward America can be seen symbolically on the cover of Irving Howe's collection of radical and socialistic pieces drawn from the journal *Dissent*. The title of the book, *Twenty-Five Years of Dissent: An American Tradition*, demonstrates how even the opponents of so-called dominant political beliefs and values still see themselves as modern Jeremiahs working within an American tradition that makes them part of the American Way in its broadest and most meaningful sense.[5] One of the first and most important examples of this phenomenon can be found in the life and career of Abraham Cahan. As a writer, intellectual, and activist, Cahan represents something of a paradigm for the Jewish man of ideas and letters whose original opposition to American culture evolves into a more complicated prophetic position of advocacy for the ideals of the American Way and of criticism for the failure to live up to them. In many ways, Cahan provides a model for the Jewish intellectual who begins as an alien to America but turns into a convert while even being a critic. The great depth and breadth to Cahan's understanding of the American experience can be found in his novel *The Rise of David Levinsky*. A classic study of immigration and success, the novel dramatizes the meaning to a generation and a culture of the myth of America as the new promised land. It shows the shift from European experiences and ways of thought to the adoption of the American way of life. The novel further dramatizes the psychological, sexual, sociological, and intellectual roots within both American and Jewish culture of the corruption of the American idea. Thus, Cahan uses the persona of David Levinsky in order to take the traditional stance of a modern-day Jeremiah attacking those who have lost their faith or cheat in their proper observance of the ideals of the American idea. As such the novel is more than an important literary work and cultural document. It forms part of the traditional ritual of renewal of the American Way.

Abraham Cahan was a man of many conflicts and aspects. As Louis

Harap says, "at the core his personality was a set of contradictions."[6] Indeed, he was born into a world of cultural contradictions on July 6, 1860, in the town of Podberezy, situated about twenty miles from Vilna, the city Napoleon called the "Jerusalem of Lithuania." This was also Cahan's Jerusalem under siege by new ideas, institutions, and philosophies that reflected the enormous social and economic forces changing modern Jewish life. As the grandson of a famous rabbi, Cahan was expected to maintain that tradition. However, by the time he arrived in Philadelphia in early June of 1882, socialism had for several years become a new religion to him. His flight to America as a revolutionary was made to avoid arrest by czarist police. In his later years, Cahan recalled the confidence with which he and his friends in Europe emphasized socialism over Judaism, even in the wake of the pogroms that followed the assassination of Alexander II in 1881. He writes, "Even though the pogrom brought dread into the heart of every Jew, I must admit that the members of my group were not disturbed by it. We regarded ourselves as human beings, not as Jews. There was only one remedy for the world's ills and that was socialism."[7] In spite of such youthful bravado, Cahan never actually lost his concern as a Jew over matters relating to Jewish welfare, although there remained a lingering tension between his religious roots and his belief in a universal socialism. Thus Ronald Sanders notes that in his fiction "Cahan seems to have been unable to find the proper control of his own ambivalences about Jewishness."[8] Almost immediately upon his arrival in America this conflict between religion and politics was compounded by another conflict of loyalties between the revolutionary cause in Russia and political realities in America. In his first speech to Jews and Socialists that made him by his own account "the hero of the day," Cahan said: "'We have come to seek a home in a land that is relatively free,' I began. 'But we must not forget the great struggle for freedom that continues in our old homeland. While we are concerned with our own problems, our comrades, our heroes, our martyrs are carrying on the struggle, languishing in Russian prisons, suffering at hard labor in Siberia. There is little we can do from this distance,' I continued. 'We can raise money to aid the sacred cause. And we must keep the memory of that struggle fresh in our minds'" (*EAC*, p. 236). Throughout his life, attitudes and policies toward Russia were to consume a considerable amount of Cahan's attention.

In America there also developed a split between Cahan's work in Yiddish and his writings in English. Indeed, Cahan the Yiddish journalist and socialist leader at times seems to be a different person from the Cahan who wrote both fiction and journalism in English. From his first days in America, Cahan became a force within the Jewish community. Throughout the 1880s and 1890s, he wrote for the Yiddish journals, *Di Neie Tseit*, the *Arbeiter Tseitung*, the Yiddish weekly of the Socialist Labor party, and *Di Tsukunft*. In 1897, however, in helping to form the *Jewish Daily Forward*, Cahan took the most important step in his journalistic career. After heated dealings with other editors and managers that caused him on various occasions to leave the paper, Cahan finally returned in 1903 as editor with unqualified authority. Editing the *Forward* became his major work. "Cahan's greatest achievement," writes Leon Stein, "was the *Jewish Daily Forward*" (*EAC*, p. viii), while Jules Chametzky says that "Cahan's lifework was the great Yiddish newspaper, the *Jewish Daily Forward*."[9] The newspaper was a leading force in the Yiddish community in shaping political attitudes, supporting socialism and social welfare measures, and establishing and maintaining the garment unions. It also participated in the daily life and activities of the Jewish community through its editorial features such as the *Bintel Brief* (a "Bundle of Letters" section that created a dialogue with the people of the ghetto about the most intimate and personal of problems) and its political and social commentary. In this paper Cahan exercised a direct influence on the daily customs, habits, and attitudes of Jews in the community.

However, his progress as a writer in English seems no less remarkable than his success as a Yiddish writer. He moved quickly from using *Appleton's English Grammar* to teaching himself English to writing sketches and pieces in English for various papers and journals. His most important experience on an English-language newspaper occurred from 1897 to 1901 when he worked on the *Commercial Advertiser*. Lincoln Steffens was the editor, and the staff consisted of talented writers such as Hutchins Hapgood. On the newspaper he learned the basics of modern journalism that helped him so much in his later work as the editor of the *Forward*. Around this time he also began to write fiction in English, publishing his first story, "A Providential Match," in 1895 and his first novel, *Yekl: A Tale of the Ghetto*, in 1896. The latter provided the basis for the contemporary movie *Hester Street*. Cahan was encouraged to pursue his work in fiction by William Dean Howells, who was interested in Cahan both as a young realistic writer and as an expert on the Jewish Lower East Side. For his part, Cahan, according to Ronald Sanders, "still considered Howells to be the greatest living American author, but he had never met him, nor did he ever dream that he would." Cahan also ranked Howells with Henry James as a leader in the "avant-garde" (*EAC*, p. 351). Howells had first heard of Cahan's work as editor of the *Arbeiter Tseitung* and paid a surprise visit to Cahan's office. Not finding him there, Howells also missed Cahan at a neighborhood café called Sussman and Goldstein's that Jewish intellectuals frequented. He followed this excursion with an invitation to Cahan to visit him at home on East 17th Street and Second Avenue. "Cahan's visit here," writes Sanders, "provided him with his first glimpse of the upper-class life of an established American writer."[10] Howells tried to help Cahan in important ways, including finding a publisher for the English version of *Yekl*. He then favorably reviewed the book along with Stephen Crane's *George's Mother* on the front page of the literary section of the *New York World* of July 26, 1896.

As a socialist critic of both European and American literature who had his own literary ambitions, Cahan developed a theory of realism that attempts to establish a connection between his work as a writer of fiction and his experiences as a journalist and active socialist. This theory of literary criticism and social values was presented first as a lecture before a cultural group of the Socialist Labor party. It was printed later on March 15, 1889, in the *Workmen's Advocate* as an article entitled "Realism." The article reflects Cahan's devoted readings of Howells as well as his admiration for Tolstoy. In this piece Cahan advocates a literature of realism on the grounds that the accurate portrayal of social conditions inevitably would lead to social change and revolution.[11] Writing retrospectively in his autobiography, Cahan admitted the naiveté of some of his ideas about art as expressed in "Realism." He also described his confusion between art and propaganda. "In the portion of the article dealing with the social question," he writes, "much of the language is straight propaganda and creates an impression that undermines my own integrity. Now, it is easy for me to separate the passages that were written from the heart, with conviction, from those which were written as propaganda, from a sense of duty. We used propaganda for an honest purpose, and there are still socialists who feel that this should be done. Almost all that I wrote at that time suffered from this fault" (*EAC*, p. 405).

Cahan's literary production in English constitutes a measure of his success in overcoming his initial tendency to confuse propaganda with art. After writing *Yekl*, his stories such as "The Imported Bridegroom," "A Providential Match," "Circumstances," "A Sweat Shop Romance," "A Ghetto Wedding," and "Tzinchadzi of the Catskills" appeared in the *Atlantic, Cosmopolitan, Short Stories, Century*, and *Scribner's*. Thus, by 1913 when *McClure's Magazine* asked him to write an article about the economic success of American Jews, he already was an important figure both in the Jewish community and in New York literary and intellectual circles. Just three years before the request from *McClure's*, the celebration of his fiftieth birthday filled Carnegie Hall. The work he produced for *McClure's* was a four-part series entitled "The Autobiography of an American Jew." Described sensationalistically on the cover as "The Confessions of a Jew," the articles were written in the form of fiction but really were more on the order of a modern "documentary." The series provided the basis for his novel *The Rise of David Levinsky*.[12]

Cahan's willingness to see himself as a writer rather than as a propagandist for socialism follows his critical reexamination upon reaching America of the political ideology that inspired his early years of intellectual development. Almost immediately the experience of America and the American ideology tended to challenge the rigid socialism that Cahan like others brought from Russia. Thus, Cahan states that "for the first four or five years of my life in America I had no answers—only perplexities" (*EAC*, p. 225). Among the greatest perplexities was his immediate impression that America was a new kind of political and cultural enterprise. He writes, "The anarchists and even the socialists argued that there was no more freedom in America than in Russia. But that was just talk, I concluded. After all, in America there was no Czar, there were no gendarmes, no political spies. You could speak and write what you wanted! The President was elected, the governor was elected, even the congressmen who made the laws were elected." At the same time he also could perceive that "some things were strange, ridiculous, wild, sometimes even disgusting" (*EAC*, p. 282). The imbroglio of conflicting beliefs and perceptions that Cahan faced led him to feel that "what I considered to be my convictions were in truth a mishmash of ideas" (*EAC*, p. 314). Out of this percolation of new ideas and impressions emerged a fresh analysis from Cahan of European political philosophers and thinkers such as Proudhon, Johann

Most, William Frey, Bakunin, Kropotkin, and Herbert Spencer (*EAC*, pp. 330–37).

Cahan's sense of the importance of America to the future of the Jews helped him ultimately to moderate his socialism and to give priority to the American ideology over other systems of belief. Thus, upon seeing America as a real refuge for the world's Jews, he reversed his early inclination to prefer socialism over Judaism. By converting to Americanism, Jews could survive as a people and as free individuals. As early as 1890, he understood that "we have no Jewish question in America. The only question we recognize is the question of how to prevent the emergence of 'Jewish questions' here."[13] In addition, Cahan saw that America offered the average Jew a way of life that seemed inconceivable in Europe. "The life of the Jewish sweatshop worker was hard," he writes. "Still the average Jewish immigrant felt that in comparison with what he had suffered in the old country, America was paradise. The worker ate better and was better clothed than in the old country" (*EAC*, p. 400). The benefits of this life, according to Cahan, were apparent even in the physiques of the younger generation. He writes, "The immigrant family began to understand the difference between the old and new lands when it looked upon its children, who grew tall and strong and were better built than their parents. It was not uncommon to see a sixteen-year-old boy towering over his father" (*EAC*, pp. 400–401). To Cahan, however, it was freedom in America that was of the greatest importance to the American Jew. "And what value there was in political freedom!," writes Cahan. "Here, one was a human being. My friend Alter, who always worked hard but barely made a living and considered himself to be a failure, once said to me with a resigned smile, 'Never mind. In the old country I kept my head bowed and my back bent. Here I keep my head high and my back is straight'" (*EAC*, p. 401). Cahan was especially impressed by the fact that Jews could participate so freely in the political process in contrast to Russia where "Jews were denied even the small rights granted to their gentile neighbors. But here in America all enjoyed the same rights, whether Jew or gentile. And for us the right to vote should have been even more precious than for our Christian fellow Americans" (*EAC*, p. 290).

In assuming this commitment to the American ideology, Cahan in effect was accepting the inevitable. He recognized that the mass movement of Jews from the oppression of Europe to the freedom and opportunity of

America dramatized an inexorable shift in the direction and meaning of modern Jewish history. There is a touching moment in his autobiography when Cahan discovers that he is part of forces larger than himself. During his escape from Russia, he realizes that on roads all over Eastern Europe other Jews also are on the move toward America. This happens to him as he boards a train at the Kiev station and sees how many other Jews are also traveling. "On that Saturday night there began the broad stream of Jewish migration that was to continue for almost two generations," he writes. "It was to make America the major center of Jewish population. The course of Jewish history would be changed by it." He notes that "soon every emigrating Jew moving westward realized he was involved in something more than a personal expedition. Every Jew, even the most ignorant emigrant, came to feel that he was part of a historic event in the life of the Jewish people. Ordinary, common Jews became as idealistic and enthusiastic as the intellectuals. Even Jewish workers and small tradesmen who had managed fairly well sold their belongings and joined the exodus from Russia and the move westward to start a new Jewish life in America. They did so with religious fervor and often with inspiring self-sacrifice" (*EAC*, p. 196).

Cahan realized that the socialism in which he believed so strongly would not be as acceptable to many of his fellow immigrants. He saw that even before arriving in America many Jews forgot their radicalism as their expectations about America grew. Thus, while still in the European phase of his journey to America, Cahan remembers that he was "bitterly disappointed at not finding more socialists. In fact, in the seething tumult of Brody [the first city on the Austro-Galician side of the Russian border] even some who had considered themselves socialists in their hometowns began to have doubts about the political meaning of their journey to America" (*EAC*, pp. 204–5).

However, even while criticizing the abandonment of radical doctrine, Cahan himself fell victim to the excitement of going to America. He felt the enthusiasm for achieving a new life and identity in accordance with the myth of America. In spite of his radicalism, Cahan, like so many others, saw himself as a new man in the new American garden. Cahan writes, "America! To go to America! To re-establish the Garden of Eden in that distant land. My spirit soared. All my other plans dissolved. I was for America!" (*EAC*, p. 187) It is this mythic sense of America as a new land that dominates Cahan's novel *The Rise of David Levinsky*. The idea of America as a unique culture offering a new way of life constitutes the book's central concern; it is not a discussion of political principles and ideologies disguised as a novel.

The story of America in *The Rise of David Levinsky* can be compared with that in F. Scott Fitzgerald's *The Great Gatsby*. Fitzgerald writes, "And as the moon rose higher the inessential houses began to melt away until gradually I became aware of the old island here that flowered once for Dutch sailors' eyes—a fresh, green breast of the new world. Its vanished trees, the trees that had made way for Gatsby's house, had once pandered in whispers to the last and greatest of all human dreams; for a transitory enchanted moment man must have held his breath in the presence of this continent, compelled into an aesthetic contemplation he neither understood nor desired, face to face for the last time in history with something commensurate to his capacity for wonder."[14] Years before Fitzgerald, Cahan describes the same kind of experience for Levinsky. Cahan's language is far more literal than Fitzgerald's. Indeed, his language at times approaches sociology. Nevertheless, like Fitzgerald, Cahan attempts to relate fact to symbol as they merge in the psychology of one individual who comes to represent a people, a generation, and a culture in one moment in history. Both Fitzgerald and Cahan dramatize the myth of America through their portrayals of men who are propelled by their "vision" of what America could mean to them. And like Fitzgerald, Cahan shows how the concept of America translates itself into perceptions of the landscape. This projection of the self onto the landscape in turn reflects back onto the self with a force that inspires a belief in self-transformation.

Accordingly, to Levinsky America is a place of awe and wonder. "The United States lured me not merely as a land of milk and honey," he says, "but also, and perhaps chiefly, as one of mystery, of fantastic experiences, of marvelous transformations. To leave my native place and to seek my fortune in that distant, weird world seemed to be just the kind of sensational adventure my heart was hankering for."[15] Based on his own first view as an immigrant of New York, Cahan describes David Levinsky's vision of the city "as something not of this earth" until he glimpses a cat. The reality of the cat brings America back to earth—somewhat. "For a moment," Levinsky says, "the little animal made America real to me" (*RDL*, p. 88). The wonder of America creates a physical and psychological reaction in Levinsky. Levinsky, Cahan notes, "was in a trance or in some-thing closely resembling one" upon actually seeing "the hostile glamour of America." His feelings of "ecstasy" and "transport" contribute to his "sense of helplessness and awe." Such emotions result in the immigrant's belief in his own rebirth. "The immigrant's arrival in his new home," writes Cahan, "is like a second birth to him. Imagine a new-born babe in possession of a fully developed intellect. Would it ever forget its entry into the world? Neither does the immigrant ever forget his entry into a country which is, to him, a new world in the profoundest sense of the term and in which he expects to pass the rest of his life" (*RDL*, pp. 86–87). For Levinsky, the transformation is so complete that he thinks of it as a meta-morphosis. "Sometimes," he says, "when I think of my past in a superfi-cial, casual way, the metamorphosis I have gone through strikes me as nothing short of a miracle" (*RDL*, p. 3). A similar change seems to occur for the Jewish people as a whole as they participate in "the great New Exodus" to America (*RDL*, p. 61).

Although the novel focuses on graphic and momentous transforma-tions, it also dramatizes the significance of the idea of regeneration through a woman who denies herself the opportunity to achieve a new life because of fear and inexperience. In some ways, the meaning of the chance for a new life becomes most palpable in this woman who seems compelled to suffer the constraints of the life she has but wants to change. The misery and self-sacrifice of Dora Margolis emphasize the importance of giving people the opportunity to create their own futures. In love with David but unable to escape from her marriage, she feels "'buried alive'" (*RDL*, p. 301) and decides that her only alternative is to live vicariously through her daughter. "'I want to know everything about her. Every-thing. I wish I could get right into her. I wish I could be a child like her.'" Mostly she wishes that life would give her the opportunity for a second chance. "'Oh,'" she asks Levinsky, "'why can't a person be born over again?'" (*RDL*, p. 276) The intensity of her lament greatens by contrast the dimensions of Levinsky's own rebirth in America.

Unfortunately, Levinsky's transformation in the New World garden seems more diabolical than miraculous. He becomes The Great Levinsky, a grotesque perversion of the American dream whose enormous economic success leaves him feeling homeless. Like Gatsby, he is without any real sense of identity or place as he comes to embody the corruption of the myth that brought him to America in the first place. As Levinsky the immigrant is transformed into The Great Levinsky the giant of the cloak and suit trade, we see the myth of regeneration and new life transmogrified into the "gospel of success." Levinsky represents a Jewish version of the rags-to-riches myth in America in which success and power are values in and of themselves. Thus, Levinsky notes how people who congratulate him on his achievements "were inspired by genuine admiration for my enterprise and energy." He goes on to say, "All of them had genuine admiration for my success. Success! Success! Success! It was the almighty goddess of the hour. Thousands of new fortunes were advertising her gaudy splendors. Newspapers, magazines, and public speeches were full of her glory, and he who found favor in her eyes found favor in the eyes of man" (*RDL*, pp. 444–45). The deification of success for Levinsky into what William James called "the bitch goddess" indicates his ready adaptability to a world in which there are no greater ideals than power over others. Students of American culture such as John Cawelti and Moses Rischin have pointed out how the myth of success reaches far back into our history. Originally, success in the form of wealth and power often were considered symbolic of righteousness and strong character.[16] In this novel, however, success becomes its own justification and establishes a new ideology that counters the more traditional democratic values of the ideology of the American Way. As a member of this new ideology, Levinsky finds himself with the rest of American culture on the brink of an abyss from which no higher values and beliefs can be seen. In the novel Tevkin the old poet summarizes this situation by condemning America as a cage of the spirit. Levinsky, who admires the poet, is shocked by "'the idea of America being likened to a prison.'" The poet, however, tells him that Russia is a "'freer country, too—for the spirit, at least'" (*RDL*, p. 459). Levinsky's own values seem to prove the poet's point. For Levinsky develops a world view based on his business experience in the garment industry and his reading of Darwin and Spencer. His philosophy goes back to a comment made by a friend who compares the world to "'a big barn-yard full of chickens'" in which all the chickens are "'scratching one another, and scrambling over one another'" in their greed for shares of "'little heaps of grain'" scattered in the yard (*RDL*, p. 272). Levinsky identifies himself with the fittest and develops a concomitant contempt for workers and the poor. He says, "A working-man, and every one else who was poor, was an object of contempt to me—a misfit, a weakling, a failure, one of the ruck" (*RDL*, p. 283). His experience in business teaches him that life is a jungle. "My business life had fostered the conviction in me that, outside of the family, the human world was as brutally selfish as the jungle, and that it was worm-eaten with hypocrisy into the bargain" (*RDL*, p. 380). With faith only in success and power, Levinsky espouses a philosophy of nihilism that starkly contrasts with the idealism and wonder of his original idea of America. "I had no creed," he says. "I knew of no ideals. The only thing I believed in was the cold, drab theory of the struggle for existence and the survival of the fittest" (*RDL*, p. 380).

The ideology of success changes the emphasis in the idea of being American from a question of inner values, ideals, and strengths to a matter of images. However, because appearances are inherently ephemeral and contingent upon others' perceptions, it condemns one to continual frustration. Thus, success, as Levinsky perceives it, is simply a part of never-ending failure. In the novel, the road becomes an important metaphor for this aspect of American life. It dramatizes how American mobility and change inspire both alienation and adventure. As noted earlier in this study, on the road Levinsky learns how to disguise his shame and uncertainty about being Jewish through his adoption of the style and manners of the dominant culture. Thus, he sees the road as a "great school of business and life" that brings out and develops "the 'real American' quality" in him as opposed to New York, which he comes to see as "not an American city at all" (*RDL*, p. 325). He becomes self-conscious about his mannerisms, "trying to make them as 'American' as possible," and attempts to overcome his "Talmudic gesticulations, a habit that worried me like a physical defect." Instead of simply seeing himself as different from others, he feels deformed because such Jewish gestures were "so distressingly un-American." He says, "I struggled hard against it. I had made efforts to speak with my hands in my pockets; I had devised other means for keeping them from participating in my speech. All of no avail. I still gesticulate a great deal, though much less than I used to" (*RDL*, pp. 326, 327). Thus, attempts to literally shackle himself and to stifle the Jewish self within him fail, leaving him feeling always out of place and inferior. Guilt over such reactions compounds the complexity of his feelings. Literally a man divided against himself, he laughs publicly over another Jew's jokes about Jews. "I laughed with the others," he says, "but I felt like a cripple who is forced to make fun of his own deformity. It seemed to me as though Loeb, who was a Jew, was holding up our whole race to the ridicule of Gentiles" (*RDL*, p. 328).

However, the contrast between the appearance of being American and the inner reality of the values below the surface startles Levinsky when he realizes that one of the most American-looking travelers is in fact a butcher, a gentile who undoubtedly deals in unkosher meat, which is an abomination to orthodox Jews. Levinsky says, "He fascinated me. His cultured English and ways conflicted in my mind with the character of his business. I could not help thinking of raw beef, bones, and congested blood. I said to myself, 'It takes a country like America to produce butchers who look and speak like noblemen.' The United States was still full of surprises for me. I was still discovering America" (*RDL*, p. 330). Thus, the road teaches him about the brutality of shaping and turning people into a single definition of what it takes to be an American. On the road with strangers Levinsky comes to feel at war with himself and devoid of any reality or sense of self beyond what others see in him. " 'Can it be that I am I?' " he asks himself. In the end he is alone and miserable. "After dinner, when we were in the smoking-room again, it seemed to me that the three Gentiles were tired of me. Had I talked too much? Had I made a nuisance of myself? I was wretched" (*RDL*, p. 330).

Levinsky's response to such insecurity is to fight even harder for success. One of the novel's frequently heralded achievements is Cahan's method of relating the psychology of the individual immigrant, as seen through Levinsky's drive to success, to the rise of the Jews as a group in the clothing and other industries. In the novel, the Jews take the lead in the national anxiety to shed one identity and assume a new one by putting on a new fashion of clothes. Through the Jewish experience in this industry, the novel documents the growing national obsession with looking a particular way labeled "American" at a time when there was a growing uncertainty over what such an identity entailed. This was, after all, the eve of the twenties when, as Robert Sklar notes, "careful self-schooling in the mass technological norms of dress, habits, manner and language" could enable the individual, especially a minority member, to establish a new identity, even if that identity made the person like everyone else. "You could change your name, ignore your religion, leave your background a thousand miles behind," writes Sklar. "But you could never afford to neglect your appearance. In the twenties Americans began their grand obsession with cosmetics. The absence of body odor mattered more than the lack of a family tree."[17] Ironically, the Jews, as Moses Rischin indicates, achieved dominance in the clothing and such other industries related to taste and style as communications, films, and media because they were so systematically excluded from participating significantly in more basic American industries.[18] Such dominance in these industries helped create a myth of Jewish power. However, there is another irony in the prominence of Jews in relatively marginal enterprises that depend so much upon public taste and fashion. Rather than setting or establishing tastes, styles, and trends, the leaders in these kinds of industries often resemble slaves to the publics they serve. This can be especially true for minority or ethnic leaders whose own self-image and ambition compel them to anticipate the desires and standards of the dominant culture. Moreover, progress in such areas often can undermine individual power because success requires participation in mass markets that tend to redefine the whole concept of taste and fashion to mean only the average, the mediocre, and the marketable. Cahan's novel dramatizes these kinds of weaknesses that lurk beneath the cover of success in America.

Levinsky becomes a perfect model of impotence masking itself as power as we get beneath the surface of his claims concerning his business success. The contrast between visible success and inner weakness grows apparent as we see that his reputed influence over fashion really reflects a demeaning readiness to trade his own sense of self for a system that imposes one standard of beauty and style upon the new market of women buyers. At one point in the novel Levinsky in a reportial voice boasts of "the advent of the Russian Jew as the head of one of the largest industries in the United States," which can, because of the Jew's leadership, provide "clothes for the American woman of moderate or humble means" (*RDL*, p. 443). Proud of this visible success he maintains that "the average American woman is the best-dressed average woman in the world, and the Russian Jew has had a good deal to do with making her one" (*RDL*, p. 444). "Indeed," says Levinsky, "the Russian Jew had made the average American girl a 'tailor-made' girl" (*RDL*, p. 443). However, the diminution of individuality implied by such appeals to the "average" have their impact upon Levinsky himself. While Levinsky does exert power over women by averaging their tastes and influencing them to tailor their buying habits and expectations, he also must place his own mind in a kind of straitjacket that will enable him to exert such leadership. To become a success, he totally accepts an external—in a sense, a foreign—set of values and standards.

With all his supposed influence over taste and standards, Levinsky finds only one ideal for beauty and charm—the Anglo-Saxon—in a way that clearly demonstrates his deep sense of ethnic inferiority. Thus, of his models he writes, "These models were all American girls of Anglo-Saxon origin, since a young woman of other stock is not likely to be built on American lines—with the exception of Scandinavian and Irish girls, who have the American figure" (*RDL*, p. 444). Of course, the idea of women as "stock" built according to certain "lines" fuses racist and sexist ways of thinking with the steady movement of American culture toward a uniformity of style and taste that fits the needs of a mass-market industry and economy. The conformity sought by Levinsky extends to more than looks. His models have to be the "right" examples of accepted and standard American behavior and thought. Thus, Levinsky, who is only too ready to sell himself for success in the system, learns how to expect others as well to sacrifice their ways of thought and patterns of behavior in order to satisfy a model created for them. Levinsky says, "But the figure alone was not enough, I thought. In selecting my model-girls, I preferred a good-looking face and good manners, and, if possible, good grammar. Experience had taught me that refinement in a model was helpful in making a sale, even in the case of the least refined of customers. Indeed, often it is even more effectual than a tempting complexion" (*RDL*, p. 444). Besides an obvious disdain for his own people and other non-Anglo-Saxons, the language of this paragraph shows Levinsky's strong animosity toward women. The man who clothes women and brags about taking care of them in fact talks about them as though they were merchandise and hates them.

Levinsky's hatred of women signals a deep sexual neurosis. Cahan connects this psychic phenomenon in Levinsky to the attitude toward clothing in both Jews and other Americans. For Cahan, the obsession with style and the need to dress up the self and the body dramatize a problematic attitude toward sexuality. The neurosis vitiates the opportunity within both cultures to achieve autonomy and individuality. Moreover, each culture in its own way nurtures the psychic causes for the individual's ambivalence toward women. Accordingly, Cahan couples this basic psychic discontent toward women with institutions and behavioral patterns in both cultures that tend to turn Levinsky into a psychic and social outcast. Aspects of Levinsky's life as both a Jew and an American, some of which already have been described, interiorize a sense of inferiority and inadequacy in him that strengthens the immutability of his alienation. Thus, both cultures contribute to Levinsky's misery and unhappiness. Both share responsibility for the corruption of his character and for his unrealized regeneration. This attempt to demonstrate partial responsibility within Jewish culture itself for Levinsky's suffering and moral failure is contrary to most interpretations of the novel. While Irving Howe notes that Cahan was concerned about Jewish "*alrightniks*," or parvenus, other critics tend to place the burden of the blame for Levinsky's problems and unhappiness upon materialistic America.[19] These critics believe that American values encouraged Levinsky to abandon more spiritual Talmudic and intellectual pursuits. Thus, John Higham says, "But David Levinsky's 'rise' is simultaneously a fall, and the reader participates in both. . . . In any case, the American experience, so stimulating and manifold in its possibilities, coarsened Levinsky's character in the very process of liberating it. Since he could not forget what he had betrayed, the path of commercial achievement ended in spiritual loss and emptiness."[20] In an indispensable study of Cahan and his fiction, Jules Chametzky writes, "Rich in the things of this world, he [Levinsky] finds at last that he has purchased them at the expense of his inner spirit. At the end Levinsky yearns for more spiritually satisfying fare than business and the success ethic. He envies those of his brethren who have distinguished themselves in science, music, art, and he says that if he had it to do all over again, he would *not* think of a business career. At the heart of whatever is self-serving rationalization in that statement, we must discern a legitimate and despairing hope for an elusive center that would stabilize and legitimate his American life."[21]

Aspects of the novel certainly support Chametzky's interpretation. For example, in the last paragraph Levinsky says, "I cannot escape from my old self. My past and my present do not comport well. David, the poor lad swinging over a Talmud volume at the Preacher's Synagogue, seems to have more in common with my inner identity than David Levinsky, the well-known cloak-manufacturer" (*RDL*, p. 530). This paragraph repeats an important theme of yearning for the past that appears throughout

Cahan's writings. It also suggests, as Chametzky notes, a longing for the kind of center Levinsky thinks once existed in his life. However, this interpretation also exaggerates the significance and solidity of Levinsky's earlier identity and implies too great a discontinuity between the old David of Europe and The Great Levinsky of America. In fact they are, as Isaac Rosenfeld and David Engel suggest, very much the same person.[22] Both have the same roots in a diminished and miserable sense of self, a self that derives from Levinsky's cultural origins as a poor Jew in Russia, which in turn involve his ambivalent psychosexual relationship to his mother.

However, before describing one basic source of his misery in his pathological relationship to his mother, I wish to discuss how his origins in Russia helped to make Levinsky a man of great loneliness and despair. Levinsky grew up in an atmosphere of poverty, misery, and worldly ignorance that cultivates the psychic insecurity and ambivalence of his relationship with his mother. Born in northwest Russia, David becomes the archetypal Jew: an alien among aliens, an outcast among a dispersed nation of pariahs. He yearns for the past because in sentimentally recalling the circumstances of his youth he can explain his current state of despair without accepting responsibility for it. "I love," he says, "to brood over my youth. The dearest days in one's life are those that seem very far and very near at once" (*RDL*, p. 3). The very next line, however, indicates that beneath this sentiment are feelings that associate his youth with a form of sickness. He says, "My wretched boyhood appeals to me as a sick child does to its mother" (*RDL*, p. 4). Throughout the novel, he describes this inner identity, this center of his existence, in images of sickness and desolation. His mother also saw his situation in pathetic terms, at least since his second year when his father died. From that moment his mother regarded him as an orphan. "Sometimes," he remembers, "when she seemed to be crushed by the miseries of her life, she would call me, 'My poor little orphan'" (*RDL*, p. 4). In fact, the absence of a father creates a vacuum in his life that helps to shape his view of the world. "I scarcely remembered my father, yet I missed him keenly," he says. "I was ever awake to the fact that other little boys had fathers and that I was a melancholy exception; that most married women had husbands, while my mother had to bear her burden unaided. In my dim childish way I knew that there was a great blank in our family nest, that it was a widow's nest; and the feeling of it seemed to color all my other feelings" (*RDL*, pp. 4–5).

Thus, the key to Levinsky's character lies not in his solid sense of be-

longing and identity during his youth in Europe but in the exact opposite—a pervading sense of destitution and deprivation. Moreover, because
of their poverty David and his mother are made to feel like the black sheep
of the community. Unable to pay as much as others for his Hebrew education, his mother perennially fights to give him opportunities they cannot
afford. At school the teachers vent their frustrations on David so that at
one point he compares himself to a friend who is always abused at home.
He says, "She was the outcast of the family just as I was the outcast of her
father's school" (*RDL*, p. 21). The event that turns Levinsky into a permanent outcast with a deprived and inferior sense of self is the violent
death of his mother at the hands of neighborhood bullies. This occurs
when Levinsky is attacked and beaten by a group of gentiles who are
amused at his Orthodox style of dressing in a "long-skirted coat" and his
Orthodox appearance with his hair grown out into "side-locks" over his
ears. Upon seeing her son bloodied and disheveled, the mother races out
of the house to attack the bullies and is killed by them. Since he is in
his late teens at this time, her overly protective reaction indicates his
prolonged adolescence.

His mother's death reduces David to a condition of mendicancy and
despair. The impact of her death and the horrible manner in which it
occurred together with the resulting state of isolation, insecurity, and misery mark the climax of the processes that shaped his character from the
beginning. Describing his situation after her death, he says, "Nothing
really interested me except the fact that I had not enough to eat, that
mother was no more, that I was all alone in the world" (*RDL*, p. 56). He
notes how the "shock of the catastrophe" had altered his outlook and way
of relating to people. "My incessant broodings," he says, "and the corrod-
ing sense of my great irreparable loss and of my desolation had made a
nerveless, listless wreck of me, a mere shadow of my former self. I was
incapable of sustained thinking" (*RDL*, p. 56). Throughout the rest of the
novel, Levinsky continues to feel essentially the same way.

American conditions nurture the insecurity of Levinsky's youth. "'You
are all alone in the world!,'" he says to himself in the midst of his rise to
success in the clothing industry (*RDL*, p. 356). He also describes himself
as "a lonely man" (*RDL*, p. 357). A friend says to him, "'You feel more
alone than any bachelor I ever knew. You're an orphan, poor thing. You
have a fine business and plenty of money and all sorts of nice times, but

you are an orphan, just the same. You're still a child. You need a mother'"
(*RDL*, p. 358). By the end of the novel, he still says of himself, "I am
lonely," and he adds that, even after having a good time, "I suffer a gnaw-
ing aftermath of loneliness and desolation" (*RDL*, p. 526). As a permanent pariah and outsider, Levinsky's relationships with people always
awaken his feelings of inadequacy and misery. Thus, he feels sure that a
condescending gentile merchant believes him to be "his inferior, all the
same—a Jew, a social pariah. At the bottom of my heart I considered
myself his superior, finding an amusing discrepancy between his professional face and the crudity of his intellectual interests; but he was a Gentile, and an American, and a much wealthier man than I, so I looked up to
him" (*RDL*, p. 502). He fails to see the contradiction of "looking up" to a
man whose condescension amuses him. Similar feelings occur even in his
dealings with other Jews. A Jewish sculptor doing a head of Levinsky
arouses a comparable sense of inadequacy in him. Levinsky says of the
sculptor, "His demeanor toward me was all that could have been desired.
We even cracked Yiddish jokes together and he hummed bits of synagogue music over his work, but I never left his studio without feeling
cheap and wretched" (*RDL*, p. 530). The problem obviously resides more
in Levinsky's head than in the sculptor's.

Given his background and the nature of his developing values, The
Great Levinsky can only feel "cheap and wretched." His debilitated sense
of self makes it impossible for Levinsky ever to consider himself worthy of
love or able to love successfully. Although he has a long series of infatuations and affairs, he can neither establish a solid and permanent relationship nor find a real home for himself. As David Engel says in his brilliant
study of the novel, Levinsky "is nowhere at home." Levinsky's "real affliction," writes Engel, "is lovelessness. He makes no true friend, has no
family, and is welcome in no home."[23] Thus, as a boarder during the early
days of immigration, Levinsky pursues the married woman from whom
he rents. After years of infatuations, he becomes engaged to a woman he
does not love but who promises him a Jewish home. However, he falls in
love with another woman so intellectually and emotionally removed from
him that the lesson of this unhappy relationship can clearly be attributed
to his penchant for hurting and punishing himself.

At the core of Levinsky's diminished sense of self is a pathological attitude toward women that goes back to his relationship to his mother. In

what has been a neglected aspect of this novel, Cahan shows how family and culture prime Levinsky for an ambivalence toward women and sexuality that receives added reenforcement in his life in America. In her provocative discussion of the role of mothers in shaping attitudes toward life and sexuality, Dorothy Dinnerstein uses Freud and Norman O. Brown to provide an important model for gaining insight into the formation of Levinsky's character. She argues that the mother as the "first parent" receives the first love of the child but also the burden of the first hatred for being the apparent cause of life's initial pain of separation. The mother, therefore, also introduces the first intimation of death. Dinnerstein writes, "As Brown, following Freud, maintains, the adult's grief at mortality is preceded and preformed by the infant's grief at its lost sense of oneness with the first parent: The later knowledge that we will die resonates with the pain of our earliest discovery of helplessness, vulnerability, isolation; with the terrified sorrow of the first, and worst, separation." The logical extension of this fear of death and separation is the denial of the vulnerability of the flesh that in turn requires a denial of the flesh itself. The mother as the first parent operates at the center of these drives. "Freud has pointed out," Dinnerstein argues, "how the child tries to console itself for the first great loss by mastery, by the exercise of competence and will: Torn from what he calls the 'oceanic feeling' that it enjoyed at the outset, from the passive infinite power that lay in unity with the all-providing mother, it explores the active, the finite but steadily growing, powers of its newly isolated self." In order to gain a sense of "control" over the ineluctable forces of separation, the child and then the adult renounce "the fundamental, primitive joy of the body."[24] Dinnerstein maintains that this revolt against the flesh to achieve through denial control over death also amounts to a revolt against women because the entire process occurs "under all-female auspices."[25] "The relation," she writes, "between our sexual arrangements and our unresolved carnal ambivalence begins with this fact: when the child first discovers the mystical joys and the humiliating constraints of carnality, it makes this discovery in contact with a woman. The mix of feelings toward the body that forms at this early stage, under female auspices, merges with our later-acquired knowledge of the body's transience, and the flavor of this early mix remains the most vivid ingredient of that unassimilable eventual knowledge."[26] This ambivalence turns woman into a magical goddess with both a life-giving power and a shame-ridden carnal body that invites death. "Woman, by and large," writes Dinnerstein, "meekly carries this burden of shame and sacredness, relying on man to represent matter-of-fact spiritual self-respect, clean, world-conquering humanity."[27]

Dinnerstein's analysis of Freud and Brown describes very well the psychology of Levinsky's attitude toward women and sexuality. Without the influence of a strong father, caught in a culture of poverty and alienation, characterized almost from birth as an orphan, Levinsky develops an abnormal dependence upon his mother. The heightened intensity of the relationship demonstrates contradictory feelings of both love and hate. In Levinsky's case, the initial feeling of death associated with the first separation from the mother merges psychologically with the physical death first of the father and then of the mother. In spite of the separation in time of these events, the second death confirms the domination of death and isolation in his childhood. Moreover, the manner of the mother's death on the son's behalf and the guilt it engenders further intensify their love-hate relationship. She died for him. Therefore, she not only acts as the vehicle for his knowledge of separation and death but she also helps to make him feel responsible for her death. Thus, he shares death with her. So while Levinsky throughout the novel indicates his love and grief for his mother, he also demonstrates a calculating ability to exploit her in a manner that implies deep-seated hostility toward her. In a scene suggesting true grief immediately after her death Levinsky says, "I had been in an excited, hazy state of mind, more conscious of being the central figure of a great sensation than of my loss. As I went to bed on the synagogue bench, however, instead of in my old bunk at what had been my home, the fact that my mother was dead and would never be alive again smote me with crushing violence. It was as though I had just discovered it. I shall never forget that terrible night. At the end of the first thirty days of mourning I visited mother's grave. 'Mamma! Mamma!' I shrieked, throwing myself upon the mound in a wild paroxysm of grief" (*RDL*, pp. 53–54).

Later in his life, however, the authentic quality of his grief seems to change. The artificiality of his emotions—what Engel characterizes as his penchant for "bogus emotion"—dramatizes Levinsky's ambivalence toward his mother as he lights a memorial candle for her. He remembers that "as I gazed at that huge candle commemorating the day when my mother gave her life for me, I felt as though its light was part of her spirit.

The gentle flutter of its flame seemed to be speaking in the sacred whisper of a graveyard. 'Mother dear! Mother dear!' my heart was saying" (*RDL*, p. 389). This, of course, is the language of sentimental popular music and the stage. It is filled with stock images and emotions. Such language and thought patterns enable Levinsky to avoid confronting his complex and contradictory feelings toward his mother. However, his actions in other parts of the book also demonstrate his confused emotions. Levinsky exploits the drama of his mother's death to gain the attention and favor of his first benefactor in America. The man offers to take Levinsky to a restaurant for a meal. Levinsky says, "On our way there I told him of my mother's violent death, vaguely hoping that it would add to his interest in me. It did—even more than I had expected. To my pleasant surprise, he proved to be familiar with the incident. It appeared that because our section lay far outside the region of pogroms, or anti-Jewish riots, the killing of my mother by a Gentile mob had attracted considerable attention. I was thrilled to find myself in the lime-light of world-wide publicity. I almost felt like a hero" (*RDL*, p. 100). Calling him "'My poor orphan boy!,'" the man asks for additional details about the incident. Levinsky says, "I made it as appallingly vivid as I knew how. He was so absorbed and moved that he repeatedly made me stop in the middle of the sidewalk so as to look me in the face as he listened" (*RDL*, p. 100). Transparent exploitation of his mother's death, however, does not always work for Levinsky. To his great dismay, he learns that not everyone knows of her or cares. There was only a "murmur of curiosity and sympathy" among worshipers in a synagogue when he identifies himself and tells the story of his mother (*RDL*, p. 107). The congregation is interested in other things and Levinsky must operate on his own.

Levinsky's contradictory feelings toward his mother dramatize the pattern of ambivalence that Dinnerstein delineates. Moreover, the drive that Dinnerstein describes which denies the flesh as a response to the mother and to death finds significant reenforcement in the Orthodox religion and culture of Levinsky's background. In fact, the theme of God, sex, and women dominates an early chapter of the novel. As a Talmudic student prior to his mother's death in Antomir, Levinsky receives instruction in the absolute opposition of sex and religion. He says, "In the relations between men and women it is largely a case of forbidden fruit and the mystery of distance. The great barrier that religion, law, and convention have placed between the sexes adds to the joys and poetry of love, but it is responsible also for much of the suffering, degradation, and crime that spring from it." Levinsky adds that in his case "this barrier was of special magnitude" (*RDL*, p. 42). Levinsky is taught about women in a way that guarantees his perpetual distrust of them. "In the eye of the spiritual law that governed my life women were intended for two purposes only: for the continuation of the human species and to serve as an instrument in the hands of Satan for tempting the stronger sex to sin" (*RDL*, pp. 42–43). This attack on women as instruments of sin and the embodiment of evil ultimately constitutes an attack on masculine flesh as well. When Levinsky's teacher, Reb Sender, catches him eyeing an attractive woman, he tells him about Satan and refers him to a lesson in the Talmud of Rabbi Mathia. The rabbi " 'had nails and fire brought him and gouged out his own eyes' " because of Satan's effort to tempt him with the image of a naked woman (*RDL*, p. 40). The vision of the rabbi "gouging out his eyes supplanted the nude figure" that had been in Levinsky's mind (*RDL*, p. 40). An ideology that places women in an inferior status and a religious orthodoxy that preaches self-mutilation to suppress sexuality intensify Levinsky's ambivalence toward sex and women. Both ideological and religious restrictions tend to intensify his confusion and curiosity concerning sex and the flesh. "But at present," he says, "all this merely deepened the bewitching of the forbidden sex in my young blood. And Satan, wide awake and sharp-eyed as ever, was not slow to perceive the change that had come over me and made the most of it" (*RDL*, p. 43).

A girl from Levinsky's youth serves as a symbol throughout the novel of his uncertainty about sexuality, women, and the body. Her family is one of four that crowd into the basement in which the Levinskys live. Her name of Red Esther refers not only to the color of her hair but also suggests his fear of sexuality and the female body. Throughout his life, female sexuality arouses in him the feelings and associations he had toward Red Esther. This is true of his relationship with Matilda Shiphrah, the daughter of a woman who adopts him for a brief time following the death of his mother. Matilda's situation as a divorcée and her name fascinate him. "Her Gentile name had a world of charm for my ear," he says (*RDL*, p. 67). These factors give her a quality of forbidden experience that tantalizes him. Her flirtations and teasings remind him of Red Esther and conjure up an aura of Eve. "A thought of little Red Esther of my childhood days flashed through my brain, of the way she would force me to 'sin' and then gloat over my 'fall,'" he says (*RDL*, p. 75).

All of the sexual images and contradictions that operate in Levinsky's mind come together in the American landlady who serves as his surrogate mother. As though to drive home the point of Levinsky's lingering sexual obsession with his mother, Cahan awkwardly names this woman Mrs. Levinsky. Levinsky takes his room and board with her and notes, "The curious thing about her was that her name was Mrs. Levinsky, though we were not related in the remotest degree" (*RDL*, p. 109). Of course, a relationship does exist, but on a deep psychological level that indicates how well Dinnerstein's theory explains Levinsky's condition. The relationship with the landlady dramatizes his neurosis as a pattern of contradictory attitudes that dehumanizes women by turning them into either whores or goddesses. Subconscious drives propel him toward this woman while hidden needs to overcome the flesh and sensuality cause him to hate her. He manifests a self-destructive cycle with her that typifies his relationships with all women. Thus, while observing Mrs. Levinsky one morning, he thinks: "'I don't like this woman at all,' I said to myself, looking at her. 'In fact, I abhor her. Why, then, am I so crazy to carry on with her?'" Levinsky follows this question about his compulsion with a statement that indicates a continuity of contradiction in his relationships that begins with his mother and carries forward to all future experiences with women. "It was the same question that I had once asked myself concerning my contradictory feelings for Red Esther, but my knowledge of life had grown considerably since then" (*RDL*, p. 119). The irony, of course, of this increased knowledge is that it simply adds more female names to the same pattern of love and hate, a pattern he is never able to break and which keeps him so unhappy. Thus, while dealing with Mrs. Levinsky, he thinks of Matilda in a way that seems new to him. In reality, however, his thoughts of Matilda as having fallen from a pedestal only reflect the same pattern of his relationships with other women who as goddesses must fall because they cannot escape their flesh. Accordingly, in the midst of his flirtations with the innocent Mrs. Levinsky he thinks, "I saw Matilda from a new angle. It was as if she had suddenly slipped off her pedestal. Instead of lamenting my fallen idol, however, I gloated over her fall. And, instead of growing cold to her, I felt that she was nearer to me than ever, nearer and dearer" (*RDL*, p. 120). Levinsky gloats because her imagined fall helps to justify his own sexuality. At one point Matilda had called him a "'devil with side-locks'" (*RDL*, p. 78), but Levinsky never learns to confront and cope with that devil within himself and the flesh of the women he wants to both possess and idolize.

Levinsky's neurosis becomes a social pathology when he moves into the clothing industry. The Great Levinsky's personal problem achieves institutionalization in this business. His rise documents the growing dominance of a special social phenomenon of outward success based on self-deprecation, mass conformity, and the values of prejudice. Levinsky's story indicates that such success sustains the denigration of women, the debasement of the body, and the dehumanization of the spirit. Cahan's social criticism and his lines of attack anticipate by several decades the arguments and theories of many later social theorists. There is a direct link, for example, between his understanding of the social significance of the clothing industry and Marshall McLuhan's analysis much later of modern advertising. For McLuhan, the world of advertising constitutes another layer of signs and symbols that reenforce the messages of the world of fashion as rendered by Cahan. McLuhan's interpretation of advertising demonstrates the continued relevance and significance of Cahan's portrait of modern American character. McLuhan believes that advertising turns women into "mannequins" of "competitive display" as opposed to real persons of "spontaneous sensuality."[28] He argues that advertisements demonstrate that men are threatened by the power women exercise in order to move between the contradictory images of whore and goddess. Such power heightens masculine hostility and suspicion and arouses feelings of violent detachment. This situation, according to McLuhan, creates "the view of the human body as a sort of love-machine capable merely of specific thrills." Levinsky's sexual life with women, who do not even rate a name, exemplifies such mechanical sexuality. For McLuhan, these values further debilitate the qualities of inner character and strength that are necessary for democracy.[29] Thus, he suggests, "we would do well to strengthen those inner resources, which we still undoubtedly exert, to resist the mechanism of mass delirium and collective irrationalism."[30]

Precisely such "inner resources" are dissipated in Levinsky. In addition, the inner weakness that Cahan's novel describes goes beyond simply constituting an attack on business and commercialism. The character of David Levinsky, who feels himself to be of little worth in a world that defiles man's greatest dreams and ideals, finds duplication in other characters far removed from the garment industry. In other words, Levinsky's belief that he would be a happier man in a more established and prestigious intellectual, professional, or academic position seems to be another example of self-deception and rationalization. Levinsky's character and background, his sexual pathology, his place in both Jewish and American culture suggest that he would feel unhappy, insecure, and unworthy in any situation in contemporary American culture. Moreover, if we accept Isaac Rosenfeld's insight that *The Rise of David Levinsky* "consists of an extended commentary . . . somewhat in the manner of Talmud" from the opening paragraph of the novel, we can say that many Jewish writers since Cahan continue that Talmudic commentary.[31]

Like Cahan himself, David Levinsky became a convert to the American Way. However, in his search for the "real" America, he turned to the artificial and superficial as substitutes for values of independence and inner strength. This amounted to a turn against himself and his potential. As the story of a Jewish immigrant's journey on the wrong road to the "real" America, *The Rise of David Levinsky* serves as Cahan's vehicle for an attack against those social, ideological, and psychological factors undermining the promise of America. Cahan viewed the corruption and perversion of the American idea from the vantage point of his own culture of Yiddish life and thought. To such Jews there seemed a possibility of losing two cultures at once. As their own world of Yiddish changed and moved more into the mainstream of American life, they also could imagine the America of their hopes losing its way in a world of reactionary and violent totalitarian "isms." At the same time, the belief in the importance of America to the future welfare and survival of the Jews added to the sense of Jewish investment in the idea of America. Rather than opposition to American politics and alienation from American life, Cahan's public career as a political leader and editor increasingly demonstrated a growing commitment to and participation in the American Way. Along with union leaders Sidney Hillman and David Dubinsky, he was instrumental in putting Jews at the center of the liberal consensus of the New Deal in the mid-1930s. However, examples of such personal achievement and national consensus are generally missing from *The Rise of David Levinsky*. The novel intends, instead, to uncover the other side of the American dream, to expose the nightmare of conformity, materialism, and dehu-manization that corrupts the idea of America. In effect, Cahan gives us this story of America to help revivify the moral imagination of all the people. Like the traditional jeremiad, the story functions as a warning and an attack. Moreover, this jeremiad achieves special immediacy and inten-sity because it is rendered through the perspective of a lost generation. Engel correctly articulates Levinsky's dual tragedy by claiming that "there is simply no viable world to which one can return" and that there can be "no easy faith in progress."[32] The moral rhetoric of the story, however, mitigates such pessimism by insisting that "modernity" may complicate but does not automatically eliminate the moral vision of America. A myth of regeneration and a rhetoric of moral responsibility in Cahan's novel suggest the possibility of a future of choices that were unavailable to the oppressed cultures of the past.

PART III

The Ghetto: Shelter and Prison

Chapter 5

A Portrait of the Artist
as a Young Luther
Henry Roth

The ghetto had been a way of life for Jews in Europe ever since the Middle Ages.[1] In America, however, the European experience for Jews was reversed—the ghettos followed a history of liberation and freedom. The ghettos that emerged in the major cities of the Northeast and Midwest were the result of the immigration of millions of East European Jews from 1880 to the mid-1920s. The statistics on immigration and population growth speak for themselves. In 1880, there were 280,000 Jews living in America. By 1925, the population rose to 4.5 million Jews while the total national population only more than doubled to 115,000,000. In this period, 2,378,000 Jews immigrated to America.[2] For the millions of Jews who came here, the ghettos symbolized conflicting feelings about America. As Peter Rose says, "Despite the repeated mutterings of *a klug tzu Columbus* (a curse on Columbus), one could make it here—and many did. The Jews' ghetto, unlike the Negroes', was a gateway. It served to help them get in rather than to keep them locked out."[3] The ghettos provided not only opportunity mixed with pain but also an intensity of life that brought to a boil the kinds of conflicts and contradictions that might merely have simmered in easier environments. On the streets and in the tenements Jewish family life, love, learning, religion, and culture battled disease, poverty, crime, violence, and desperate overcrowding. Abraham Cahan encountered these forces as a grown man recently arrived in America. However, for many prospective Jewish writers and intellectuals, the ghetto was a place for growing up. At a time when the ghetto reflected a changing America, one was initiated into the ways of Jewish culture and life in anticipation of a later initiation into American life as a whole. In effect, life came to require at least a double initiation for the Jewish writer and intellectual. The desire to leave —perhaps "escape" would be a more fitting term for some—inspired the drive toward maturity.

Henry Roth's *Call It Sleep* and Anzia Yezierska's *Bread Givers* are two important novels dealing with this process of maturation. They are significant not only for dramatizing individual growth but also for rendering a particular period when most of the Jews in America were living in ghettos of one kind or another. Roth's David Schearl and Yezierska's Sara Smolinsky are male and female counterparts of the same story of struggle and survival in the ghetto. While Roth and Yezierska describe the searing and brutalizing impact of external conditions upon their characters, in the final analysis both are more concerned with the ghetto as a state of mind than with the physical environment. Similarly, Philip Roth emphasizes the internalization of the ghetto in the form of values and attitudes. Thus, some of the same themes, challenges, and problems connect these writers. In all three writers the psychology of the ghetto functions as a way of being in and relating to America.

Henry Roth's novel *Call It Sleep* constitutes a major step toward establishing the tradition of the New Covenant between Jewish writers and intellectuals and the American idea. Published seventeen years after *The Rise of David Levinsky*, Roth's *Call It Sleep* functions as the paradigmatic Jewish novel of initiation of a boy whose imagination, brilliance, and sensitivity make him an archetype for the Jewish hero of thought. As the story of a youth's rebirth on the streets of New York, the novel takes the American frontier narrative myth of regeneration and moves it to the hostile urban environment. Moreover, the novel also moves inexorably toward a conclusion that rearticulates the rhetoric of the myth of America. In the closing section of the novel when David slowly awakens after his near-fatal electrocution on trolley tracks, he emerges as a new American consciousness, a prophetic Jewish "kup" dramatizing in a modern setting the cultural democracy and pluralism of the American idea. The conclusion of the novel strongly suggests the importance of Jewish voices in expressing a revivified form of the myth and ideology of America.

This argument about the novel contradicts much of what the author himself has said about his own work. It also runs counter to a good deal of what Roth believes now or has believed in the past about various issues ranging from communism and the potential hostility of America toward the Jews to his sudden passion for Israel in the late 1960s. His marked change of political views and his drastic loss of interest in literary matters for most of the years after writing the novel may help to explain his long silence as a writer, and even as a serious intellectual and man of ideas, since the novel's appearance. In any case, he tends to prove D. H. Lawrence's famous dictum: "Never trust the artist. Trust the tale." Lawrence maintains that his "business" in his "studies" of American literature was to save "the American tale from the American artist."[4] Similarly, it also is necessary to save the American meaning in Roth's modernistic Jewish novel.

After nearly three decades of relative obscurity, *Call It Sleep* has become something of a modern classic in the past twenty years. An impressive array of critics including Alfred Kazin, Irving Howe, Leslie Fiedler, Walter Rideout, and Walter Allen all participated in the book's revival through their enthusiastic reviews and articles.[5] In these and in the many other articles that followed, the novel has been given the full treatment of contemporary critical analysis. It has been studied in terms of its psychological, religious, political, symbolic, mystical, and mythic significance. All of these elements are in the novel. For example, Fiedler writes, "There is surely no more Jewish book among American novels." Fiedler asserts that Schearl "is portrayed not only as a small boy and a Jew but also as a 'mystic,' a naive adept visited by visions he scarcely understands until a phrase from the sixth chapter of Isaiah illuminates for him his own improbable prophetic initiation."[6] While Fiedler's comments reflect the enthusiasm of those who rediscovered the novel, a more recent critic suggests a very different reading. Gary Epstein challenges the conventional critical view that the book is about the creative awakening through a mystical experience of a young Jewish hero. Instead, he argues that "the evidence of the book suggests an exactly opposite conclusion." He maintains that "the 'sleep' of the novel's title is symbolic of a spiritual death" from which David does not arise and that "the ending of this novel, carefully read, may go a long way in explaining Roth's future inability to complete another one."[7]

Epstein's controversial interpretation receives important confirmation from the author himself. In an interview, Roth indicates that the conclusion of the book signals the end of any creative life for David and anticipates the death of Roth's creativity. Roth states, "The experiences themselves, on the rail and on the water—these were epiphanies if you like, creative moments, but the short-circuiting at the end seems to me an end of that kind of creativity. David's problem, as I saw it, would be to reconcile himself to a more ordinary form of existence from now on. I don't know what he'd do after that, perhaps go off and teach elementary school somewhere. But his special gift was gone. I didn't see a creative life in store for the boy, and in that sense again I see it as prophetic." In the same interview, Roth dismisses other critical readings of the novel, including those espousing the importance of the Freudian view, at least in his own mind at the time of writing it. After being told about the "obviously" Freudian aspects of the book, Roth replied: "Of course, I knew about Freud, but I had only a smattering of it. I knew only what almost everyone knew of Freud, and that wasn't a great deal. Don't forget this was more than 35 years ago, and Freud didn't have the currency then that he was to have later. I guess I must have occasionally thought about the relationships in Freudian terms, but I wouldn't say I was following Freud. Of course that's what an artist does. If he's good, and if he's working right, he doesn't need to be told. He senses these things on his own." Roth also denigrated the Jewish aspect of the novel by saying that the "Jewishness isn't very important. They're only Jewish because that's the life I knew best, but they might have been almost anything."[8] In another interview with Bonnie Lyons, Roth dismisses the significance of politics in the novel. "Even as a young man," he said, "I had no interest in political involvement. I grew up at a time when politics was looked down upon completely."[9]

Thus, Roth at various times has dismissed most of the major critical interpretations of the novel. However, he claims that he was inspired in his youth by literary modernism—what he calls "art for art's sake." In his interview with Bonnie Lyons, Roth said that it was Joyce's *Ulysses* that "opened my eyes to the fact that the material for literature was all around you. That you didn't have to go to the Yukon with Jack London. That life was a junkyard, that your environment was a junkheap, and you just picked up the pieces of junk. That language and art was the way you transmuted it."[10] Lyons, who has written extensively about Roth, points out how much of the novel reflects Joyce's influence. The novelistic techniques of stream of consciousness and foreshortening and the use of recurring motifs all suggest Joyce. In addition, the almost anthropological concern for archetypal patterns of initiation and mythological uses of symbolism show the influence not only of Joyce but also of Roth's relationship to Eda Lou Walton, the New York anthropologist who supported and nurtured him for so long.[11] After *Call It Sleep*, Roth wrote about a hundred pages of a second novel that was greeted with much enthusiasm by Maxwell Perkins of Scribner's. However, Roth was unable to complete the novel and has written nothing but occasional short pieces since then.

In spite of Epstein's persuasive thesis and Roth's own remarks, I believe a case can still be made for reading *Call It Sleep* as a novel of regeneration. I also think one of the ways to make this case is through the use of a Freudian approach to the book, even though Roth himself discounts the importance of Freud as an influence upon him. A psychoanalytical study of David Schearl's character can do much to explain his symbolic significance both in the novel and in the development of the role of the Jewish writer and intellectual in America. My model for this psychoanalysis comes from Norman Brown's controversial study of Martin Luther. Brown considers Luther a revolutionary force partly because of his method of reaching radical religious doctrines through a form of psychoanalysis that proffers a triumph over repression and death-in-life with the concomitant promise of a resurrection of the body. Luther, according to Brown, anticipates Freud's insight into the connection between sublimation, repression, and higher spiritual and artistic creativity. Like Freud, Luther linked the psychology of so-called higher religious and spiritual experiences with basic biological functions. However, Luther's special contribution, according to Brown, was the recognition of a "middle term" of the devil as a black figure who represented a form of anality that connected religion, money, and character. This linkage could explain the significance of Luther's account of his realization of the doctrine of justification by faith while using the privy of the Wittenberg tower.[12] Luther, however, achieves an additional insight by reaffirming the central role played by the devil in Protestantism. "But Protestantism," writes Brown, "and its social and psychological implications must be understood as a new relation to the Devil, a relation which explains the new relation to God. . . . For Luther, as for John Wesley, 'No Devil, no God.' . . . The psychological premise of Protestantism is conviction of sin. Protestantism, as a new relation to God, is a response to a new experience of evil. The novelty consists first in the scope and intensity of the evil experienced, and second in the sense of absolute powerlessness in the face of it. . . . In Luther this experience of omnipresent and uncontrollable evil generates the theological novelty that this world, in all its outward manifestations, is ruled not by God but by the Devil."[13] For Luther, Brown argues, the devil's control over the material world and the flesh becomes a Protestant version of the death instinct. "It would be hard to find a clearer illustration of the actuality and effective power of that death instinct which Freud postulated and which the non-Freudian world has ridiculed," writes Brown. "For hell, Luther said, is not a place, but is the experience of death, and Luther's devil is ultimately personified death."[14]

Brown's study of Luther helps to explain the meaning of the pattern of images and ideas in the mind of David Schearl that associates death with anality and religion. However, in David's mind the middle term of the devil as the symbol of filth and death becomes his conception of the Jew. This idea makes particularly pertinent a famous epigram by C. M. Doughty that "the Semites are like to a man sitting in a cloaca to the eyes, and whose brows touch heaven." Both Walter Allen and Leslie Fiedler emphasize the relevance of this statement to an understanding of *Call It Sleep*.[15] The association of excrement with David's Aunt Bertha and his father, Albert, helps to establish the theme in the novel of the Jew as the middle term of the devil. Soon after her appearance, Bertha antagonizes her severely critical and authoritarian brother-in-law Albert by making a joke about how the word cocaine in English sounds like the Yiddish word for excrement. Following her trip to the dentist, she says that in the old country "'they say that 'kockin' will clear the brow of pain. But here in America—didn't he call it that? 'Kockin'?—will clear the mouth of pain.'"[16] The joke, of course, disturbs Albert, for the hidden meanings in Bertha's teasing suggest that Albert needs to be relieved of internal pressures of both a psychological and physical sort. Thus, the father personifies the repressed and neurotic souls that concern Norman Brown. Roth writes that at one point when David sees his father, "it was as though his whole body were smouldering, a stark, throbbing, curdling emanation flowed from him, a dark corrosive haze that was all the more fearful because David sensed how thin an aura it was of the terrific volcano clamped within" (*CS*, p. 127). In addition, in her attitude toward money, Bertha exemplifies anality as Brown interprets its capitalistic aspects. "'I don't care where we live,' said Aunt Bertha, 'as long as we make money. Money, cursed money! What if it is a little uncomfortable. I never refused pot-roast because it got between my teeth. Now is the time to save. Later when we've sold the store and made a little money, we'll talk again'" (*CS*, p. 185).

David's version of Brown's thesis of the middle term coheres in *cheder*, or Hebrew school, with Reb Yidel Pankower. In cheder one day, the rabbi prepares a student for his bar mitzvah, the religious ceremony marking adulthood at the age of thirteen. For the boy it will require reading from Books 6, 7, and 9 of Isaiah, which is his Haftorah, or the additional reading for the day of his bar mitzvah. "'Now,' said the rabbi stroking his beard, 'this is the 'Haftorah' to Jethro—something you will read at your bar mitzvah, if you live that long'" (*CS*, p. 225). As the boy Mendel reads, young David listens. The passage explains how God cleans Isaiah's lips with coal. In his translation and explanation of the passage, the rabbi says, "'I, common man, have seen the Almighty, I, unclean one have seen him! Behold, my lips are unclean and I live in a land unclean—for the Jews at that time were sinful—'" (*CS*, p. 227). In awe of the power of the coal, David also is shocked at the notion of the Jews as dirty. He thinks, "—Clean? Light? Wonder if—? Wish I could ask him why the Jews were dirty. What did they do?" (*CS*, p. 227). As he mulls over these impressions and tries to assimilate the conflicting ideas and images surrounding the use of coal for purifying an unholy and filthy people, the other boys mutter a continuous whisper of street language and vulgarities that invade his own thoughts. To his horror he finds himself thinking the same words even as he ponders the religious significance of the Isaiah passage. He thinks, "—Some place Isaiah saw Him, just like that. I bet! He was sitting on a chair. So he's got chairs, so he can sit. Gee! Sit Shit! Sh! Please God, I didn't mean it! Please God, somebody else said it! Please—" (*CS*, p. 230). In resisting the temptation to think of these words, he naturally finds that the very effort calls up the same words so that his own thought processes trap him. Listening to the cacophony around him, he thinks, "—He said dirty words, I bet. Shit, pee, fuckenbestit—Stop! You're sayin' it yourself. It's a sin again! That's why he—Gee! I didn't mean it. But your mouth don't get dirty. I don't feel no dirt" (*CS*, p. 231). Thus, David not only connects the Jews with filth but also identifies himself as contributing to that filth. Moreover, the rabbi both confirms this relationship and introduces another aspect of death-in-life in the form of repression. After David fails to respond to a call to recite, the rabbi accuses him of being like the other boys. Roth writes, "He glared at David accusingly. 'You too? Is your head full of turds like the rest of them? Speak!'" (*CS*, p. 233). After David completes a brilliantly successful recitation, the rabbi beams proudly at him and gives him an unprecedented reward of a penny. The rabbi says, "'Because you have a true Yiddish head'" (*CS*, p. 234), meaning one that is filled with God's word rather than with the filth that seemingly permeates the thoughts of the other Jewish boys and, secretly of course, David's as well. The rabbi thus urges the repression and sublimation of the flesh and body in the interests of achieving a higher religious awareness.

Repression, however, cannot keep David from seeing relationships that his mind, body, and experience thrust him toward. He feels forced to confront the paradox of reconciling the religious vision of being Jewish with the idea of the Jews as unclean and evil. Although he does not actually connect the words *devil* and *Jew*, he makes such an association when told by his first gentile friend, a Polish boy named Leo Dugovka, that the Jews are the killers of Christ. "'Jews?' David repeated, horrified and incredulous" after Leo tells him (*CS*, p. 323). "'Sure,'" Leo answers. "'Jews is de Chris'-killers. Dey put 'im up dere'" (*CS*, p. 323). David confesses his ignorance of the story of Jesus. "A hundred other questions clamored at his tongue," writes Roth, "but fearful of further revelations, he stifled them" (*CS*, p. 323). The impact of the news of Jesus is greatened because David receives it in Leo's apartment in the midst of his first exposure to paintings of Christ and of Christian artifacts. Awed by a painting showing Jesus' sacred heart as luminous, David cannot help but compare the power of that light to the light he seeks from Isaiah's coal. Leo says, "'Dat's Christchin light—it's way bigger. Bigger den Jew light'" (*CS*, p. 322). In his admiration for the independence, freedom, and strength of the Christian boy, David seems only too ready to accept this inferior status as a Jew. Thus, in an earlier scene, David compounds his own anxiety about being Jewish by mocking the Jews in order to entertain and please Leo. Insecurity yields to a sense of guilt over his identity. Roth writes, "He had felt a slight qualm of guilt, yes, guilt because he was betraying all the Jews in his house who had Mezuzehs above their doors; but if Leo thought it was funny, then it was funny and it didn't matter" (*CS*, p. 306). (A mezuzah is a small box that contains words from the Pentateuch and is attached to the doorpost of a Jewish home.) For David, the challenge to grow up requires that he overcome his intense dependence upon his mother and his fear of his father while attempting to cope with all the complexities and contradictions of his identity as a Jew in the modern world. Throughout the novel, biological and emotional repression reenforces David's proclivity to alienate himself from his own Jewishness. His initial flight from his Jewish identity toward Christian light represents a basic flight from his own body and life. The novel builds toward a climactic moment of reconciliation and growth when he manages to assert himself by confronting and accepting his existence as a living being and as a Jew.

In Norman Brown's terms, David must learn how to live other than through sublimation. In the first place, Brown protests, sublimation dooms itself to failure because "no matter how anality is sublimated, human nature remains essentially filthy." For Brown, all "psychic energy taking the form of sublimation" becomes deadening through its emphasis on "self-sacrifice and instinctual renunciation." Brown writes, "It follows that what we call historical progress, or higher civilization, means an increase in the domain of the death instinct at the expense of the life instinct. Sublimation is a mortification of the body and a sequestration of the life of the body into dead things."[17] Brown further argues that mankind has taken "the path of sublimation" to "the end of this road" where death awaits for the individual and the race. "The path of sublimation," he writes, "which mankind has religiously followed at least since the foundation of the first cities, is no way out of the human neurosis, but, on the contrary, leads to its aggravation. Psychoanalytical theory and the bitter facts of contemporary history suggest that mankind is reaching the end of this road. Psychoanalytical theory declares that the end of the road is the dominion of death-in-life. History has brought mankind to that pinnacle on which the total obliteration of mankind is at last a practical possibility."[18] He argues that a true resurrection of the body can occur first by understanding and then by overcoming repressions and sublimations by which means death has dominion over life. By rejecting sublimation and accepting death and the body, the death and life instincts function together to create new life.

David's history of sublimation is basic to a pattern of fear and anxiety that makes his existence a form of death-in-life from the beginning of the novel's first section entitled "The Cellar." The cellar of the first building in which he lives in Brownsville functions as a symbol for such fears and for the deep psychological drives within him. With its rats, darkness, and odors, the cellar is a nightmare, but other parts of the world are also terrifying. On the street his language and religion separate him from others and invite abuse from neighborhood bullies. At home his ferocious father persecutes him with suspicion and distrust. Even his mother's love seems compromised by the secrets of her past in Europe that work to separate her from David. Moreover, her love affair, which certainly seems justified as a response to her despair, appears to be an act of betrayal to David. It arouses the same visions of death that Dorothy Dinnerstein describes in *The Mermaid and the Minotaur* as the natural result of the child's separation from the mother. Dinnerstein's interpretation of Freud and Brown once again helps to explain the sense of dread and death that dominates much of David Schearl's imagination and sensibility. Early in the novel he observes a funeral, and his mother explains death to him as an eternal sleep. She says, " 'They are cold; they are still. They shut their eyes in sleep eternal years' " (*CS*, p. 69). This establishes the death theme in the novel as David faces eternal sleep-in-life because of the world of anxieties and sublimations that control his emotional life and physical environment.

In a mystical moment for David, the novel anticipates how he will achieve freedom. The event takes place significantly on the morning of Passover eve, the holiday marking the freedom of the Jews and, by extension, freedom for all oppressed peoples. David goes out to perform a religious ritual, the burning of the *chumitz*, the last of the household bread that must be destroyed to mark the demand to eat only matzoh or unleavened bread for the holiday. (During the exodus from slavery in Egypt, the Jews had time to make only unleavened bread.) Watching the burning of the chumitz prepares David for a charged moment of ecstasy. "—No more chumitz," he thinks. "All burned black. See God, I was good? Now only white Matzohs are left" (*CS*, p. 246). He walks down to the river and the effect of the sunlight on the water mystifies him. "The brilliance," writes Roth, "was hypnotic. He could not take his eyes away. His spirit yielded, melted into light" (*CS*, p. 247). In his near trance-like state, David does not realize how close he is to the water and does not fully sense the approach of a tugboat with a man on board. "'Wake up, Kid!'" the man shouts, startling David from his reverie (*CS*, p. 248). The totality of the day's experiences constitutes a promise for a form of spiritual journey for David in the future.

The message for David to wake up does not really get answered until the end of the novel when the tugboat reappears in David's mind as he tries to survive the shock on the trolley tracks. There are several important aspects to this part of the novel as David rests in an unconscious state, absorbing all the voices and sounds that abound around him and remembering an array of images and symbols of significance to his story, including the words of his mother concerning "eternal years." The incident presents David struggling to wake from a sleep that obviously symbolizes the deathlike quality of his life. Onlookers say, "'He's woikin' hard!'" "'Oy! Soll im Gott helfin!'" and "'He no waka'" (*CS*, p. 426). However, as the images and memories pour through his mind, David's energy and will return. Roth writes, "On the dark and broken sidewalk, the limp body gasped, quivered. The interne lifted him, said sharply to the officer. 'Hold his arms! He'll fight!'" (*CS*, p. 431). After so much fear and self-doubt, the idea of David's willingness to fight, especially under the circumstance of the easy alternative of a final sleep, is of major importance. David emerges with a revivified Jewish identity. Through his mind runs biblical images, religious memories, thoughts of cheder and synagogue. Moreover, witnesses looking at him say, "'Unh! Looks Jewish t' me.'" Another witness responds, "'Yeah, map o' Jerusalem, all right'" (*CS*, p. 427).

Throughout this scene of David's fight for his life, the onlookers and witnesses to his injury form a chorus of American voices mixing accents and languages. The words and dialects circulate through David's head so that he becomes a unifying consciousness bringing the sounds and the people together in a single entity and perspective. He thus anticipates and fulfills the reponsibility of the writer and intellectual to participate in the re-creation of American culture and life through the renewal of language. Ironically, Rabbi Pankower, a staunch defender of orthodoxy, uses words reminiscent of Crèvecoeur to predict this transformation of all Jewish youth into a "new breed" of Americans. Pankower thinks: "'A curse on them!' He glared about him at the children and half-grown boys and girls who crowded the stoops and overflowed into the sidewalks and gutter.

'The devil take them! What was going to become of Yiddish youth? What would become of this new breed? These Americans? This sidewalk-and-gutter generation?'" (*CS*, pp. 373–74).

As the consciousness of this transformation of Jewish youth into a "new breed" that mixes with other "foreign" and native voices, David's mind focuses on the Statue of Liberty as a symbol of the powerful forces and ambiguities involved in such a change in people and culture. The growing complexity of his relationship to America is symbolized by the changing persona he assigns to the Statue of Liberty. In the novel's prologue, David and his mother arrive in America and first see the Statue of Liberty as rather ominous and forbidding, more of a sign of their dread and alienation than of their hopes for freedom in a new land. In this scene, the Statue of Liberty reenforces the fear aroused by David's father who waits to greet mother and son in the new land. Roth writes, "And before them, rising on her high pedestal from the scaling swarmy brilliance of sunlit water to the west, Liberty. The spinning disk of the late afternoon sun slanted behind her, and to those on board who gazed, her features were charred with shadow, her depths exhausted, her masses ironed to one single plane. Against the luminous sky the ray of her halo were spikes of darkness roweling the air; shadow flattened the torch she bore to a black cross against flawless light—the blackened hilt of a broken sword. Liberty. The child and his mother stared again at the massive figure in wonder" (*CS*, p. 14). In the concluding pages of the novel, however, the Statue of Liberty appears as a female figure to be possessed as a symbol of America. Roth writes, "Above the even enthusiasm of the kindly faced American woman: 'And do you know, you can go all the way up inside her for twenty-five cents. For only twenty-five cents, mind you! Every American man, woman and child ought to go up inside her, it's a thrilling experience. The Statue of Liberty is—'" (*CS*, p. 415). The teasing sexual references to the Statue of Liberty foreshadow a sense of confidence about America in David's mind. Such sarcasm deflates a proclivity toward self-righteousness and knocks the Statue of Liberty, so to speak, off its pedestal.

David returns to consciousness remembering the sound of the whistle from the man on the tugboat who had called out to him to wake up. The odor of ammonia brought to him to arouse his consciousness reminds him of the smell of the synagogue on Yom Kippur, the Day of Atonement following Rosh Hashanah, the Jewish New Year. On that day, Jews atone for their sins and hope to do better during the forthcoming year. The total combination of images and symbols powerfully suggest that David's awakening marks his resurrection as a Jew from a living death.

Fighting to live for David Schearl means accepting himself as a Jew and overcoming the fears and sublimations that have made life a form of death-in-life for him. His success can be seen in the emergence of the Jewish writer and of Jewish sensibility as basic forces in American life and thought. Reborn on the street, he serves as a central consciousness for a chorus of American voices and identities. Moreover, when seen in the light of Norman Brown's interpretation of Luther and psychoanalysis, David's rebirth can be understood as a triumph of the life instinct. His new freedom includes the opening of human consciousness to eros. In terms of the Jewish writer's relationship to American culture as a whole, David's struggle to achieve the autonomy and integrity of his imagination makes him a young Luther in the religion of modern American democracy. Through the symbolic achievement of his own freedom, he becomes a prophet of freedom for others.

David's awakening with its promise of his integration into the community as a complete individual contradicts Roth's own sense of personal, political, and cultural alienation during the mid-1930s when his commitment to the ideology of the left deepened. His uncompleted second novel expressed his leftist thought through the character of a proletarian hero from the Midwest who turns to communism. In the succeeding years, Roth never proved able to find an adequate artistic structure for his left-wing ideology. Such silence, of course, does not diminish the significance of his one great achievement, a novel about the attempt of one boy to overcome the various forms of psychological and cultural repression in the ghetto.

Chapter 6

"Blut-und-Eisen"
Anzia Yezierska and the
New Self-made Woman

The conflict between literary imagination and ideology that stifled Henry Roth did not bother Anzia Yezierska. A double ideology drove Yezierska's personal life and sustained her writing. This ideology consisted of a belief in America as a land of hope and new life along with a passionate feminist consciousness that anticipated aspects of the women's movement today. The union of the American Way and feminism in the context of Jewish culture and the ghetto make Yezierska special to the tradition of the New Covenant. She saw herself as a mediator between American and Jewish cultures, explaining each world to the other in terms related to her fight for identity, respect, and freedom as a woman.

Yezierska's attitude toward America as both a woman and a Jewish immigrant from Plinsk in Russian Poland is succinctly expressed in two of her stories published originally in different collections in the early twenties and republished in a new collection edited by Alice Kessler-Harris. In "The Miracle," the heroine discovers through the help of an American teacher what the new Jewish immigrants can contribute to America. Up to that moment she felt isolated and disappointed in the broken promises of America. The teacher says, "'If you would only know how much you can teach us Americans. You are the promise of the centuries to come. You are the heart, the creative pulse of America to be.'"[1] The responsibility to be the creative impulse of the "America to be" puts the Jewish writer at the heart of American culture. Many Jewish writers could be expected to relish this responsibility because it also implies an official expectation to fulfill one's self as an individual and as a Jew. Thus, in her story, "America and I," Yezierska argues that the Jews are the new Pilgrims of America. Perhaps such a linkage—a Jewish girl from a shtetl and the Pilgrim Mothers—seems ludicrous. On the other hand, this election of herself and the Jews to such prominence makes even more sense in some ways for Yezierska than it does for other Jews like Brandeis and Straus. Yezierska's romanticization in "America and I" of the Pilgrims and her identification with them dramatize the immigrant's anxious attempt to structure and render meaning to her existence in a new country. Moreover, the immigrant's belief in America as a promised land along with the desperate need for an opportunity for a new life provide a psychological justification for seeing the common values in both cultures of work, individuality, and achievement as a means of fusing Jewish and American identities.

Yezierska delineates a function of myth as a tool in the service of acculturation by showing how the immigrant's consciousness and experience adopt and internalize an important part of national history for her own needs and uses. In her story, the example of the Pilgrims becomes a vehicle for entrance into American culture. The Pilgrims' story personalizes America for the narrator and helps her to re-create her own identity. She says, "I began to read the American history. I found from the first pages that America started with a band of Courageous Pilgrims. They had left their native country as I had left mine. They had crossed an unknown ocean and landed in an unknown country, as I" (*OC*, p. 32).

Furthermore, the narrator's understanding of the myth of the Pilgrims provides the psychic machinery that enables her to translate her unwarranted sense of guilt as a foreigner into a program of action for personal change and growth. She expresses her feelings of guilt in various ways. She says, "But the great difference between the first Pilgrims and me was that they expected to make America, build America, create their own world of liberty. I wanted to find it ready made" (*OC*, p. 32). Blaming herself for being a stranger, she exaggerates the achievements and strengths of the dominant culture as rendered through the story of the Pilgrims. "I read on," the narrator says. "I delved deeper down into the American history. I saw how the Pilgrim Fathers came to a rocky desert country, surrounded by Indian savages on all sides. But undaunted, they pressed on—through danger—through famine, pestilence, and want—they pressed on. They did not ask the Indians for sympathy, for understanding. They made no demands on anybody, but on their own indomitable spirit of persistence" (*OC*, p. 32). In comparison with such bravery on the part of the Pilgrims, she says of herself: "And I—I was forever begging a crumb of sympathy, a gleam of understanding from strangers who could not understand" (*OC*, p. 32). The narrator seems to create an impassable gap between herself and the Pilgrims; in fact, however, her story of the Pilgrims becomes her own. Through the story she adopts the psychology of the jeremiad for the purpose of transforming and regenerating herself. She uses the moral rhetoric of self-reproach for self-elevation. Centuries and cultures apart, the Pilgrim and the Jew in her story become one in terms of values and ethos.

The immigrant, as Yezierska describes her, not only feels inferior for being different but also feels guilty for feeling guilty about being herself and a Jew. Thus, the immigrant appears trapped between wanting to be American and not wishing to betray her background and ties. Although it creates this trap for the immigrant, the ideology constructs an escape that Yezierska quickly perceives as another indication of how America creates unprecedented opportunity for Jews. It consists of the idea elaborated upon by Brandeis and others that with honesty about being Jewish one can be faithful to the principles of pluralism and diversity that ultimately bring all people together as Americans. By being true to herself as a Jew, she can set an example of what it means to be an American. She must compromise enough to achieve so-called Americanization but not change so much as to lose her ethnic identity. Thus, the story ends with her adoption of an ideology that encourages Jewish participation in the continued making of America without surrendering Jewish identity. She says, "Then came a light—a great revelation! I saw America—a big idea—a deathless hope—a world still in the making. I saw that it was the glory of America that it was not yet finished. And I, the last comer, had her share to give, small or great, to the making of America, like those Pilgrims who came in the *Mayflower*" (*OC*, p. 33). She even sees what her role will be in that project of building America. Her personal mission as a writer involves concentrating on herself and her culture in a way that assures her inclusion in American life. She says, "I began to build a bridge of understanding between the American-born and myself. . . . In only writing about the Ghetto I found America" (*OC*, p. 33). This story, with its use of the subjective first person pronoun in the title—"America and I"—reflects a commitment to action and optimism.

However, insofar as the narrative voice of these stories is a projection of Yezierska herself, it also represents the author's process of self-alienation in the form of the objectification of her own identity. In a sense, therefore, the stories dramatize a kind of self-petrification in the interests of literary creation. The damage inflicted by such self-sacrifice for the purpose of change receives consideration in a story entitled "Bread and Wine in the Wilderness," published almost thirty years later in 1950, in which many of the same themes of adjustment and cultural accommodation are treated with greater pessimism and ambiguity. In this story the narrator attends a Thanksgiving Day celebration given by strangers. She identifies with the Pilgrims who "had been dissenters and immigrants like me" (*OC*, p. 201), but she cannot feel comfortable with the people at the dinner who seem distant in their rural and formal ways. The effect of this story, especially when published with her earlier pieces, is to emphasize the impossibility of burying the immigrant and alien self. The story illustrates the cost to the individual of the attempt to change so much so quickly.

The ideology of the individual self at the core of Yezierska's writings represents basic American attitudes toward freedom, success, and culture. This philosophy of the individual self finds expression in simple, populistic terms throughout her work. In the story "The Miracle" it comes down to a phrase: " 'Make a person of yourself' " (*OC*, p. 14). The idea of being a person or making one's self into a person rather than a slave or a victim appears repeatedly in Yezierska's work. Moreover, the achievement of selfhood informs Yezierska's concept of success in America. However, her idea of success differs markedly from such models as Cahan's in *The Rise of David Levinsky*, Norman Podhoretz's in *Making It*, and Joseph Epstein's in *Ambition: The Secret Passion*.[2] For Yezierska, as for John Cawelti, success is "tied to individual fulfillment and social progress rather than to wealth and status."[3] The form of success that I associate with Yezierska goes back in America at least to Benjamin Franklin and Thomas Jefferson. Franklin and Jefferson represented, says Cawelti, "the belief that the individual's place in society should be defined by his ability to perform useful actions and not by his rank in the traditional hierarchy."[4]

As a Jewish immigrant, Yezierska's brave effort to achieve the Franklinian and Jeffersonian ideals of self-improvement and self-fulfillment seems impressive. However, as a Jewish woman, her fight to realize such ideals makes her truly exceptional because she had to overcome both Jewish and American hostility to her ambitions. Yezierska came to America in the 1890s, when life for all Jews under the czar was a form of imprisonment within the Pale of Settlement. For Jewish men and women, America was a refuge. However, for Jewish women a second prison moved with them to America in the form of their status within Jewish culture itself. America potentially served as a double rescue from their traditional roles of subservience as daughters, wives, and mothers to the men who were elevated by religious law to study Torah. America gave women the opportunity to break their dependence on men and to work for themselves. Yezierska, according to Alice Kessler-Harris, fought so hard for such freedom that her efforts can be described as "revolutionary." Kessler-Harris writes that "when a woman's autonomy involved the search for personal fulfillment, it became nothing short of revolutionary. It violated a basic tenet of Jewish family structure: that women were merely the servants of men, the extensions of their husbands. Anzia Yezierska was, in that sense, a revolutionary. Passionately convinced that her life was her own, she deliberately rejected traditional home and family roles."[5]

The most important target of Yezierska's attack for female independence is the figure of the father in her novel *Bread Givers*. Seeing her father "as a tyrant more terrible than the Tsar from Russia," the heroine of the novel, Sara Smolinsky, says, "Wild with all that was choked in me since I was born, my eyes burned into my father's eyes. 'My will is as strong as yours. I'm going to live my own life. Nobody can stop me. I'm not from the old country. I'm American!'"[6] From her early youth, Sara saw the structure of religion as designed to keep women in their place. She says, "The prayers of his daughters didn't count because God didn't listen to women. Heaven and the next world were only for men. Women could get into Heaven because they were wives and daughters of men. Women had no brains for the study of God's Torah, but they could be the servants of men who studied the Torah. Only if they cooked for the men, and washed for the men, and didn't nag or curse the men out of their homes; only if they let the men study the Torah in peace, then, maybe, they could push themselves into Heaven with the men, to wait on them there" (*BG*, pp. 9–10). She believed that men simply continued to assume authoritarian power over women in marriage. Thus, she watches her sisters escape from her father by entering equally miserable marriages. She insists on living alone and fighting for an education so that she will not have to suffer a "'boss of a husband to crush the spirit in me'" (*BG*, p. 177). During one point of her struggle for independence she comes close to marrying a man whose affections really touch her. At the end of her relationship with him, however, she thinks, "To him, a wife would only be another piece of property" (*BG*, p. 199).

Hatred of the idea of women as property becomes one of the most powerful forces behind Smolinsky's feminism. She maintains that dependence breeds only contempt and lack of interest in husbands and obsequiousness in women. Moreover, the implication of a promise in marriage of economic if not emotional security proves to be a cruel hoax. Sara sees that marriage for her sisters often results in economically impoverished and physically brutal living conditions. Thus, the title *Bread Givers* can be taken ironically. It refers to her sisters' husbands and to all men who brutalize women. Those husbands are not providers and bread givers but grudging, selfish, and ugly tyrants. One sister says, "'With Moe for my bread giver I'm too dirt-poor to help you'" (*BG*, p. 147). For Yezierska, women without economic power will never achieve freedom. In *Bread Givers*, Sara learns this lesson early in life when her family faces eviction because of her father's refusal to work. She invests in a quarter's worth of herring to sell for a profit on the streets. "'I want to go into business like a person,'" she says. "'I must buy what I got to sell'" (*BG*, p. 21). However, it is not just in marriage that she finds women treated unfairly. In one incident in the novel, she complains about the practice of a cafeteria that serves larger portions of meat to men than to women (*BG*, p. 169).

As a modern, educated feminist who rebels against her father by refusing to accede to his authoritarian demands, Sara seems to be not only his arch enemy but his exact opposite in terms of values and ideals. In fact, however, they are most like each other as character types. He dubs her "'*Blut-und-Eisen*'" (*BG*, p. 20)—blood and iron—qualities of character that most resemble him. Whereas the other sisters are generally obedient, even subservient before him, only she manifests his iron will and independence. Her sisters, therefore, recognize their father in Sara. "'You hard heart,'" one sister named Fania says. "'Come, Bessie,'" she says to a second sister, "'Let's leave her to her mad education. She's worse than Father with his Holy Torah'" (*BG*, p. 178). More important, she herself comes to recognize how much she respects his commitment and solidity in spite of his terribly tyrannical and selfish way of being. She says, "In a world where all is changed, he alone remained unchanged—as tragically isolate as the rocks. All that he had left of life was his fanatical adherence to his traditions. It was within my power to keep lighted the flickering candle of his life for him. Could I deny him this poor service? Unconsciously, my hand reached out for his" (*BG*, p. 296). She alone effectively challenges her father's authoritarianism but also becomes the only daughter capable of internalizing and accepting responsibility for his model of authority. Only she incorporates his moral authority within herself. She can function with her own superego and conscience.

Thus, Sara Smolinsky develops the inner strengths that are necessary for the sort of independent personality essential for a democracy. In this novel, therefore, Yezierska anticipates the concerns expressed by cultural critics such as Christopher Lasch who fear our failure as a culture to fill the gap created by the collapse of paternal authority. Lasch writes, "Modern man faces the world without the protection of kings, priests, and other more or less benevolent father-figures; but he could accept their loss if it had helped him to develop inner resources of his own. Unable to internalize authority, however, he projects forbidden impulses outward and transforms the world into a nightmare. Authorities, inevitably modeled on the divided father, present themselves as either incompetent or malevolent."[7] Both Yezierska and Lasch see a social need for the middle-class character type that exemplifies values of intensity, depth, independence, and authority.

Moreover, through her development of Sara Smolinsky as a modern woman and a heroic figure, Yezierska anticipates the efforts of some contemporary feminist writers such as Juliet Mitchell, Elizabeth Janeway, and Jean Strouse. These writers suggest the possibility of new paradigms to transcend old patterns of love and authority and old stereotypes of masculinity and femininity.[8] They consider and develop Freud's theory of the psychology of women in terms of his understanding of the relationship between biology, intrapsychic structure, and culture. However, they also confront his patriarchal perspective by suggesting that women can achieve autonomy and moral responsibility for themselves. It seems to me, therefore, that Sara Smolinsky is a character worthy of their consideration. Yezierska's Sara contradicts Freud's argument that women generally develop passive natures with weakened superegos as a result of their need to find refuge in their fathers following the loss of their mothers during the Oedipal phase of development. Independent and ambitious during her youth, Sara overcomes her father's domination to establish her own sense of moral authority. She sees that in his absolute self-centeredness her father personifies the cruelty of an ideology that condemns women to a purely domestic sphere of existence whether for economic, religious, social, or cultural reasons. In fact, in her attempt to make this ideological statement, Yezierska probably exaggerates the father's unmitigated selfishness. The portrayal of the father as so utterly spoiled in effect challenges the credibility of Sara's final act of kindness toward him. Since she has spent so many years fighting him, her act of ultimate support and help for her father seems somewhat unreal. At the same time, however, Sara's kindness toward her father is meant to constitute a moral triumph of her own values, will, and authority. Like her mother and her sisters, she finally acquiesces to her father in his miserable last days. In contrast to them, however, she does so out of strength not weakness. She fulfills a sense of her own moral authority as an independent woman and not as a slave. Furthermore, Sara also provides an interesting contrast with Henry Roth's David Schearl. David, in Norman Brown's sense of the terms, learns to sublimate less in order to live more. Sara, on the other hand, counters cultural prejudices and expectations by sublimating her energies to develop her own internal moral resources. Thus, Yezierska's portrayal of Sara represents an important attempt to proffer a feminist challenge to conventional ideology.

Just as Yezierska was a leader in developing new roles for women in her fiction, she also was an innovator in her use of language and in her presentation of immigrant character. Many critics have commented on the power of Henry Roth's style in capturing Yiddish speech and dialect and in dramatizing the world of language as the embodiment of cultural identity. However, with the exception of Jules Chametzky, few appreciate Yezierska's own strengths in this area. Like her various fictional selves, she was a pioneer as a writer. She not only re-created the myth of America to include Jews and women but she also saw the importance of authenticity in depicting Jewish language and culture. She, therefore, became a true leader of linguistic innovation in her successful attempt to render the excitement of immigrant speech and dialect. Although writing in English, her tone and phrasing were perfect for conveying the flavor of the Yiddish character and vernacular, especially under the pressure-cooker conditions of the immigrant experience. As her daughter reports in an afterword to

The Open Cage, Yezierska was able to achieve this effect only after working consciously to make her style suitable for the setting and circumstances of her stories (*OC*, pp. 256–57). Through such effort, she was able to create the impression, especially in her earliest stories, of an almost direct rendering of the immigrant experience and consciousness. For example, in the opening paragraphs of "The Miracle," she writes, "I was a poor Melamid's daughter in Savel, Poland. In my village, a girl without a dowry was a dead one. The only kind of a man that would give a look on a girl without money was a widower with a dozen children, or someone with a hump or on crutches" (*OC*, p. 3). Such language not only conveys the life of the immigrant but it also evokes the sense of a true Yiddish folk culture with its own legends, superstitions, and rituals. In the same story, Yezierska shows how excitement to go to America developed after the receipt of a letter from the New World. She writes, "Gewalt! What an excitement began to burn through the whole village when they heard of Hannah Hayyeh's luck! The ticket agents from the ship companies seeing how Hanna Hayyeh's letter was working like yeast in the air for America, posted up big signs by all the market fairs: 'Go to America, the New World. Fifty rubles a ticket.' . . . Oi weh! How I was hungering to go to America after that! By day and by night I was tearing and turning over the earth, how to get to my lover on the other side of the world" (*OC*, p. 5). Of course, upon her arrival in America she initially feels great disappointment and loneliness. "Nu," she says, "I got to America" (*OC*, p. 11). She then proceeds to describe her trials and tribulations, including an encounter with a wretched matchmaker. She asks him, " 'Can't I get a man in America without money?' " and records his response: "He gave a look on me with his sharp eyes. Gottuniu! What a look! I thought I was sinking into the floor" (*OC*, p. 13).

Such stories that are written in the vernacular style helped to make Yezierska quite successful and widely known in the twenties. Born around 1880—the exact date is not known—she fought for success in America like one of the characters in her stories and books. A rebel and nonconformist by nature, it is possible that her instinctively individualistic attitude toward American culture received encouragement through her brief but intense relationship with the philosopher John Dewey (*OC*, pp. 259–60). She achieved great notoriety when Sam Goldwyn of Hollywood bought *Hungry Hearts* (1920), her first collection of short stories that included "The Fat of the Land," which won the important Edward J. O'Brien prize as the best short story of 1919. It was the first of six books published between 1920 and 1932. Although she continued to write until her death in 1970, she fell into relative obscurity in the 1930s and never recovered her former popularity. In a brief discussion of Yezierska that has been vital to the revival of her reputation, Allen Guttmann notes that along with Samuel Ornitz—(*Haunch Paunch and Jowl: An Autobiography* [1923])—she has been "almost completely forgotten."[9] Fortunately, Kessler-Harris's recent criticism and editions of Yezierska's work have done much to correct the neglect Guttmann describes by bringing new recognition to Yezierska's importance as a Jewish writer and woman. An early critic said Yezierska wrote as though "she dipped her pen in her heart" (*OC*, p. v). It was a style she never gave up.

Chapter 7

The Jew as Underground Man
Philip Roth

Anzia Yezierska fought with "blut-und-eisen" to find her identity and freedom as a woman and Jew in America, and Philip Roth, in our own time, has struggled to establish his identity as a Jewish writer and man. Perhaps no other modern American writer has done so much to challenge old stereotypes and concepts about masculinity. Roth has written almost compulsively about achieving independence, authority, and maturity as an artist and man in America. The fact that his heroes are multiple guises of a single mythic consciousness of the modern urban Jew both complicates and enriches his fiction and vision of American culture. Like Yezierska's Sara, Roth's hero finds himself encaptured in a ghetto of the mind. This theme of finding one's self unable to escape the past and unable to overcome a perennial perspective from a psychic ghetto pervades most of Roth's fiction. However, another important part of his perspective as a writer is Roth's definite sense of himself as an American writer. From the beginning of his career, Roth has expressed concern about the need to understand the meaning of the American experience, and, in this sense, Roth is a major contributor to the tradition of the New Covenant. In fact, along with Bellow and Mailer, Roth has written intensively about the responsibilities of the writer to explore the American idea and explain contemporary American culture. Moreover, he has also asserted the importance of Jewish writers in developing new literary styles and tastes as both a response to their situation as Jews in America and as a way of fulfilling their artistic and literary promise. Roth, in effect, claims for Jewish writers the kind of linguistic initiative and leadership that characterizes the writers of the New Covenant. In Roth, one finds justification for the argument that the Jewish writer and thinker is a linguistic innovator who develops the rhetorical and narrative structures of the myth and ideology of America while maintaining the role of the modern Jewish hero of thought. After reading what Roth says about fiction and literature, it becomes easier to understand that he wants his own fiction to lead the literary and intellectual effort to help liberate people from the bonds and shackles that they put on themselves. Roth's sentiments on such matters indicate a depth of concern that many miss in the creator of Alexander Portnoy.

In his famous essay of 1960 on "Writing American Fiction," Roth argues that "the American writer in the middle of the twentieth century has his hands full in trying to understand, describe, and then make *credible* much of American reality. It stupefies, it sickens, it infuriates, and finally it is even a kind of embarrassment to one's one meager imagination. The actuality is continually outdoing our talents, and the culture tosses up figures almost daily that are the envy of any novelist."[1] However, in spite of Roth's complaint about the intractability of American reality, his greater complaint goes against those who avoid the challenge. Thus, he expresses concern in 1960 because Norman Mailer "seems for the time being to have given up on making an imaginative assault upon the American experience" (*RM*, p. 123). He also attacks both the beat writers who deal in cynicism and the best sellers who peddle platitudes for ultimately committing the same crime of not taking either America or their own roles as writers seriously. He writes, "The attitude of the Beats (if such a phrase has meaning) is not entirely without appeal. The whole thing is a joke, America, ha-ha. But that doesn't put very much distance between Beatdom and its sworn enemy, best-sellerdom—not much more than what it takes to get from one side of a nickel to the other: for is America, ha-ha, really any more than America, hoo-ray, stood upon its head?" (*RM*, p. 125).

Roth's dismay at trying to reflect reality in America eventually develops into an affirmation of the writer's role. He carves out a special territory based not merely on his view of contemporary literature and culture but also on his understanding of the American literary tradition. A student of both American and European literature who received a master's degree from the University of Chicago, Roth realizes that he is not the first writer to confront the difficulty of rendering American reality. In a self-interview on *The Great American Novel*, he says:

Later I also became a disciple of certain literature professors and
their favorite texts. For instance, reading *The Wings of the Dove* all
afternoon long in the graduate-school library at the University of
Chicago, I would find myself as transfixed by James's linguistic tact
and moral scrupulosity as I had ever been by the coarseness, reck-
lessness, and vulgar, aggressive clowning with which I was so taken
during those afternoons and evenings in "my" booth at the corner
candy store. As I now see it, one of my continuing problems as a
writer has been to find the means to be true to these seemingly in-
imical realms of experience that I am strongly attached to by temperament and training—the aggressive, the crude, and the obscene,
at one extreme, and something a good deal more subtle and, in
every sense, refined, at the other. But that problem is not unique to
any single American writer, certainly not in this day and age. (*RM*,
p. 82)

Roth sees himself as trying to bridge what he goes on to describe in Philip
Rahv's terms as the worlds of the serious "paleface" writer and the spontaneous and more vernacular "redskin."

For Roth, this contrast between the styles and sensibilities of the "paleface" as opposed to the more aggressive "redskin" is complicated by being
Jewish, which automatically enlists one in the ranks of the "redskin." The
contrast between genteel sensibilities and the "redskin" reality of Jewish
ethnicity and class origins creates acute tensions for the Jewish writer and
intellectual. The Jewish writer has to face "being *fundamentally ill at ease
in, and at odds with, both worlds*." Roth continues, "In short: neither the
redskin one was in the days of innocence, nor the paleface one could never
be in a million (or, to be precise, 5,733) years, but rather, at least in my
own case, what I would describe as a 'redface'" (*RM*, p. 83). To the
Jewish writer, however, such tension can encourage discomfort with ordinary stylistic conventions and make one "alert to the inexhaustible number of intriguing postures that the awkward may assume in public, and the
strange means that the uneasy come upon to express themselves" (*RM*,
p. 83). In "Writing American Fiction," Roth more specifically identifies
the characteristics of this innovative Jewish style and the forces that help
to shape it. He writes:

When writers who do not feel much of a connection to Lord Ches-
terfield begin to realize that they are under no real obligation to try

and write like that distinguished old stylist, they are likely enough to go out and be bouncy. Also, there is the matter of the spoken language which these writers have heard, as our statesmen might put it, in the schools, the homes, the churches and the synagogues of the nation. I would even say that when the bouncy style is not an attempt to dazzle the reader, or one's self, but to incorporate into American literary prose the rhythms, nuances, and emphases of urban and immigrant speech, the result can sometimes be a language of new and rich emotional subtleties, with a kind of back-handed charm and irony all its own, as in Grace Paley's book of stories *The Little Disturbances of Man*. But whether the practitioner is Gold, Bellow, or Paley, there is a further point to make about the bounciness: it is an expression of pleasure." (*RM*, p. 131)

For Roth, therefore, his Jewish background provides an important source for creative literary and linguistic invention.

In contrast to Henry Roth, Philip Roth's sense of participation in a literary movement of modern Jewish writers is consistent with his acknowledged sense of himself as inexorably Jewish in terms of experience and thought. In an interview with George Plimpton about *Portnoy's Complaint*, Roth said, "I have always been far more pleased by my good fortune in being born a Jew than my critics may begin to imagine. It's a complicated, interesting, morally demanding, and very singular experience, and I like that. I find myself in the historic predicament of being Jewish, with all its implications. Who could ask for more?" (*RM*, p. 20). Although he has written fiction about non-Jews, such as *When She Was Good*, he clearly feels that his own experience as a Jew largely dictates his perception and understanding of the moral and psychological themes that dominate his work. Thus, in a discussion about one of his earlier and most controversial stories called "Defender of the Faith," which is about two Jewish soldiers, Roth, in "Writing about Jews," says, "Yet, though the moral complexities are not exclusively a Jew's, I never for a moment considered that the characters in the story should be anything other than Jews. Someone else might have written a story embodying the same themes, and similar events perhaps, and had at its center Negroes or Irishmen; for me there was no choice" (*RM*, p. 157).

In terms of cultural geography, the Jewish environment that nurtured Roth was not so far removed from the experiences of Henry Roth and

Anzia Yezierska a generation earlier. Moreover, in psychological terms, Roth's Newark also seems close to the earlier ghetto of the Lower East Side. Roth describes a community of his youth that considers itself under perennial siege. In trying "to transform into fiction something of the small world in which I had spent the first eighteen years of my life," Roth says that his early stories drew upon "the ethos of my highly self-conscious Jewish neighborhood, which had been squeezed like some embattled little nation in among ethnic rivals and antagonists, peoples equally proud, ambitious, and xenophobic, and equally baffled and exhilarated by the experience of being fused into a melting pot." "It was," he says in "The Story of Three Stories," "to this nation-neighborhood—this demi-Israel in a Newark that was our volatile Middle East—that I instinctively turned for material at the beginning of my writing career, and to which I returned, ten years later, when I tried to distill from that Newark Jewish community the fictional, or folkloric, family that I called the Portnoys" (*RM*, p. 172). Ironically, Portnoy's mental state, as a reflection of this kind of environment, in some ways typifies the thinking of many of Roth's Jewish critics, who resent his uses of Jewish materials. In "Writing about Jews," Roth characterizes one of these critics as an individual who prefers "to remain a victim in a country where he does not have to live like one if he chooses" and says others prefer to hear "the oratory of self-congratulation and self-pity" (*RM*, pp. 165, 169) as opposed to more serious and honest expressions of the life of the Jews in America.

The presence in Roth's work of this ghetto mentality is obvious. However, Roth's fiction since *Portnoy* shows the growing importance of another force—literary modernism. In fact, his essays and fiction in this period sound almost like a reader of the modernist movement in literature. Although the strongest influences are Kafka and Chekhov, there are also continual references to Flaubert, Joyce, Dostoyevsky, Tolstoy. The importance of modernism to Roth is clear in his early description of fiction as "something like a religious calling, and literature a kind of sacrament." "I might turn out," he says in "On *The Great American Novel*," "to be a bad artist, or no artist at all, but having declared myself *for* art—the art of Tolstoy, James, Flaubert, and Mann, whose appeal was as much in their heroic literary integrity as in their work—I imagined I had sealed myself off from being a morally unacceptable person, in others' eyes as well as my own" (*RM*, pp. 77, 78). In style, subject matter, and sensibility,

Roth's *My Life as a Man*, *The Professor of Desire*, and *The Ghost Writer*, as well as his own critical writings, all reflect the intensity of this modernist impulse. In addition, his editorship of Penguin's series of books entitled "Writers from the Other Europe" further demonstrates the importance to Roth today of European themes and thought. In responding to the triad of modernism, American culture, and Jewish life in America, Roth juxtaposes the American drive for individual freedom with the psychology of the ghetto and what Sanford Pinsker calls the "reflexive mode" of modernism.[2]

Roth's special style as a writer—what we have come to think of as his unique contribution to the linguistic achievement of Jewish writers in general—derives from his insights into the styles associated with the different cultural perspectives of literary modernism, Americanism, and Judaism. The tensions, conflicts, and incongruities involved in bringing these perspectives together often account for the devastating but humorous social and cultural criticism of his prose. The different styles reflect different modes of thought and ways of life. As such they operate as checks and critical perspectives on one another—Jew vs. American, middle-class conformist vs. modernistic rebel. Brought together by Roth into one consistent style, they become the ironic consciousness and multiperspective of the modern urban Jew. A character named Nathan Zuckerman and the epithets that are used to describe him best epitomize Roth's effort. Zuckerman, who is from Newark, would like to be a Jewish James Joyce. However, when Roth refers to him as Nathan Dedalus in *The Ghost Writer* and as "Zuckerman Unbound" in a later novel, Zuckerman's hopes are properly deflated by the dramatic tension between his middle-class Jewish background and the combination of creativity and nihilism implied in his ambitions to be a writer who can revolutionize the consciousness of his times. Earlier in his career Roth referred in an interview to the social and cultural roots of this dilemma for the Jewish writer who wants to rebel against parents who will not only protect him but will adore him to the point of expressing pride even in his rebelliousness. As a youth, he used "millions of words" as the way to fight his parents. The knowledge of his parents' undiminished love, however, effectively countered the vehemence of his rebellion. It was fear of the "broken heart" rather than of physical punishment that kept him at bay so that "even in post-adolescence, when I began to find reasons to oppose them, it never occurred to me that as a consequence I might lose their love" (*RM*, p. 5). The difficulty that Zuckerman encounters in breaking away from such loving parents by establishing true independence from them signifies the schlemiel's prolonged adolescence that undermines any authority to his rebellion.

Like Alexander Portnoy, Nathan Zuckerman learns that even while trying to make his escape from his parents he will find them waiting for him somewhere, usually in a corner of his own psyche. The problem, he discovers, is that not only does guilt keep him close to home but being Jewish in America creates the kinds of anxieties and doubts that naturally send one back to one's roots. Thus, in his desire for independence as both a man and a writer, Zuckerman in *The Ghost Writer* psychologically disowns his father and sees an older, famous writer named E. I. Lonoff as an adopted literary father figure. However, in Lonoff's writings Zuckerman discovers his own background. Thus, Zuckerman notes that "Lonoff's canon . . . had done more to make me realize how much I was still my family's Jewish offspring than anything I had carried forward to the University of Chicago from childhood Hebrew lessons, or mother's kitchen, or the discussions I used to hear among my parents and our relatives about the perils of intermarriage, the problem of Santa Claus, and the injustice of medical-school quotas." Through Lonoff's fiction, Zuckerman finds himself able to identify with "the same burden of exclusion and confinement that still weighed upon the lives of those who had raised me."[3] Zuckerman's condescension toward his real father and his desperate search for a new father figure dramatize how completely the insecurities of his past carry forward into his adult life.

The image of the Jew that emerges in Roth reflects modern literary sensibility, Jewish insecurity, and American ambivalence. Through these tensions Roth continues the pattern of the Jewish hero of thought. However, in Roth the Jewish hero of thought becomes a kind of underground man, a symbol of perennial Jewish isolation advanced to represent, in a manner more like Kafka than Dostoyevsky, the alienated condition of modern man.[4] Roth relates this hero to Ralph Ellison's *Invisible Man*. In discussing Ellison's novel, he compares "the image of his hero" with Bellow's Henderson and finds the former more relevant to his own vision of the world. In "Writing American Fiction," Roth says, "For here too the hero is left with the simple stark fact of himself. He is as alone as a man can be. Not that he hasn't gone out into the world; he has gone into it, and out into it, and out into it—but at the end he chooses to go underground, to live there and wait. And it does not seem to him a cause for celebration either" (*RM*, p. 135). The heroes of Roth's fiction are often these men from the underground even though they frequently function on the surface as seemingly successful and bright young Jewish men. They—David Kepesh, Nathan Zuckerman, Peter Tarnapol—dramatize the situation of being Jewish, modern, and American all at once.

As an underground man, Roth's modern Jewish hero is engaged in a perennial search for identity and masculinity. Roth's development of his fiction as a continuous search for a center or a "real" author conforms with the desperate search of his characters for a sense of self. An example of Roth's experiment to combine this technique of fiction and his theme of the lost or uncertain self can be found in *My Life as a Man*. In this novel, two stories, "Salad Days" and "Courting Disaster," are entitled together "Useful Fictions" and concern the character of Zuckerman. Both stories and Zuckerman himself are deemed the creation of Peter Tarnapol, the hero of the "autobiographical" third part of the novel which is called "My True Story." Thus, the fictional process of creating a "real" self is sustained by the attempt in the novel to find the real author. Roth further explains this method of searching through the self to find a real self by having Zuckerman quote to a bored class from Joseph Conrad's introduction to the *Nigger of the Narcissus*. The opening words of the quote indicate an important part of Roth's artistic creed and method: "'the artist descends within himself, and in that lonely region of stress and strife, if he be deserving and fortunate, he finds the terms of his appeal.'"[5] Roth's heroes not only want new identities and fathers, but they also exhibit what Tarnapol's (and Portnoy's) psychiatrist, Dr. Otto Spielvogel, terms the narcissism of the artist, thus adding to the significance of Zuckerman's reading from Conrad. The same problems also face David Kepesh, the young Jewish professor of literature who appears first in *The Breast* and then again in *The Professor of Desire*, the later novel that anticipates the physical transformation in the first book.

Dr. Spielvogel's perceptions are important because for Roth art and psychology collaborate to mitigate the authority of an omniscient, all-powerful "authorial" presence. The multiplication of selves challenges the existence of a superior self resting in security somewhere in control of the story. Thus, Zuckerman as the creation of Tarnapol in *My Life as a Man* suggests Tarnapol's strength—until we get the true story of Tarnapol. The movement toward a true and superior writer or poet reflects the wish for a realm of objective authority and security where none exists, Roth seems to say, in either art or life. In "Salad Days" Zuckerman refers to the "amused, Olympian point of view" of the author—presumably meaning Tarnapol— and in "Courting Disaster" he discusses "the decorousness, the orderliness, the underlying sobriety, that 'responsible' manner that I continue to affect" as perhaps "the funniest thing of all, or perhaps the strangest" part of the story (*MLM*, pp. 31, 81). While dramatizing the wish to create such a detached and final authorial presence, Roth simultaneously demonstrates how such a self demolishes itself through the ironic and inevitable process of reflection that undermines the claims of autonomy and authority through the creation of another level of critical consciousness. There is, therefore, no omniscient self either in literature or life that offers an ultimate assurance of security.

Without a final source of truth or an ultimate moral authority, fiction and reality for Roth's heroes become interchangeable. Zuckerman says that "my life was coming to resemble one of those texts upon which certain literary critics . . . used to enjoy venting their ingenuity" (*MLM*, p. 72). Similarly, Peter Tarnapol, as he tells his own story in *My Life as a Man*, justifies his decision to marry the woman he believes has ruined him by seeing himself in terms of the meaning and ethics of literary modernism. "It seemed then," he says, "that I was making one of those moral decisions that I had heard so much about in college literature courses. But how different it all had been up in the Ivy League when it was happening to Lord Jim and Kate Croy and Ivan Karamazov instead of to me. Oh, what an authority on dilemmas I had been in the senior honors seminar!" (*MLM*, p. 193). He says that he wanted his "intractable existence [to] take place at an appropriately lofty moral attitude, an elevation somewhere, say, between *The Brothers Karamazov* and *The Wings of the Dove*" (*MLM*, pp. 194–95). Tarnapol becomes a victim of his ambition for ultimate experience and of his literary philosophy, neither of which distinguishes between what he is and what he reads. He says, "Stuffed to the gills with great fiction—entranced not by cheap romances, like Madame Bovary, but by *Madame Bovary*—I now expected to find in everyday experience that same sense of the difficult and the deadly earnest that informed the novels I admired most. My model of reality, deduced from reading the

masters, had at its heart *intractability*. And here it was, a reality as obdurate and recalcitrant and (in addition) as awful as any I could have wished
for in my most bookish dreams" (*MLM*, p. 194). Tarnapol's prose often
parodies and reflects a particular style of literary criticism. His vocabulary
indicates that his model for such writing comes from the essays of Lionel
Trilling while the subject matter suggests a particular Trilling essay entitled "On the Teaching of Modern Literature." In the essay Trilling discusses the implications of teaching literary modernism from the perspective of the academic and cultural establishment. While Roth's mimicry of
Trilling's vocabulary (obdurate, recalcitrant, intractability) contributes to
the humor of the piece and makes Tarnapol seem even more artificial, the
clever connection to Trilling lends credibility to Roth's subject.[6] Tarnapol
illustrates the moral, educational, and intellectual issues in Trilling's essay,
including the question of how the violence, nihilism, and alienation of
modern literature operate upon students from conventional and stable
backgrounds.

Tarnapol's confusion between his own life and the lives of various characters in great literature enables Roth to mix up the worlds of fiction and
reality in a way that turns his works into studies of the issue of fiction and
the fiction-making process. His recent novels dramatize some of the questions concerning fiction and reality that have been raised by such critical
theorists as Gerald Graff.[7] The title of *The Ghost Writer* symbolizes his
concern for the subject through its suggestion that behind each fiction is
another story writer or another fiction. Roth's penchant for including a
great deal of his public self and autobiography in his novels further blurs
the distinctions between fiction and reality. Thus, when Nathan Zuckerman complains in *Zuckerman Unbound* that people keep confusing him,
the successful author, with the creations of his novels, we can assume that
Roth is joking. In the novel Zuckerman must contend with a public who
will not let him forget that he wrote a sensational book that sounds very
much like *Portnoy's Complaint*. *Zuckerman Unbound* therefore confirms
Roth's intention to diminish the barrier between fiction and reality. In
Zuckerman Unbound a stranger says to Zuckerman about his book that
"'they arrest people for that.'" Zuckerman in turn thinks of people like the
offensive stranger: "They had mistaken impersonation for confession and
were calling out to a character who lived in a book."[8]

As we have seen, however, it is precisely the line between impersonation and confession that Roth so humorously exploits in his works. He develops the tension between fiction and the real self in a way that elevates his fictional hero to the level of cultural myth. The identity of this hero emerges from Roth's public self and literary self. By writing into his recent fiction so many brilliant, internal variations of a single fictive self that so closely resembles himself, he creates a hero that lives in both literature and public life. In effect, Roth achieves a modern-day bridge in the tradition of Whitman that connects the public Roth with the literary self that searches in his novels for a solid center. As both a Jew and a modernist, Roth projects a mythic self onto American culture that seems nothing less than revolutionary in its departure from the historic model of the hero in American literature and culture. At the same time, the receptivity to such a heroic figure by the general public conveys something of the revolution in values, tastes, and style that the culture as a whole has undergone in the past several decades.

The most lasting and pervasive model for Roth of that mythic self that represents the new version of the modern American male as the underground man comes not from native grounds but from Europe in the figure of Franz Kafka. Kafka epitomizes for Roth both modern consciousness and the archetypal modern Jewish sensibility. Roth also sees in Kafka an important ability to understand the humor in the absurdity of modern man's alienated and self-destructive condition. In an interview, Roth told George Plimpton that he was "strongly influenced by a sit-down comic named Franz Kafka and a very funny bit he does called 'The Metamorphosis'" (*RM*, p. 21).[9] What Roth seeks to give us is an Americanized version of Kafka. In 1973, Roth wrote a story called "Looking at Kafka" in which he imagines Kafka's immigration to America to escape the Holocaust. In order to survive in America, Kafka in Roth's imagination becomes a Hebrew-school teacher, and, of course, the results for Kafka's life and work are disastrous. For example, among other things he is called "Dr. Kishka" by his students (*RM*, p. 258). Roth returns to Kafka as a subject in his fiction by making his memory the object of Professor David Kepesh's devotion in *The Professor of Desire*. Kepesh's reverence for Kafka is part of his overall commitment to literary modernism, on which subject he shares many attitudes and ideas with Zuckerman and Tarnapol in *My Life as a Man*. Thus, in remarks Kepesh prepares for the opening of his college class he tells his students of his "'insistence upon the connections between the novels you read for this class, even the most eccentric and off-putting of novels, and what you know so far of life. You will discover (and not all will approve) that I do not hold with certain of my colleagues who tell us that literature, in its most valuable and intriguing moments, is "fundamentally non-referential." '"[10] To Kepesh, literature and the individual's experience of life are so related that he confidently says to his students, "'I present myself to you young strangers in the guise not of your teacher but as the first of this semester's texts'" (*PD*, p. 184). Roth takes Kepesh's belief in the interaction of fiction and reality to its most ludicrous extreme in *The Breast*, a story modeled after Kafka's "The Metamorphosis." In *The Breast* Kepesh asks himself how it came to be that he turned into a breast. *"Did* fiction do this to me?" he asks.[11]

The Professor of Desire, as already noted, was published five years after *The Breast*, but its action takes place before Kepesh's change. In the later novel Kepesh only goes so far as to visit Kafka's grave in Prague. The visit occurs with the same reverence pilgrims demonstrate on journeys to Mecca and Jerusalem. Roth prepares us for the importance of this moment through a conversation between Kepesh and Professor Soska, his Czech guide who was fired from an academic position for political reasons. For Soska, understanding and loving Kafka help him tolerate the humiliation of life under Communist totalitarianism. Kepesh, on the other hand, appreciates Kafka for helping him to understand another kind of oppression. He says to Soska, "'Of course you are the one on intimate terms with totalitarianism—but if you'll permit me, I can only compare the body's utter singlemindedness, its cold indifference and absolute contempt for the well-being of the spirit, to some unyielding, authoritarian regime. And you can petition it all you like, offer up the most heartfelt and dignified and logical sort of appeal—and get no response at all. If anything, a kind of laugh is what you get'" (*PD*, pp. 171–72). Both men realize that great literature can have such highly personal uses. "'To each obstructed citizen his own Kafka,'" says Soska to Kepesh (*PD*, p. 173). At Soska's suggestion, Kepesh goes on to Kafka's gravesite where Kepesh sees a monument to his own anguish and suffering. Roth writes, "Of all things, marking Kafka's remains—and unlike anything else in sight—a stout, elongated, whitish rock, tapering upward to its pointed glans, a tombstone phallus" (*PD*, p. 175). The stone for Kepesh symbolizes his own problem, while the actual grave goes deeper, so to speak, and indicates the unconscious forces that propel it. Examining the grave, Kepesh evidences surprise that "the family-haunted son is buried forever—still!—between the mother and the father who outlived him" (*PD*, p. 175). Even in death Kafka seems caught between his mother and father, realizing in his tomb a permanence to the pain he suffered in life. Kepesh's sense of Kafka's affliction and his understanding of Kafka's role as a Jewish artist make him feel closer to Kafka than to his own father. Showing Kafka a level of respect he denies his real family, Kepesh affects a Kafkaesque sensibility and style of alienation. At the same time, Kepesh stands in awe at this gravesite of all the Jewish dead around him, many of whom died in the Holocaust. He feels an inevitable link with these Jewish dead. As he looks at the names on the monuments, he realizes that they sound as familiar as the names in his "own address book" (*PD*, p. 175). However, even during a touching moment of realizing a bond with these dead, he finally cannot maintain his sense of relationship with this aspect of his past and identity.

As a modern sensibility and consciousness in the tradition of Kafka, Kepesh finds it impossible to achieve the solidity of a single well-centered self of the middle class. He cannot be like his father in this book or like other fathers in Roth who function with basic beliefs and have loyalties to their Jewish families and friends who see them through life. Life cannot be dealt with simply for Kepesh in commonsensical terms designed to assure security and success. Roth sympathetically portrays Kepesh's father as an example of sensitive and responsible masculinity and as a model of middle-class authority. He describes the father during a moment when he confronts both the imminent death of his wife and the weakness of his son. "He puts a hand over his eyes and quietly begins to cry. With his other hand he makes a fist which he waves at me. 'This is what I have had to be all my life! *Without* psychiatrists, *without* happy pills! I am a man who has never said die!'" (*PD*, p. 115). In contrast to his father, Kepesh seems unable to live. He verges on a perennial death condition that makes basic functions and actions impossible to achieve. In this sense, Roth's vision relates to an earlier Jewish writer in America, Nathanael West, whose characters such as "Miss Lonelyhearts" and Tod Hackett and Homer Simpson seem to be dying men in a dying land.

Kepesh's condition of immaturity can be compared with Tarnapol's hysteria in *My Life as a Man*. Both men resist the manhood they claim to seek. In one fight scene Tarnapol puts on his wife's clothes to show her that he wears the "'panties in this family'" (*MLM*, p. 246) out of a need to take what Roth called, in an interview with Joyce Carol Oates, "a sex *break*" (*RM*, p. 110). Later Tarnapol asks, "How do I ever get to be what is described in the literature as *a man*? I had so wanted to be one, too— why then is it always beyond me?" (*MLM*, p. 299). At the end of *My Life as a Man* Tarnapol learns of his wife's death and wants to believe that he is "free." However, Dr. Spielvogel quickly corrects him. "'Released is the word you are looking for,'" says Spielvogel. "'You have been released'" (*MLM*, p. 327). Freedom is another issue beyond Tarnapol. His wife's death has released him from one imprisoning situation, but clearly he will not find any kind of freedom until he stops inventing new prisons for himself.

In his discussion with Oates about *My Life as a Man*, Roth seems to confirm a pessimistic view of the book's conclusion. "If there is an ironic acceptance of anything at the conclusion of *My Life as a Man* (or even along the way), it is of *the determined self*. And angry frustration, a deeply vexing sense of characterological enslavement, is strongly infused in that ironic acceptance" (*RM*, p. 108). In elaborating upon this idea, Roth refers once again to Kafka—this time to the scene in *The Trial* when K looks up in hope at a priest in the cathedral. For Roth, the great irony comes through the discovery that "the man in the pulpit turns out to be oneself" (*RM*, p. 108). The chains we put on ourselves are our greatest obstacles to freedom. He writes, "If only one *could* quit one's pulpit, one might well obtain decisive and acceptable counsel. How to devise a mode of living completely outside the jurisdiction of the Court when the Court is of one's own devising?" (*RM*, p. 108). Roth's pessimism about man's potential for achieving freedom and his use of Jews as examples of self-bondage unite many critics in their objections to his work. Writers as different politically as Irving Howe and Norman Podhoretz tend to be more sanguine than Roth in their views of human nature and freedom. Moreover, both men also chafe under Roth's depiction of Jewish life and mores.[12] Roth has survived such attacks and refuses to modify his views in spite of the feelings and sensitivities of others. He has continued to emphasize the perennial frustration of the individual's drive for freedom.

Roth, according to Bernard F. Rodgers, Jr., also continues an important American literary tradition. "American writers," says Rodgers, "are dedicated to the effort to liberate consciousness—an effort with which Roth allied himself early in his career."[13] Roth has at times spoken of himself and his work in such heroic terms. For example, in an interview he once said: "I sometimes think of my generation of men as the first wave of determined D-Day invaders, over whose bloody, wounded carcasses the flower children subsequently stepped ashore to advance triumphantly toward that libidinous Paris we had dreamed of liberating as we inched inland on our bellies, firing into the dark. 'Daddy,' the youngsters ask, 'what did you do in the war?' I humbly submit they could do worse than read *Portnoy's Complaint* to find out" (*RM*, p. 8). However, Roth is usually more pessimistic about man's capacity for freedom than this quote would indicate. Often in Roth's fiction when imprisoning walls around men collapse, others rise soon after to replace them. Almost always such new walls are constructed by the prisoners themselves. However, as a writer in the tradition of the New Covenant, Roth contributes significantly to our understanding of the nature and psychology of freedom in America.

PART IV

The Book of America

Chapter 8

Song of Him-Self
Norman Mailer

The interest in the American idea that so fascinates other Jewish writers reaches a new intensity in the writings of Norman Mailer and E. L. Doctorow. Their attempts to produce a literature that is synonymous with American culture and history results in works that are considered by many to be new literary forms. Other writers offer fiction that expresses their perspectives on the American experience. For Mailer and Doctorow that experience, as manifested in historical moments, contemporary events, and public figures, undergoes a transmutation into literature.

Thus, Mailer's work in the field of new journalism and Doctorow's experiments with the historical novel represent their efforts to synthesize literature with American history and life. Through these ventures into new forms of literary experience, they attempt to change contemporary consciousness by revivifying our literary and cultural imagination.

This fascination with and concentration upon American history and culture means that Mailer and Doctorow write what Hayden White calls "metahistory." As noted earlier in this study, White's theory proposes to analyze the linguistic or poetic roots of historical writings.[1]

Thus, Mailer, as our most provocative student of "history as a novel" and "the novel as history," and Doctorow, as our most interesting innovator of the historical novel, write a version of metahistory. In a sense, they are the ultimate metahistorians because they concentrate upon the poetic acts from which more sophisticated and conscious historical interpretations emerge. Their linguistic strategies as writers coincide with their innovative development of the narrative and rhetorical structures that express the American idea. In Mailer and Doctorow metahistory merges with the poetics of the American idea as manifested in the evolving forms of the myth and ideology of America.

Of all the Jewish writers in the tradition of the New Covenant, Norman Mailer stands out as the most self-conscious in his performance of the role of the New Jeremiah by acting as the moral consciousness of his culture. His moral fervor cannot be separated from an almost mystical belief in the myth of America as the land of deliverance for those heroic and strong enough to answer its existential challenge to create and control their own destinies. Noting that "to write was to judge," Mailer in *Of a Fire on the Moon* comes closest perhaps to literally assuming the biblical role of prophet when he declares: "It was conceivable that man was no longer ready to share the dread of the Lord."[2] However, he clearly believes that salvation for the land and its people remains possible. Thus, Benjamin Spencer notes that Mailer in effect links "a redemptive national vision to a belief in divine mystery and, like an Old Testament prophet, turned to identifying and denouncing apostates and unbelievers."[3] Similarly, Allan Wagenheim relates Mailer's moral vision to American culture. He writes, "If Mailer were not something of a middle-class Jewish intellectual, one would have to suppose he was the last remaining Devil-haunted Puritan on the modern American scene."[4] Mailer's moralistic rhetoric in the manner of the jeremiad first became an effective force in *Advertisements for Myself*, a work that he says "was the first book I wrote that had a style I thought I might be able to call my own."[5]

In *Advertisements for Myself*, which Laura Adams describes as his "literary manifesto,"[6] Mailer declares that he can "settle for nothing less than making a revolution in the consciousness of our time" (*AM*, p. 1). The language of the book's first advertisement demonstrates that moral passion and righteousness constitute the motivating force behind his revolution. He attacks the entire society for its failure to live up to his moral expectations. Mailer writes, *"We have grown up in a world more in decay than the worst of the Roman Empire, a cowardly world chasing after a good time (of which last one can approve) but chasing it without the courage to pay the hard price of full consciousness, and so losing pleasure in pips and squeaks of anxiety. We want the heats of the orgy and not its murder, the warmth of pleasure without the grip of pain, and therefore the future threatens a nightmare, and we continue to waste ourselves"* (*AM*, p. 7). However, in the rhetorical style of the jeremiad that becomes his own in this work, Mailer indicates the possibility, even in the face of his pessimism, of achieving salvation through finding the courage and strength to honestly confront the implications of one's moral vision. Moreover, in the tradition of "the American Jeremiad," he links that salvation to a sense of national destiny. He writes:

> *So, yes, it may be time to say that the Republic is in real peril, and we are the cowards who must defend courage, sex, consciousness, the beauty of the body, the search for love, and the capture of what may be, after all, an heroic destiny. But to say these words is to show how sad we are, for those of us who believe the most have spent our years writing of fear, impotence, stupidity, ugliness, self-love, and apathy, and yet it has been our act of faith, our attempt to see—to see and to see hard, to smell, even to touch, yes to capture that nerve of Being which may include all of us, that Reality whose existence may depend on the honest life of our work, the honor of ourselves which permits us to say no better than we have seen.*
> (*AM*, pp. 7–8)

Although it is tempting to dismiss such rhetorical flourishes as a cover for the absence of a perfectly clear moral vision or a consistently coherent intellectual program, it needs to be recognized that Mailer's discussions of American culture are based on extensive thought and experience. It would be difficult to find another contemporary writer of equal merit and influence who has worked so hard to experience America on so many different levels. He has made himself into an eyewitness to more than three decades of enormously complex cultural change and growth. From the psychological depths of the sexual revolution to the fascination with space-age technology, from the arenas of major sporting events to the centers of political conventions, Mailer has studied the meaning of contemporary America. This attempt to know and understand America in all its aspects has been made in both his fiction and in his new journalism. As Richard Poirier writes, "No other American writer of this period has tried so resolutely and successfully to account for the eclecticisms of contemporary life when it comes to ideas of form, of language, of culture, of political and social structures, and of the self." In trying to take the measure of Mailer's achievement as a writer, Poirier argues that works including *Advertisements for Myself*, *Why Are We in Vietnam?*, *An American Dream*, and *The Armies of the Night* "make Mailer easily the equal . . . of Fitzgerald and Hemingway, potentially of Faulkner."[7] Mailer's work and competitive attitude invite such comparisons with the major modern writers. However, in terms of his place in American literature and culture and his development of a rhetorical style that reflects his complex feelings and attitudes toward America, he should also be compared with Walt Whitman. In fact, several critics have so compared Mailer and Whitman. As Adams, for example, writes, "The vision of the 'great literatus' is Whitman's a century ago and, with reservations, Mailer's today."[8]

For Whitman and Mailer, knowledge of America becomes so personal that the idea of knowing turns into loving. Knowing and feeling about America as they do, Whitman and Mailer presume to speak to her with the attitude of a lover with moral authority over her. It is consistent with this attitude that both Mailer and Whitman emphasize the sexual basis for their cultural programs. Thus, Whitman in an important letter to Emerson that was published in the 1856 edition of *Leaves of Grass* but never mailed, lists the following as related to sex: ". . . all existence, all souls, all realization, all decency, all health, all that is worth being here for, all of woman and of man, all beauty, all purity, all sweetness, all friendship, all strength, all life, all immortality."[9] This "sex program" for Whitman reaches its peak in such poetry as "Song of Myself," "Children of Adam," and "Calamus." Just as he argues in "Song of Myself" that "a kelson of the creation is love," so he maintains that his own sexuality and freedom must provide the basis for a relationship of love between the American people and the American idea.[10] He sees himself as a mythic lover to a mythic America. He writes, "I turn the bridegroom out of bed and stay with the bride myself, / I tighten her all night to my thighs and lips."[11] As the basis for cultural democracy, such sexual freedom becomes a moral obligation for Whitman. Similarly, Mailer is perhaps as notorious in our day as Whitman was in his for espousing in such works as "The White Negro" a program for individual and cultural renewal based on "love" and "orgasm" that can enable civilized man to cease being a "sexual cripple" and to become "sexually alive" (*AM*, pp. 309, 311). More recently, Mailer's symbol for his Whitmanesque relationship to the myth of America becomes Marilyn Monroe. Seeing Monroe as both the "sweet angel of sex" and as "the last of the myths to thrive in the long evening of the American dream," Mailer says she came to embody "every man's love affair with America." She was not only the American Dream in the form of "all the cleanliness of all the clean American backyards," but she also became for American men what Daisy Buchanan was for Gatsby, a symbol of hope for an impossible future.[12] In wooing her back to life in his writings about her, Mailer performs in a microcosmic fashion what he hopes to achieve for America.

Mailer's early commitment to socialism also reflected the political dimension of his Whitmanesque belief in establishing love as a basis for human relationships in society. As Stanley Gutman writes in his discussion of Mailer, "the most important effect the failure of socialism has had on the individual is the loss of love."[13] However, Mailer's views have changed considerably since he devotedly argued in the 1950s for socialism as the moral and political solution to the world's ills (*AM*, 160–88). Actually, his views today seem much closer to the kind of synthesis that Whitman devised between radical individualism, democracy, equality, social justice, and cultural freedom. Thus, Mailer came to identify a new politics for himself. He defines himself as a "Left Conservative." He writes in *The Armies of the Night*, "Mailer was a Left Conservative. So he had his own point of view. To himself he would suggest that he tried to think in the style of Marx in order to attain certain values suggested by Edmund Burke. Since he was a conservative, he would begin at the root."[14]

A partial explanation for Mailer's move to the right can be found in *Miami and the Siege of Chicago* in his slashing attack on the left. He writes:

> The Left was not ready, the Left was years away from a vision sufficiently complex to give life to the land, the Left had not yet learned to talk across the rugged individualism of the more rugged in America, the Left was still too full of kicks and pot and the freakings of sodium amytol and orgy, the howls of electronics and LSD. The Left could also find room to grow up. If the Left had to live through a species of political exile for four or eight or twelve good years, it might even be right. They might be forced to study what was alive in the conservative dream. For certain the world could not be saved by technology or government or genetics, and much of the Left had that still to learn.[15]

Mailer further articulated his growing political conservatism during his 1969 campaign for mayor of New York City. In campaign oratory, he advocated ideas that put him even closer to a traditional vision of a democratic culture and society of free individuals. In fact, the values that he expresses, as Adams states, recall "a kind of frontier spirit." She argues that "the contention that the revival of that spirit is the means toward any future America might develop is a long-standing belief of Mailer's."[16] Thus, basically conservative American values of individualism, self-direction, and autonomy are implicit in Mailer's statement that "power to the neighborhoods would mean that any neighborhood could constitute itself on any principle, whether spiritual, emotional, economical, ideological or idealistic. . . . To the degree, however, that we have lost faith in the power of the government to conduct our lives, so too would the principle of power to the neighborhoods begin to thrive, so too would the first spiritual problem of the twentieth century—alienation from the self—be given a tool by which to rediscover oneself." Mailer goes on to assert that "life in the kind of neighborhood which contains one's belief of a possible society, is a form of marriage between one's social philosophy and one's private contract with the world."[17]

Mailer takes Whitman's urbanized version of Jefferson's idea of local control and small government and modernizes it in the hope of reviving on the frontier of the city the America of his mind. As Spencer says, "In Mailer's dream, New York became, as it were, the holy city, the birthplace of an imminent and imperative transformation of the human consciousness of which America is to be the harbinger."[18] As this vision of America solidified in Mailer's imagination, it gave structure to his moral and aesthetic consciousness. He uses the American idea to give focus and direction to the wrath of his jeremiads that in the fifties often struck out in blind rage. Feeling more comfortable with a philosophy of left conservatism that recognizes the human possibilities in individual freedom, Mailer during the years of national turmoil in the middle and late sixties, formalized his commitment to the same religion of American democracy that so captivated Whitman's imagination. The target of Mailer's condemnation became any force that threatens or defiles the hope offered in the American Way for regeneration and heroism. Mailer's vitriolic rhetoric matches Whitman's attacks in *Democratic Vistas* upon those who create "an atmosphere of hypocrisy throughout" American culture and who turn "our New World Democracy" into "an almost complete failure in its social aspects, and in really grand religious, moral, literary, and aesthetic results."[19]

Mailer's vision of the American idea and dream as well as his self-delegated role in shaping it comes together for him during the 1967 march on the Pentagon described in *The Armies of the Night*. At one point on that march he undergoes an almost mystical experience during which he feels as though "one stood under some mythical arch in the great vault of history, helicopters buzzing about, chop-chop, and the sense of America divided on this day now liberated some undiscovered patriotism in Mailer so that he felt a sharp searing love for his country in this moment and on this day, crossing some divide in his own mind wider than the Potomac, a love so lacerated he felt as if a marriage were being torn and children lost" (*AN*, p. 113). Fed by his belief that events of the time meant that "nothing less is involved than whether America becomes a great nation or a totalitarian tyranny" (*AN*, p. 112), Mailer's newly discovered patriotism actually reaffirms a feeling of his "love for America," which he had first encountered in what he terms "Mailer's America" in the army (*AN*, p. 48). This America, it turns out, seems very much like the democratic America of the ordinary American man and woman that Walt Whitman envisioned. Mailer writes that "he had first come to love America when he served in the U.S. Army, not the America of course of the flag, the patriotic unendurable fix of the television programs and the newspapers, no, long before he was ever aware of the institutional oleo of the most suffocating American ideas he had come to love what editorial writers were fond of calling the democratic principle with its faith in the common man" (*AN*, p. 47). Mailer's description of the common man completes his vision of the American idea. His memory of the army grounds his myth of America in the "obscenity," "language," and "humor" of the common man (*AN*, pp. 47, 48). The ideal vision of America, which arches over ordinary historical, geographical, and moral boundaries, combines with a feeling for the regular G.I. so that the combination gives Mailer a moral universe in which to operate.

Mailer's affirmation of his American identity and his related mission to save America from the forces that would dehumanize her and turn her into a "totalitarian tyranny" sharpen his moral purpose and verbal weaponry. Thus, on the Washington march, which becomes for Mailer part of his journey toward understanding America, he excoriates those who would diminish his dream and endanger the people who are worthy of it. For example, he writes, "the American corporation executive, who was after all the foremost representative of Man in the world today, was perfectly capable of burning unseen women and children in the Vietnamese jungles, yet felt a large displeasure and fairly final disapproval at the generous use of obscenity in literature and in public" (*AN*, p. 49). Armed on the march on Washington with a moral vision that enables him to identify himself as a member of the elect who can discern the enemies of America's highest principles, Mailer achieves a further sense of his own masculine identity as well. It is as though his life has been a Puritan's preparation for a moment of truth between himself and his national and cultural destiny. Noting that now "Mailer felt a confirmation of the contests of his own life on this March to the eye of the oppressor," Mailer points out the real enemies who destroy the real America—"greedy stingy dumb valve of the worst of the Wasp heart, chalice and anus of corporation land, smug, enclosed, morally blind Pentagon, destroying the future of its own nation with each day it augmented in strength" (*AN*, p. 114).

As the American hero-novelist, Mailer saves the meaning of America by seeing through the evil of technology, corporate and military power, and sanitized sexuality. Despite this corruption Mailer perceives the wonderful "mysteries of America." He challenges those who would turn her into a "dowager" by destroying the source of her life in "these liberties to dissent." Thus, Mailer fully exploits the moral psychology of the jeremiad to both condemn and extol, to castigate and challenge. He writes that "the Novelist induced on the consequence some dim unawakened knowledge of the mysteries of America buried in these liberties to dissent—What a mysterious country it was. The older he became, the more interesting he found her. Awful deadening programmatic inhuman dowager of a nation, corporation, and press—tender mysterious bitch whom no one would ever know, not even her future unfeeling Communist doctors if she died of the disease of her dowager, deadly pompous dowager who had trapped the sweet bitch" (*AN*, p. 114). Through the rhetorical structure of the jeremiad, Mailer dramatizes the distinction between America as the woman of mystery and wonder who nourishes freedom and hope and the dowager of death and decay. Mailer's use of the jeremiad not only describes but also reflects and perpetuates the moral schizophrenia that he believes to be at the heart of American consciousness. The jeremiad, especially in the hands of a force like Mailer, can become an instrument of moral terror to instill a sense of inadequacy and alienation. Such use of the jeremiad remains consistent with its history as derived from the prophets and as applied by the Puritans.

Thus, Mailer sustains both the Jewish and the American strains of the jeremiad. His use of this rhetorical apparatus as a means for perpetuating the New Covenant tradition becomes clear in his own description of how it "was left to the sons of immigrants" to write "the sort of literature" that could "explain America" as "a phenomenon never before described, indeed never before visible in the record of history."[20] One of the best illustrations of the rise to influence of this generation of immigrants' sons can be found in Mailer's adoption of the style and role in *The Armies of the Night* of Henry Adams in *The Education of Henry Adams*. While Mailer himself almost inadvertently refers to Adams in *Armies* (*AN*, p. 54), many critics have discussed the connection between Adams and Mailer in the book, partly because of Mailer's use, as Michael Cowan says, of "the third-person narrative guise."[21] However, more than style connects Adams and Mailer.[22] Mailer's assumption of the role of a modern-day Adams fulfills Adams's own personal nightmare prophecy of the increased importance of Jewish immigrants in American life. Mailer's responsibility for maintaining the rhetoric and story of the American Way embodies Adams's worst fears of Jewish influence upon American character and culture.

At the same time, Mailer's leadership in the New Covenant tradition further complicates the difficult question of his identity and role as a Jewish writer in America. His handling of Jewish characters or themes often has been ambivalent at best or negative at its worst. In spite of his interesting comments about the Jews, the devil, and Hasidism in *The Presidential Papers*, ambivalence would seem to be consistent with Mailer's admission in an interview with Steven Marcus that his "knowledge of Jewish culture is exceptionally spotty."[23] Mailer believes that such ignorance could serve as a strength in the effort to explain the reality of life to the modern Jew who also probably would be largely uninformed about Jewish life and thought. For Donald Kaufmann, however, this is a strength that Mailer does not frequently demonstrate. Kaufmann maintains that Mailer generally "has shelved his Jewish heritage" and that "even in his literary criticism, the Jew in Mailer never shows."[24] Barry Leeds emphasizes the negative qualities in two Jewish characters in Mailer's first novel, *The Naked and the Dead*. "Roth and Goldstein," Leeds writes, "are as different as two men can be. Yet they are complementary figures, making up in sum Mailer's portrait of the New York Jew."[25] Jews in subsequently published works by Mailer are also presented in generally negative ways. This is true throughout *Advertisements for Myself* of the ridiculous Jewish jock Wexler in "A Calculus at Heaven," the failed writer who is part Jewish in "The Man Who Studied Yoga," and the Jewish American Princess in "The Time of Her Time." On the other hand, Stephen Rojack in *An American Dream* also is part Jewish and clearly represents a heroic figure for Mailer.

The thrust behind Mailer's penchant for drawing uncomplimentary portraits of Jews in his fiction can be attributed at least in part, I believe, to a statement he makes in *The Armies of the Night*. Mailer asserts in *Armies* that while observing himself in a documentary film he saw "a fatal taint, a last remaining speck of the one personality he found absolutely insupportable—the nice Jewish boy from Brooklyn. Something in his adenoids gave it away—he had the softness of a man early accustomed to mother-love" (*AM*, p. 134.). The intensity of his effort to eradicate this aspect of his character—a drive somewhat similar to Philip Roth's own fictional perorations on the subject of masculinity and Jewish identity— must account at least in part for Mailer's guerilla warfare against softness or weakness or simply nice-Jewish-boyness in his fictional characters. Mailer's refusal to portray Jewish characters sentimentally or to concede their right to self-pity or weakness as an oppressed minority can create an overcompensatory drive to be masculine that indicates in itself a certain debility or borders on the comical as in the case of his guilty adenoids.

However, after a confrontation with a Nazi, who also was arrested during the march on Washington, Mailer renders a new portrait of the Jew in *The Armies of the Night*. In that book he refers to a lawyer as "a tough Jew" who not only proves that "there was no lawyer like a good Jewish lawyer" but also shows himself to be a worthy adversary of "a well-made son of Virginia gentry" (*AN*, pp. 208–9, 211). Mailer's experiences on the march in Washington and his response to them indicate that he may not be quite as "released from his ethnic identity" as Allen Guttmann believes.[26] Certainly, his remarks about the situation of minorities in America indicate sensitivity to the inherent alienation implicit in minority membership. He writes:

> What characterizes a member of a minority group is that he is forced to see himself as both exceptional and insignificant, marvelous and awful, good and evil. So far as he listens to the world outside he is in danger of going insane. The only way he may relieve the unendurable tension which surrounds any sense of his own

identity is to define his nature by his own acts. . . . What characterizes the sensation of being a member of a minority group is that
one's emotions are forever locked in the chains of ambivalence—the
expression of an emotion forever releasing its opposite—the ego in
perpetual transit from the tower to the dungeon and back again.[27]

Mailer almost undermines the significance of this statement by asserting
that "by this definition nearly everyone in America is a member of a minority group, alienated from the self by a double sense of identity and so
at the mercy of a self which demands action and more action to define the
most rudimentary borders of identity." In spite of this generalization, his
comments about minority identity and alienation obviously can be seen as
a reflection of his own experiences as a Jew in America.

In *The Armies of the Night*, Mailer's promulgation of the myth of
America through his development of the rhetoric of the jeremiad coin-
cides with his experimentation with narrative form as a new journalist.
While Mailer's belief in the moral schizophrenia of America justifies and
propels the jeremiad, the narrative form dramatizes the moral condition
through its combination of a literary and journalistic account of the march
on Washington. The book proceeds on at least two planes—a vertical one
of ascendance toward moral truth and a horizontal one of story toward
emotional and aesthetic truth. On both planes Mailer mixes metaphor and
fact as he integrates the roles of novelist and historian/journalist. As John
Hollowell says, "Each of Mailer's nonfiction novels of the sixties relies
upon the apocalyptic metaphors of his fictional vision to provide a larger
context for specific events. To write well, Mailer must fit disparate experiences into a larger pattern of interlocking metaphors."[28] Hollowell's
study is one of several that discusses Mailer's work in detail, especially *The
Armies of the Night*, as part of the phenomenon of the nonfiction novel.
And Mas'ud Zavarzadeh concludes that *The Armies of the Night* "is full of
references to the schizophrenia of America. The narrative is indeed a
literalization of a metaphor—Mailer acting out his interpretations and
comments—not a metaphorization of the literal, which is the strategy
used in the fictive novel."[29] To Zavarzadeh, the book represents the modern assault on traditional fiction and develops the "puzzling merging of
the fictional and the factual" into a new mode that he calls "the *fictual*: a
zone of experience where the factual is not secure or unequivocal but
seems preternaturally strange and eerie, and where the fictional seems not

at all that fictitious, remote and alien, but bears an uncanny resemblance to daily experience."[30] *Armies* also follows Zavarzadeh's theory of how the fictual combines the narrative modes of fiction and fact by integrating their "referential" methods of validating experience. He says fiction is "in-referential," meaning that its referent is "an internal unified field of fiction mapped out within the book," and fact is "out-referential," meaning that its referent is "an external configuration of facts verifiable outside the book." Although both forms are "mono-referential," the new fictual mode of the nonfiction novel of which Mailer is a prime example becomes "bi-referential" in its narrative form.[31] To Zavarzadeh, *The Armies of the Night* constitutes the continuation of an effort started in *Advertisements for Myself* in which Mailer "purported to tame American reality by an amalgamation of all literary genres. The very form of the book is a commentary on the impossibility of squeezing American experience into a fictive novel."[32]

Although Zavarzadeh believes that both books ultimately fail, *The Armies of the Night* marks Mailer's most sustained and persuasive attempt up to that point to capture the American experience in an immediate and total sense through the development of a new "fictual" form that also dramatizes the traditional rhetorical structure of the jeremiad. As an important achievement, therefore, in the development of what I have been calling the New Covenant, it is worth noting how this work by Mailer touches base, so to speak, with Doctorow, who also tries through the form of the historical novel to connect the rhetorical and narrative structures of the American idea. Mailer and Doctorow come together in *The Book of Daniel*, where Doctorow, as the experimental historical novelist, injects Mailer into his novel. The connection occurs during the march on Washington. Daniel sees Mailer sitting on the steps of the Pentagon, no doubt thinking about how to record the events in his forthcoming non-fiction novel.[33] This scene in which two writers explore and play with such notions as the continuity of fiction, history, and reality is an interesting moment of self-consciousness. It shows both writers approaching a particular moment in history from very different angles but finally coming together in the common effort to present and influence American history and culture. Mailer's recent "true life novel" about Gary Gilmore, *The Executioner's Song*, entails further experimentation with narrative forms that integrate fact and fiction in a way that elucidates the American idea.

The Executioner's Song concerns Gilmore's successful fight against groups opposed to his execution in Utah in January 1977 for the murder of two men. Several reviews emphasize how the thematic roots for this book go far back into Mailer's earlier work.[34] The most obvious connection between this book and his others is his continuing interest in the psychopath. Mailer's fascination with the subject of psychopathic violence is expressed in a particular form of modernistic sensibility and thought that constitutes one of his most visible breaks with the tradition of the nineteenth century represented by Walt Whitman. The theme of the psychopath dominates Mailer's essay "The White Negro" in *Advertisements for Myself*, and the clinical description of Gilmore in *The Executioner's Song* continues the discussion. Mailer writes, "Of course, Gary did fit into a psychiatric category. There was a medical term for moral insanity, criminality, uncontrolled animality—call it what you will. Psychiatrists called it 'psychopathic personality,' or, same thing, 'sociopathic personality.' It meant you were antisocial. In terms of accountability before the law, it was equal to sanity. The law saw a great difference between the psychotic and the psychopathic personality."[35] As a psychopathic or antisocial personality, Gilmore was interesting to Mailer partly because of Gilmore's verbal intensity and ability as a writer and his demonstrated artistic talent. In a poem called "The Executioner's Song" that appears in *Cannibals and Christians*, Mailer anticipates the connection between verbal expression, artistic creativity, and murder that was to be embodied by Gilmore. In the poem Mailer writes of his interest in becoming "an executioner" who could spend time "digging graves." Mailer connects this interest in death to an internal condition of "flatulence" or gastric gas and bad bowels that he blames on an obsession with sex. Both problems could be cured, he suggests, through neatly executed murder.[36] Mailer then describes how he would perform an execution and burial in a style and manner that reminds one of Hemingway's attitude toward bullfighting and boxing. Presumably, such devotion to ceremony dignifies the dead, honors the living, and sanctifies the executioner. Mailer suggests that such clean killing is an expression of the freedom that encourages poetic creativity. As a murderer, the poet achieves a control over life and his own emotions that enables him to write great poetry. Such a murderer-poet, Mailer says, could create a poem equal to "the Lord's creation."[37] The poem, therefore, celebrates murder as an aid to the creative process and could, in fact, stand as Gary Gilmore's "executioner's song" of the psychopath. The poem further exposes the roots within Mailer's own consciousness of the moral and aesthetic questions that Gilmore's story raises.

The psychopath also appears in *An American Dream* in a way that anticipates *The Executioner's Song*, to a certain extent. In *An American Dream*, the hero, Stephen Rojack, goes on a psychopathic journey that culminates in murder, orgy, and existential battle with forces of evil. A reference at the conclusion of the book to the "new breed" in the West helps to make the novel relevant to Gilmore. At the end of his amazing ordeal, Rojack prepares to leave New York for the West to help complete his destiny before moving on to regions south of the country. Mailer writes, "Nobody knew that the deserts of the West, the arid empty wild blind deserts, were producing again a new breed of man."[38] In the novel this suggestion of "a new breed of man" seems somewhat nebulous and superficial. The idea functions as an afterthought that Mailer abandons in works that immediately follow the novel in order to undergo, as Benjamin Spencer suggests, new exploratory journeys whose literary forms tend to feature himself. Spencer says, "Having ventured through Rojack into the psychopathic jungle of the unconscious and having emerged with only a vacuous new breed of desert men, Mailer in effect became his own protagonist in a new kind of non-fictional novel wherein he could imaginatively test his American existentialism in the tensions of national politics and exhibit his courage in more socially fruitful action than teetering on parapets or murdering women."[39] When Mailer returns to the West in *The Executioner's Song*, this idea of a new breed of man achieves specificity in the form of Gilmore. Moreover, he goes beyond what once had been in Spencer's words "a new kind of non-fiction novel" by removing himself as a protagonist in his later version of the genre. Mailer does not appear as a central consciousness in the Gilmore story but concentrates on dramatizing and recording the lives of the participants, especially those of Gilmore and his girlfriend, Nicole Baker, as derived primarily from interviews and materials gathered by Lawrence Schiller, a producer and journalist, who functioned as a kind of producer for the book itself.

Moreover, Mailer dramatizes these lives in the context of his sensitivity toward Gilmore's right to determine how and when he should die. Statements by Mailer during his campaign for mayor suggest that part of his sympathy for Gilmore reflects his left conservative philosophy. Mailer writes, "Who is to say that the religious heart is not right to think the need of every man and woman alive may be to die in a state of grace, a grace which for atheists and agnostics may reside in the basic art of having done one's best, of having found some part of a destiny to approach, and having worked for the view of it?"[40] Mailer connects this religious vision to his political program. He says, "So power to these poor neighborhoods still speaks to conservative principles, for it recognizes that a man must have the opportunity to work out his own destiny, or he will never know the dimensions of himself, he will be alienated from any sense of whether he is acting for good or evil."[41] Thus, Mailer wishes to achieve in his politics and philosophy nothing less than a return of the individual to himself. He says, "Our authority has been handed over to the federal power. . . . We are like wards in an orphan asylum. . . . So our condition is spiritless. We wait for abstract impersonal powers to save us, we despise the abstractness of those powers, we loathe ourselves for our own apathy. Orphans."[42] It would seem that in Gilmore's struggle to control his own death Mailer sees the embodiment of his brand of antiauthoritarian and anti-institutional existential individualism.

The Executioner's Song represents an important intellectual and literary feat for Mailer based upon years of earlier work and thought. It continues his endeavor to construct an original literary structure that presents America to itself and revolutionizes its understanding of itself. In the book he builds upon the synthesis of journalistic and literary modes of earlier works by incorporating through interviews and tapes a new dimension of social and oral history. This addition strengthens his importance as a cultural historian without diminishing his novelist's powers as the creative intelligence behind this story of America. With his disciplined personal absence from the activities of the book, the rhetorical stress of *The Armies of the Night* grows somewhat more muted as he emphasizes the strategy of letting America speak for itself. In *The Executioner's Song*, the structure of the jeremiad is less important as a unifying device than the new strategy of almost laying out the American psyche for examination in a manner that resembles the gruesome description of Gilmore's autopsy at the end of the book. Mailer divides the book into two parts called "Eastern Voices" and "Western Voices," which coincide with what he perceives as the geographical division of American consciousness between western violence, irrationality, and innocence and eastern exploitation, manipulation, inhibitions, intellect, and conscience. The western voices, of course, belong to Gilmore, his family, people, friends, and victims. The eastern media voices are generally heard through Larry Schiller's spreading network of control over the Gilmore story, or as part of the raging battle between the state and the antideath-penalty forces. Although so different in so many ways, the two sections are comparable because self-destruction and self-torture seem to dominate the lives of the people in both sections. Mailer's double achievement in the "true life novel," therefore, is his continued success at uniting journalism and literature into a new form through which to present America while also arousing some hope for individual and national regeneration through love and art.

One important shortcoming of the book rests in its almost palpable insensitivity and near indifference to Gilmore's victims who are boring by Mailer's standards. Such indifference to the victims of crime seems to conflict with the conservative thrust of Mailer's left-conservative position and is one of the many contradictions in his thought. Both murdered men and their wives represent the epitome of Mormon and American middle-class values. Max and Colleen Jensen and Ben and Debbie Bushnell were young newlyweds hoping to reach the same kind of conventional success and security as had their friends and families. Because of their absence of intense inner lives or originality, Mailer cannot take them very seriously, and this inability represents a failure of moral and artistic imagination on his part. At one point, in what are relatively brief descriptions of the victims' lives, Mailer writes sardonically of the Jensens: "Of course, they also had fun. Stuff like shaving-cream fights. Throwing glasses of water at each other" (*ES*, p. 213). Pretty tame stuff compared with what Gilmore and Nicole did to each other and to other people. Rather than express the proper and thoroughly undangerous piety about Gilmore's obvious cruelty and the clear innocence of his victims, Mailer focuses on the killer whose evil seems to merge with the death that emanates from the lives of those in the East and the West.

In a sense, Mailer's neglect of the victims constitutes a double sacrifice of them—first to Gilmore's rage and secondly to Mailer's moral and aesthetic ambitions. Mailer's position, therefore, not only indicates his proximity to Gilmore's own situation but it also further dramatizes the inherent danger of his nihilism. At a point early in *Advertisements for Myself*, Mailer wrote of "the desire to be destructive and therefore useful" (*AM*, p. 2). This line succinctly summarizes the dilemma intrinsic to Mailer's philosophy. How do you balance the value of creativity against the destructive cost it often entails? In *The Executioner's Song*, Mailer seems to find this balance for himself. He sees Gilmore as a symbol of self-destruction and death in America and makes him a target for his own concerns about national regeneration. The challenge to confront and convert that death in Gilmore into a life force proves irresistible to Mailer and becomes one of his most interesting studies of American life. Some of the same issues were dramatized again for Mailer with tragic results in the Jack Abbott case of 1981. Mailer and others had helped to obtain Abbott's parole from prison in Utah partly on the grounds that he was a special literary talent. However, that talent, as evidenced in his book about prison life entitled *In the Belly of the Beast*, did not prevent him from being accused of committing a murder on New York's Lower East Side. The case constitutes the fulfillment of some of the implications of Mailer's attitudes toward violence, freedom, and personality. Such views have been part of Mailer's thought and work for years and are an important aspect of *The Executioner's Song*. In fact, the book represents a sad foreshadowing of the Abbott story.[43]

The artistic power of *The Executioner's Song* derives to a considerable extent from the sustained impression of genuine American lives in a dramatic context that is filled with important symbolic and mythic meaning for American culture as a whole. Mailer maintains the illusion throughout the book of being only a mere transmitter for the voices of the participants, whereas, of course, his creation of the structure and organization of the book in fact brings them all to life. Mailer, as the Pulitzer Prize-winning author of *The Executioner's Song*, must receive credit for the basic division of the book between the East and the West, the subsequent construction of seven parts in each of the divisions, the additional subdivisions throughout the parts, the organization and presentation of the vast amount of material and detail, and the adherence to just the right tone, diction, and phrasing necessary to capture the language, speech, and thought of the characters. He also understood the potential of his material in the characters, especially of Gilmore, Nicole Baker, and Larry Schiller. Mailer had usually invented his psychopathic heroes, from Sergeant Croft in *The Naked and the Dead* to Stephen Rojack in *An American Dream*. Gilmore demands that Mailer give new life to real events. Both Gilmore and Nicole Baker are genuine western types for Mailer, but their story becomes relevant to any physical setting in America where there are people whose uncontrolled emotions and violence make life impossible and death a haven. Although Gary Gilmore thought about escape from prison up until his last hours, the impulse toward death remains strong in him and in Nicole. For both, a wish for death, enforced by a grotesque belief in a form of reincarnation, becomes a means for final escape from a life they could not handle. Moreover, Mailer brilliantly connects their wish for death to their place in the American social substrata of the lost and the hopeless. In spite of intelligence—Gary's I.Q. is "supposedly about 130" (*ES*, p. 798)—and creativity, both Gary and Nicole cannot find emotional sustenance from their environments. They become part of the permanently homeless, except for the prisons they create for themselves.

At the time of their meeting, Gary is thirty-five, Nicole is nineteen, and he has spent eighteen years of his life in prison while she has two children and a history of promiscuity that challenges her memory. Seduced at the age of eleven or twelve by her father's friend Uncle Lee, committed at thirteen to "half a nuthouse and half a Reform School," married once and then remarried in a black dress provided by her mother, Nicole sounds like a case study of neglect (*ES*, pp. 89, 92–93). She remembers, "Her mother gave her a black dress to be married in. It was short and slit at the sides. That really affected Nicole. She didn't feel it was appropriate to get married in a black dress at 15" (*ES*, p. 98). At the same time she remains thoroughly innocent of other aspects of life. Thus, of one of the many men who find her beautiful, she recalls, "She had never known a fellow who wore a suit to the job every day, and it tickled her" (*ES*, p. 178). Also, a local reporter who gets to know Nicole "began to realize that Nicole, in a funny way, was kind of sheltered and didn't know a lot about certain aspects of life like music and backpacking in Oregon, or even rap sessions like this" (*ES*, p. 558). Such innocence appears most dramatically in the language of the will she prepares in anticipation of her planned joint suicide with Gary. She endeavors to explain the paternity of her children, to insist upon conditions for their care, to dispose of her belongings, and to make arrangements for the funeral. She writes, "*As to the care custody and welfare of my children—I am not only desireing* [sic] *but demanding* [underlined] *that the responsibility of them and any decisions concerning them—be placed directly and immeadiatly* [sic] *into the hands of Thomas Giles Barrett* [underlined] *and/or Marie Barret* [underlined] *of Springville, Utah.*

If the Barretts so wish to adopt my children—they have my willing consent" (*ES*, p. 569). Concerning *"a pearl ring in hock in the bowling alley in Springville,"* she *"would really like for someone to get it out and give it to my little Sister— April L. Baker"* (*ES*, p. 569).

If Nicole's black wedding dress can stand as a symbol of her life, then Gary's "Guardian Angel" is his. Gary tells Nicole:

> Once when he was 3, and his brother was 4, his father and mother stopped to have dinner in a restaurant in Santa Barbara. Then his father said he had to get some change. He'd be right back. He didn't come back for 3 months. His mother was alone with no money and two little boys. So she started hitchhiking to Provo. They got stuck on the Humboldt Sink in Nevada. Could have died in the desert. They had no money and had not eaten for the second day in a row. Then a man came walking down the road with a brown sack in his hand, and he said, Well, my wife has fixed a lunch for me, but it's more than I can eat. Would you like some? His mother said, Well, yes, we'd be very grateful. The man gave her the sack and walked on. . . . Bessie turned to thank him but the man had disappeared. This was on a long flat stretch of Nevada high-way." (*ES*, pp. 104–5)

Gary came to think of the man as his Guardian Angel who would always protect him. He extends that belief into an illusion of his immunity from pain. He writes, *"I once thought that I'd really been through some rough things, that I was immune to pain"* (*ES*, p. 327). However, such artificial defense mechanisms crumble before the onrush of Gary's own emotions and reality. There was, as Schiller comes to recognize, "a streak of childish vengefulness" in Gary (*ES*, p. 749) not too dissimilar from his immature inability to resist the temptation to get an overpriced truck because "he had fallen in love with a paint job" (*ES*, p. 217). Unable to deal with frustration or choice, Gary confesses after his murders that "I can't keep up with life" (*ES*, p. 292). Seeking immunity from pain, inventing illusory defenses against the difficulties of life, searching for love by acting out neurotic patterns that deny love, both Nicole and Gary in their own way really suffer a form of death-in-life.

Ironically, the love they feel for each other only makes life even more impossible. They cannot survive their own passion and need for each other. Gary's erratic actions and bizarre temperament, which are aggravated by her vagarious emotions, help drive Nicole away. He finds that he cannot tolerate this kind of pain and compares it to the relative security of prison. He says, "This is the first time I've experienced a pain I can't take. I used to be able to handle anything that came up, didn't matter how bad, but it's tougher out here" (*ES*, p. 195). Later, in a letter to Nicole from prison, he says, "*I have no defense for what I feel for you*" (*ES*, p. 359). Throughout his story, he attributes his murderous action to the frustration of his love for Nicole. He says, "*I killed Jenkins and Bushnell because I did not want to kill Nicole*" (*ES*, p. 691). The only way he can handle his love for her is as a prisoner. And her love for him similarly finds its expression in a choice for death. Unsure of her ability to ever meet Gary's demands for faithfulness, she desperately acquiesces to his appeals to join him in death through a second suicide attempt (*ES*, pp. 473, 480). The position of Gary and Nicole in society and their failure to survive their emotions make them, as one crass observer says, a "democratic Romeo and Juliet" (*ES*, p. 627). In the West of Gary and Nicole, love has become impossible, leaving only death and the ironic alternative of accepting death to overcome it and prove their love. Through execution and attempted suicide, they kill the death within themselves in order to achieve the love that they kill through their own violence and instability.

For Mailer, the correspondence between Gary and Nicole helps to turn their story into a kind of modern-day tragedy. Gary's ability to sing, so to speak, his own executioner's song and to instruct Nicole in achieving her own voice in their duet gives them an additional dimension. Gary's power with words parallels his talent as an artist. Mailer makes note of people's impression that Gary drew "like a real artist" and that "everything Gary painted was sharp as a razor. If he painted a bird, you could see every feather as though under a magnifying glass" (*ES*, pp. 82, 165). Gary presumes a sincerity and seriousness about art. He writes to Nicole:

> *I would really like you to see a picture of that sculpture "Ecstasy of St. Therese." I believe the sculptor is Bernini. I've never seen any great works of art in person but I guess I'm familiar with most European Art through books I've studied. I once saw a picture of Christ by a Russian artist that really haunted me for a long time. Christ didn't look anything like the popular beaming Western Christian version of the kind shepherd we're used to. He looked like a man, with a gaunt, lean, sort of*

haunted face with deep set large dark eyes. . . . Just this extraordinary
man—this ordinary human being who made himself extra-ordinary and
tried to tell us all that it was nothing more than any of us could do.
Loneliness and a hint of doubt seemed to fill the picture. I would like
to have known the man in that picture. (ES, pp. 386–87)

The force of such prison writings to Nicole derives not only from the
intensity of Gary's emotions but also from his insight into his own situation. In what appears to be his first letter to her from prison, Gary expresses his understanding of his failure to function outside of prison, his
loss of the opportunity to love her, and his need to accept death as the
only way left. He writes, "*I look at the world through eyes that suspect, doubt,*
fear, hate, cheat, mock, are selfish and vain. All things unacceptable, I see them
as natural and have even come to accept them as such. I look around the ugly
vile cell and know that I truly belong in a place this dank and dirty, for where
else should I be?" (ES, p. 305).

They write to each other of their adolescent passion in a style that feeds
their desperation. The sentimental language substitutes for the reality that
was beyond their ability to achieve. He writes, "*Remember the nite we*
met? . . . there was a wild wind blowing in my heart that nite. . . . I love you
more than God" (ES, p. 486). Nicole responds to Gary's words by developing her own excitement over words. Mailer writes, "She would put Sunny
and Jeremy to bed and then write poetry. That was all. Writing and writing at poetry" (ES, p. 513). Unsophisticated and immature as they are,
Nicole's poetry and letters demonstrate a youthful intelligence learning to
play with words in a way that enables her to live vicariously through them.
Written out of loneliness both before and during her forced stay in the
hospital that followed her suicide attempt, Nicole expresses a love that
began with infatuation and led to a total commitment to a man who
became for her a kind of cult hero with special powers. She writes, "*Touch*
my soul with your truth . . ." (ES, p. 699); "*i'm furious with the ways an wiles*
of Love Life and the Ultimate Wisdom. . . . (ES, p. 769); "*Long nights rest-*
less / Scattered thots / Wondering whats become / Of all our chances. / Nicole"
(ES, p. 769); "*So ask me no question, / Sing me no songs / Follow me no-*
where / im already gone" (ES, p. 787). In the midst of such flights, she can
also indicate a stunning sudden awareness of exactly her situation and
dilemma. She writes, "*i am in a place i dislike beyond words. My situation calls*
for me to convince a lot of intelligent important people of my desire to live and

*my capabilities to exist as a competent mother and human being. im givin it all
i got rite now"* (*ES*, pp. 786–87). About a week later fear grows when she
seems to recognize how far she has gone in her world with Gary and how
alone she will be without him. She writes to him, *"will i be nothing—if you
go away. . . . Will i be more? Will i be lost or be found?* (*ES*, p. 815). All her
expressions of love anticipate his death. In their world love and life seem
incompatible. Gilmore's escape from prison or a pardon, both of which
seem inconceivable, certainly would have resulted in a renewal of their
cycle of separation, violence, and despair.

A less romantic form of death pervades Mailer's "Eastern Voices."
While the legal debate and battle over the state's right to execute Gilmore receives considerable attention in this section, the focus of "Eastern
Voices" turns primarily on an analysis of the media. In attempting to
balance values between the law and the media, Mailer shows both sides of
the legal issue as honorable, dedicated, and obsessed with the righteousness of their positions concerning the ultimate authority for Gilmore's life
or death. Similarly, Mailer spends considerable time on portraits of media
people like Bill Moyers, David Susskind, Jimmy Breslin, and Barry Farrell.
However, the professionalism, ethical conduct, and moral standards of
such people do not always outweigh the rampant commercialism, mer-
chandizing, and exploitation that attempt to realize the full economic
potential of the Gilmore story. Mailer finds a symbol for this ghoulish
aspect of the media in the person of one national broadcaster, Geraldo
Rivera. He writes, *"Directly in front of the prison building, Geraldo Rivera,
attired in black leather jacket and jeans and looking cool, the way only Geraldo
Rivera can look cool, is shouting into his mike, 'Kill the Rona segment. Get rid
of it. Give me air. You'll be able to hear the shots. I promise. You'll be able to
hear the shots'"* (*ES*, p. 975). In an equally grotesque display, Rivera later
tries to impose himself upon a hospitalized relative of Gilmore who has
just undergone surgery in order to get a live interview with her about
Gary. Mailer writes, "Then, Geraldo Rivera called and wanted to do a live
TV interview in her hospital room. Brenda thought, How atrocious. Got
to be kidding" (*ES*, p. 999).

However, the lead voice in the section is that of Larry Schiller who
accomplishes his initial objective of gaining control of the rights to the
Gilmore story but ends by experiencing a moral reawakening as a result of
his intimate connection to the people and events surrounding the execu-

tion. Schiller grows from an entrepreneur of sorts to a moral agent. He comes to function as the moral consciousness that the book lacks in Mailer's absence. Schiller entered the Gilmore story with a dubious reputation for such previous journalistic endeavors as gaining the rights to Susan Atkins's life in the Charlie Manson case, getting the last interview with Jack Ruby, and selling a nude photograph of Marilyn Monroe to Hugh Hefner for an unprecedented $25,000. He felt that such activities weakened his case for his own seriousness. He wanted respect and recognition for what he felt was his real worth as an important journalist and producer. He blamed himself for missing an important opportunity to record history in the Atkins case and for damaging himself by letting his dealings with Atkins become a factor in her capacity to testify as a star witness for the state. Forced by the latter situation to testify in court, Schiller had to respond to the judge's query regarding his "occupation." Schiller replied, "'I believe I am a communicator.'" Mailer writes, "The courtroom laughed. They thought he was a hustler. The memory burned into the skin right under his beard" (*ES*, p. 601). Schiller comes to see the Gilmore story as a chance for him to make something new of himself. And Mailer brilliantly capitalizes on Schiller's hopes by giving him a role that involves both his own moral regeneration and the promise of elevating the Gilmore story into a cultural myth. Through Schiller's auspices, Gilmore's story becomes a tale of new life amidst the destruction of the "Western Voices" of death and the "Eastern Voices" of dehumanizing exploitation.

Schiller's vision of truth occurs in the bathroom during a moment of release of all the guilt he has accumulated by failing to live up to his own standards and expectations. Caught in the moral agony of the debate over the right to execute Gilmore and the grotesque competition for control over the story itself, Schiller makes the existential decision to be right rather than smart. Mailer writes, "He said to himself, 'I don't know any longer whether what I'm doing is morally right,' and that made him cry even more. He had been saying to himself for weeks that he was not part of the circus, that he had instincts which raised him above, a desire to record history, true history, not journalistic crap, but now he felt as if he was finally part of the circus and might even be the biggest part of it, and in the middle of crying, he went into the bathroom and took the longest fucking shit of his life. It was all diarrhea" (*ES*, p. 857). In that situation of physical, emotional, and intellectual exhaustion, he makes "the decision that in no way was he ever going to sell Gary Gilmore's execution. No. No way could anybody convince him. He would not make that fucking mistake for greed or security. No. He didn't care if he never saw a penny at the end. He had to stay by what his gut told him. He started crying again and said to himself, 'I can't even spell decently. I can't write the way I feel and want to express myself'" (*ES*, p. 858). In making such a decision, Schiller recognizes that "he was not only turning down the easiest money he had ever been offered, but was going to take a beating" because his action meant refusing to sell parts of Gary Gilmore's last days to *Time* and *Newsweek* and NBC (*ES*, p. 858). Mailer writes, "He would not deal, he would not sell. Instead, he would give it away. After the execution, he would release his private eyewitness account to all the media at once. Nobody in the bidding liked it" (*ES*, p. 859).

As an act of sacrifice and courage, Schiller's decision represents a moral triumph that renders an additional dimension of meaning to Gilmore's story. It constitutes an act of love and conscience. Schiller, in effect, becomes the conscience Gilmore never had. He represents the theme of love that emerges for many of the survivors of the experience. Thus, a memorial service for Gary is especially important to Schiller's story. Both Schiller and Barry Farrell, who worked with Schiller, attend the service. Schiller's actions symbolize the attitude of the others at the service. They choose to interpret Gary in terms of his own remark to one woman that "'All I ever wanted was a little love'" (*ES*, p. 944). For them, Gary's death and his horrible actions find meaning in their vision of him as a man of depth and pain who acted out of frustrated love but finally found the means to love. Thus, Cline Campbell, a prison official who knew Gilmore well, says, "You've gathered from those that have spoken that the thing that Gary wanted to leave was love. He probably had more capacity to love than anybody at that place. He gave to me a deep love and I want you to know that I have in me a portion of Gary Mark Gilmore that will never leave" (*ES*, p. 1020). Similarly, Vern Damico says, "I've seen the inner side of Gary, and he is human, tender, and yes, understanding, very capable of love" (*ES*, p. 1021). On the other hand, Barry Farrell saw Gilmore as a kind of existential hero capable of inventing himself. Farrell read Gary's voluminous responses to his written questions as an attempt at such self-creation. Mailer writes, "It looked to Farrell as if Gilmore was now setting out to present the particular view of himself he wanted people to keep. In that sense, he was being his own writer" (*ES*, p. 793).

Gary Gilmore became a collective creation into which Mailer's genius breathes new life. Partly because of the central role Schiller plays in events, Gilmore turns into a symbol of connection and reconciliation between western and eastern voices. Thus, Gary joins Marilyn as an important force in Mailer's conception of the continuing powers of the American myth. *The Executioner's Song* is one of Mailer's significant contributions to the tradition of the New Covenant because it further develops the narrative and rhetorical structures that keep the American idea relevant to our times. Mailer's expression of a new left-conservative political and social philosophy in both this and other nonfiction works makes him a leader in articulating the crucial shift in political consciousness that is now influencing the direction and meaning of the New Covenant.

Chapter 9

A True Radical History
E. L. Doctorow

Although E. L. Doctorow is not the same kind of public personality as Mailer, the quality of his commitment to the role of the New Jeremiah in the tradition of the New Covenant is as strong and as significant as Mailer's. Like Mailer, Doctorow writes from the perspective of a moral consciousness to reexamine the meaning of the American experience and to revivify our moral imagination. His concern for the relevance of America as a myth and ideology has led him to write a form of "metahistory" that builds upon the poetic and linguistic origins of historical understanding.[1] Moreover, it can be argued that as metahistory, in Hayden White's sense of the term, Doctorow's work can be compared with Nietzsche's philosophy of history. According to White, Nietzsche attempted "to translate history into art." Doctorow shares Nietzsche's interest in, as White says, returning "consciousness to the enjoyment of its Metaphorical powers."[2] Much of Nietzsche's discussion in *The Use and Abuse of History* of the objectives and responsibilities of the historian could serve as a model for Doctorow. Nietzsche insists that the "real value" of history "lies in inventing ingenious variations on a probably commonplace theme, in raising the popular melody to a universal symbol and showing what a world of depth, power and beauty exists in it." To achieve such a level of creativity, the historian, Nietzsche argues, must function and think like an artist. The historian, he says, must develop "above all a great artistic faculty, a creative vision from a height, the loving study of the data of experience, the free elaborating of a given type."[3] Based on this artistic theory of rendering history, Nietzsche goes on in *The Genealogy of Morals* to establish something like guidelines for an approach to history that emphasizes openness and invention.[4]

The elements of myth and symbol, as well as art and invention, are the important factors in Nietzsche's thinking about history that elucidate Doctorow's work. For Nietzsche, myth and symbol constitute the heart of a culture and its history and must, therefore, be contrasted with the fictions derived from ordinary history. History and culture without myth turn man into an abstraction. Man's loss of myth, Nietzsche writes in *The Birth of Tragedy*, leads to "abstract man stripped of myth, abstract education, abstract mores, abstract law, abstract government; the random vagaries of the artistic imagination unchanneled by any native myth; a culture without any fixed and consecrated place of origin, condemned to exhaust all possibilities and feed miserably and parasitically on every culture under the sun." In contrast to such abstraction, Nietzsche hopes to return culture to its "mythic home, the mythic womb."[5] He associates the power of myth to define the essence of culture with the power of music to stimulate men to operate and think beyond their usual capacities. Both myth and music come together for him in a truly exciting culture. Through the revivification of the metaphoric consciousness, he seeks to establish in cultural history "the mythopoeic power of true music."[6] Nietzsche's understanding of history in terms of myth, metaphor, and music is, as White says, the "notion of historical representation as pure story, fabulation, myth conceived as the verbal equivalent of the spirit of music."[7] *Ragtime* represents the most obvious example of Doctorow's attempt to develop the narrative structure of the historical novel in what can be described as a Nietzschean mode that uses music as the metaphor to best dramatize an era and a people. Thus, Doctorow indicates his interest in the idea of history as, in White's words, "pure story, fabulation, myth" when he says of *Ragtime* that "there's no more fiction or nonfiction now, there's only narrative. All the nonfiction means of communication employ narrative today."[8]

However, there are also major differences between Nietzsche and Doctorow. Most importantly, Doctorow rejects the nihilistic implications of Nietzsche's philosophy. As White indicates, in Nietzsche's "conception of history, the prospects of any *community* whatsoever are sternly rejected." "In Nietzsche," White says, "no historical grounds exist for the construction of any specific *political* posture except that of antipolitics itself. Thought is liberated from responsibility to anything outside the ego and will of the individual, whether past, future, or present."[9] Although certainly aware of such implications in contemporary thought, Doctorow remains committed to community and politics, to a moral vision that includes individual responsibility, and to history itself, meaning a belief in the necessity of trying to understand the past as a means for attempting to deal intelligently with the present and future. Such humanistic concerns also put Doctorow in opposition to a modern school of apocalyptic writers. Harry Henderson's list of these writers includes Nathanael West, John Barth, Joseph Heller, and Thomas Pynchon. Henderson believes that these writers have an "apocalyptic historical imagination" that entertains the "idea of an apocalyptic Day of Doom, an end to history that is foreshadowed by the exhaustion of the historical imagination that their parody signifies."[10] Although the ending to Doctorow's first novel, *Welcome to Hard Times*, resembles this kind of apocalyptic catastrophe, the spirit of the hero and narrator suggests a hope for human communication, truth, and love that characterizes Doctorow's literature and philosophy in general.

Welcome to Hard Times also indicates Doctorow's important interest in working with universal figures and classic motifs in a mythic pattern. In the novel Doctorow places classic western types in a traditional setting and narrative. The absence of surnames for the characters reenforces their universality. They clearly are intended to stand for general personality types that fit into the mythic scheme of "the Western." For example, the stock figure of the bad man who destroys the town of Hard Times and massacres its residents is cast simply as the Man from Bodie. The hero is known as Blue, depicting the low key, almost maudlin, mood of the piece. He is also called mayor since he assumes a kind of clerical and administrative responsibility for the town. From being a record keeper of sorts, he eventually achieves a judicial and prophetic role. His consciousness and vision make the town a community. Condemning himself for his initial cowardice in failing to stand up to the bad man, he restores the town and establishes something of a family. However, he finds himself forced to confront the return of the Bad Man from Bodie, who once again destroys everything. The mayor blames himself. He says, "I can forgive everyone but I cannot forgive myself. I told Molly we'd be ready for the Bad Man but we can never be ready. Nothing is ever buried, the earth rolls in its tracks, it never goes anywhere, it never changes, only the hope changes like morning and night, only the expectations rise and set. Why does there have to be a promise before destruction?"[11]

However, even in the face of the evil and the destructiveness of the Bad Man, Blue cannot surrender his humanistic priorities, which include at the top of the list the need to conclude his history. In spite of his awareness of what we can call the epistemological difficulties and uncertainties entailed in attempting to know and transmit the truth, Blue feels compelled to complete his project. The only meaning the events can have will be provided by Blue as the historian whose work will make them part of human consciousness. Rather than confirming the nihilism of the apocalyptic vision, the destruction of Hard Times seems to demand of Blue just the opposite of a concession to death. In spite of his fears and self-doubts, Hard Times for Blue requires a reassertion of his individual moral responsibility. He says, "And now I've put down what happened, everything that happened from one end to the other. And it scares me more than death scares me that it may show the truth." Blue admits that he cannot be sure of the final meaning of his account given the difficulty of figuring out "which minutes were important and which not." He asks, "Does the truth come out in such scrawls, so bound by my limits?"[12] His actions, however, along with his fulfillment of the obligation to record history, stand as the final moral judgment upon Blue. Thus, as he takes his last look upon the destruction of the town, he notes that wood for reconstruction remains available. He says, "And I have to allow, with great shame, I keep thinking someone will come by sometime who will want to use the wood."[13] So, even in death, he continues to be the builder, the pioneer, the American.

Blue's questions concerning his dilemma about being caught up as a man, a citizen, and a historian in the making and writing of his own history achieve brilliant elaboration and discussion in Doctorow's most successful and important novel to date, *The Book of Daniel*. Issues about history, myth, human values, and individual moral responsibility that are suggested in *Welcome to Hard Times*, and to a lesser degree in *Big as Life*,[14] reach maturity in *The Book of Daniel*, a largely neglected work that may yet receive deserving recognition as a major work of contemporary literature. There are reasons for this neglect. First of all, with the important exception of Stanley Kauffmann in the *New Republic*, most reviewers have failed to see much beyond the novel's most obvious intention of dramatizing the story of Julius and Ethel Rosenberg, who were convicted and executed by electrocution as spies for stealing atomic secrets for the Russians in the early 1950s. In the novel the names of the Rosenbergs are changed to Paul and Rochelle Isaacson, and the story is told through the consciousness of their son, Daniel Isaacson.[15] In addition, other novels in the Doctorow canon, especially *Ragtime*, have received far more critical attention from major reviewers and scholars. Doctorow's dazzling insertion of real characters in the fictional setting of *Ragtime* and his experimentation in that novel with a kind of verbal and imagistic syncopation have intrigued both popular and critical audiences, but it has also distracted them from much of the inventiveness and originality of *The Book of Daniel*, which also experiments with the form of the historical novel. In terms of sparkle and glitter, *The Book of Daniel* cannot compete with *Ragtime*'s use of such figures as Evelyn Nesbit, J. P. Morgan, Freud, Houdini, and Emma Goldman. As Barbara Foley indicates, *Ragtime* departs radically from the historical novel's practice of dealing only plausibly with historical figures. Foley writes, "Events so audaciously 'invented' as Freud's and Jung's trip through the Tunnel of Love at Coney Island or Emma Goldman's massage of Evelyn Nesbit clearly violate this canon of historical decorum. Doctorow is doing something quite different here: he is utilizing the reader's encyclopedic knowledge that a historical Freud, Jung, Goldman, and Nesbit did in fact exist in order to pose an open challenge to the reader's preconceived notions about what historical 'truth' actually is. Asked on one occasion whether Goldman and Nesbit ever really met, Doctorow has boldly replied, 'They have now!'"[16] Other critics such as Leonard Kriegel and John Seelye also have expressed their great admiration for the cleverness of Doctorow's technique in *Ragtime*. Kriegel considers the novel "intriguing" and says, "In Dos Passos' great trilogy, the biographical is used as a counterweight to the fictional. In Doctorow, the stuff of J. P. Morgan is, indeed, the stuff of fictional life." Also relating *Ragtime* to Dos Passos, Seelye notes that "perhaps Doctorow's most significant borrowing is from continental, not American literature, namely, his use of Heinrich von Kleist's historical novel *Michael Kohlhaus*." Seelye further states that *Ragtime* "manages to syncopate materials borrowed from other radically oriented novels of the '30s, including Roth's *Call It Sleep* and George Milburn's forgotten *tour de force, Catalogue*."[17]

The experimentation in *The Book of Daniel* is of a more traditional sort than in either *Ragtime* or the more recent *Loon Lake*. In *The Book of Daniel*, Doctorow, like Philip Roth, develops the idea of the self-consciousness of modern literature and art so that the process of creativity and production becomes a subject in itself. However, while Roth writes fiction about writing fiction, Doctorow writes fiction about writing history. At the beginning of the novel, we learn that Daniel Isaacson is writing his history dissertation at Columbia University and that we will be watching him watching himself as he progresses on it. In fact, Daniel's history will take the form of the very book in our hands. We also see that Doctorow, through the persona of Daniel, really writes a special kind of history that imbues Daniel's prophetic narration with the rhetoric of the jeremiad in a linguistic achievement that projects a vision of justice and truth upon American culture. In effect, then, Doctorow demands of himself a literary work of initiation that includes the stories of Daniel and his family and, for want of a better term, Daniel's inner spirit or sense of being; an intellectual and social history that establishes the ideals, values, trends, and mores of America from the period of the depression until the era of the Great Greening of America in the late 1960s; a political study of modern radical movements and thought; a moral history that lives up to the rhetorical tradition of the jeremiad. Putting all of this together—Daniel's own story plus the story of his people and their times in America—Doctorow, by adhering consistently to the complex consciousness and multidimensional point of view of his young Columbia graduate student, writes one of the great Jewish novels of our times.

Two figures are especially important examples to Daniel in his effort to write such a history—Edgar Allan Poe and the Prophet Daniel. Our Daniel—Daniel Isaacson—sees Poe as an important literary and cultural model of the power of the alienated artistic consciousness to instigate a revolution in the values and thought of his times. In Poe, art and alienation go hand in hand. Thus, Daniel calls Poe "the archetype traitor, the master subversive Poe, who wore a hole into the parchment and let the darkness pour through" by virtue of his drinking, his relationship to his thirteen-year-old cousin, and his poetry.[18] He says, "A small powerful odor arose from the Constitution; there was a wisp of smoke which exploded and quickly turned mustard yellow in color. When Poe blew this away through the resulting aperture in the parchment the darkness of the depths rose, and rises still from that small hole all these years incessantly pouring its dark hellish gases like soot, like smog, like the poisonous effulgence of combustion engines over Thrift and Virtue and Reason and Natural Law and the Rights of Man. It's Poe, not those other guys. He and he alone.

It's Poe who ruined us, that scream from the smiling face of America"
(*BD*, pp. 193–94). Daniel believes that Poe would understand him as a
complex and divided consciousness who has been trained by his parents to
be "a small criminal of perception" and "a psychic alien" (*BD*, pp. 41, 45),
meaning someone whose point of view and ideas of reality always will be
difficult and multidimensional. Daniel also believes that Poe provides an
original lesson in American culture of the cost of such a complex consciousness. Poe demonstrates how an alien vision becomes a double-edged
sword. Though a complex consciousness allows Daniel to function with
great perspicacity and imagination on many different levels and through
many creative forms, it also can be a self-destructive and nonproductive
force in the manner of much of modern nihilism. The tendency in art to
carry such alienation to its nihilistic extreme interests Daniel and becomes
an ideology in itself. Daniel finds a symbol for the nihilistic potential of
his own perspective in the mutilation of a woman's eye in "a classic sur-
realist silent film by Buñuel and Dali" (*BD*, p. 72). In the movie a man
brings his straight razor toward a woman's face and her eyeball. Daniel
says, "And just as you, the audience, have settled for this symbolic mutilation of the woman's eye, the camera cuts back to the scene, and in close-
up, shows the razor slicing into the eyeball" (*BD*, p. 73).

The counterpart to Daniel's psychological and aesthetic alienation as
represented by Poe is the moral alienation of the prophetic and righteous
visionary in a corrupt land as embodied in the biblical story of Daniel. The
biblical Daniel stands as a symbol, or a "type" in the Puritan sense of the
word, for the Daniel in the novel. His moral vision and his story establish
a standard and a pattern for our Daniel. Through Daniel the Prophet, the
novel attempts to transcend historical limitations and extends itself to a
higher realm of moral authority. However, the psychological credibility
for the moral consciousness of Daniel and his sister derives from the abra-
sive onslaught of continuous preachings from their parents. The obsessive
moralism of their parents' left-wing politics, values, and views has taught
Daniel and Susan to see even ordinary matters as ultimate moral issues.
Moreover, Daniel recognizes important parallels between his own situation and that of the biblical Daniel, of whom he says, "It is a bad time for
Daniel and his co-religionists, for they are second-class citizens, in a distinctly hostile environment. But in that peculiar kind of symbiosis of pa-
gan kings and wise subject-Jews, Daniel is apparently able to soften the

worst excesses of the rulers against his people by making himself available for interpretation of dreams, visions or apparitions in the night" (*BD*, p. 21). Similarly, as Jews and Communists, Daniel's parents consider themselves to be second-class citizens, and Daniel also feels like an alien in his own country. In addition, he sees an existential connection between himself and the biblical Daniel. As someone who inherits an awesome guilt and loss through his parents, Daniel can sympathize and identify with the biblical Daniel's feeling of having been chosen. God, according to Daniel, "enlists the help of naturally righteous humans who become messengers, or carriers of his miracles, or who deliver their people. Each age has by trial to achieve its recognition of Him—or to put it another way, every generation has to learn anew the lesson of His Existence. The drama of the Bible is always in the conflict of those who have learned with those who have not learned" (*BD*, p. 20). The biblical Book of Daniel, therefore, operates as a moral metaphor for our Daniel's history.

Daniel's moral vision achieves additional depth and specificity through the character of Susan, who functions as an alter—or more precisely a super-super—ego for Daniel, forever torturing him with ever increasing moral demands. Their intimate relationship as almost a single mind or psyche becomes solidified when circumstances unite them against the world. This special relationship emerges after the arrest and the death of their parents. Thus, she becomes capable of sending a "signal" to him "from the spasm of soul." He says, "Susan and I, we were the only ones left" (*BD*, pp. 40–41). At times he tries to treat her moral intensity facetiously, but in fact her moral authoritarianism operates as a kind of tourniquet upon his personality. He says that she has become "a dupe of the international moralist propagandist apparatus" and has been made into a "moral speed freak" (*BD*, p. 20). Significantly, her moral position is heavy with political content because she identifies ferociously with her parents and vehemently maintains a radical ideology. She attacks Daniel for defaming the memory of their parents and argues that his decision to attend graduate school is an act of cowardice and of treason against them and the left. " 'What did they die for?' " she exclaims as a curse against Daniel (*BD*, p. 94). He, of course, assumes the guilt and responsibility for her eventual breakdown and death. "There is," he says, "some evidence that she was driven finally to eradicate him from her consciousness by the radical means of eradicating her consciousness" (*BD*, p. 95).

Whereas Susan radiates radical moral righteousness, Daniel usually responds to situations with the defensive detachment of a student of radicalism. In contrast to Susan, whose radicalism recoils against herself, Daniel vents his frustration in his writing. The scattered inclusion of Daniel's interpretations of history, politics, and thought within *The Book of Daniel* is one of the novel's major accomplishments. Doctorow presents a relatively traditional Marxist historical methodology and perspective within the broader concept of history represented by the book in its entirety. By expanding upon the studies and ideas of established radical and revisionist historians such as William Appleman Williams, Daniel develops an interesting framework through which to interpret history in terms of class oppression, organized violence, bourgeois control of society's institutions, and capitalist domination of the means of economic production and distribution.[19] Daniel expounds upon this point of view in a series of statements dealing with diverse periods and events in diplomatic, political, and social history, all of which ultimately contribute to and explain the background and meaning of his parents' execution. Some of Daniel's leftist disquisitions include an explanation and justification of Stalin's leadership based on E. H. Carr's interpretation of the dictator's role in revivifying Russian nationalism (*BD*, p. 65); an argument that all men are inherently both victims and enemies of all governments because "the final existential condition is citizenship. Every man is the enemy of his own country" (*BD*, p. 85); a revisionist argument entitled "A True History of the Cold War: A Raga" that maintains that the cold war was initiated by America in the hope of using atomic weapons as a means for controlling Russia and that the Truman Doctrine and the Marshall Plan were thinly veiled disguises to protect and advance American capitalistic interests (*BD*, pp. 248—54); and a belief "that the basis of all class distinctions in society is corporal punishment. Classes are created by corporal punishment, and maintained by corporal punishment" (*BD*, p. 144). Daniel develops the latter argument along classic Marxist lines. He writes, "As societies endure in history they symbolize complex systems of corporal punishment in economic terms. That is why Marx used the word 'slavery' to define the role of the working class under capitalism" (*BD*, pp. 144—45). Daniel's obsession with the authoritarian power and brutality of the state motivates his dramatic history of civic and governmental torture and punishment that includes drawing and quartering, smoking, knouting, and burning at the stake, which he offers to strengthen the argument for the martyrdom of his electrocuted parents (*BD*, pp. 86, 122, 143, 144).

On the other hand, Daniel's personal experiences with people on the left and his proclivity to temper his radicalism and Marxism with self-criticism and pragmatic intellectualism tend to challenge Susan's ideological rigidity. Although he identifies with the left, he frequently views it ironically and critically. From his perspective the left seems more pathetic than ominous. In fact, it appears to be a danger only to those people like his parents who let their belief in it become a new kind of orthodoxy that inflates their sense of importance, disguises their vulnerability, and encourages a kind of moral myopia, which confuses immediate self-interest, personal status, and convenience with universal truth and justice. The novel offers innumerable examples of the failure of thought and character by members of the left, many of them most powerfully dramatized by his parents and their friends. His parents are filled with an enormous sense of their own importance and knowledge. They believe their access to historical truth makes them part of a psychological, moral, and intellectual elite. Ironically, such self-elevation puts them in opposition to the very masses they are supposed to serve. The fact of their political irrelevance and impotence in the face of such reputed power contributes to a sense of frustration that further increases their feeling of internal weakness and ineptitude. Thus, Daniel remembers how mixed motivations inspired the idealism of his parents. Daniel writes, "They rushed after self-esteem. If you could recognize a Humphrey Bogart movie for the cheap trash it was, you had culture. If you discovered the working class you found the roots of democracy. In social justice you discovered your own virtue. To desire social justice was a way of living without envy, which is the emotion of a loser. It was a way of transforming envy into constructive outgoing hate" (*BD*, p. 43).

Unfortunately, such hatred became a characteristic way of being in the world for his parents. He writes, "The thing about the Isaacson family, the thing about everyone in our family, is that we're not nice people" (*BD*, p. 37). The wife of the lawyer who lost his health in his tireless efforts on their behalf understandably resents the impact of the Isaacsons upon her own life. " 'I have no love for the memory of your parents,' " she tells Daniel. " 'They were Communists and they destroyed everything they touched' " (*BD*, p. 232). Accusing his parents of being unkind to everyone, she also feels that "'they were not innocent of permitting themselves to be used. And of using other people in their fanaticism'" (*BD*, p. 232). Furthermore, during the trial his own mother comes to recognize many harsh facts about the left and the people in it. She ironically fails, however, to see similarities between herself and her friends. She thinks, "My God how I hate them all, how I despise their pompous little egos and their discussions and resolutions and breast-beating; with their arrogance as they delivered to us each week the truth, the gospel according to 11th Street. Always they treated Paul like a child and with his mind! a mind so fine, so superior to theirs except in the grubby self-serving politics of the Party. He was always being censured, he was never quite in step. All he did was slave for them, believe for them. Communists have no respect for people, only for positions. . . . You blind them with your ideals and while they are looking up you stab them in the belly for the sake of your ideals" (*BD*, pp. 219–20). Thus, for Daniel, the major lesson of the left in America as rendered by his parents was self-destruction, partly through self-delusion. "But you see," he says, "I was learning. I was learning how to be an Isaacson. An Isaacson does things boldly calculated to bring self-destructive results" (*BD*, p. 222).

One of Daniel's most bitter accounts of the contrast between his parents' sense of self-importance as radicals and the reality of their pathos concerns the search of his home and the arrest of his father by the Federal Bureau of Investigation. As the FBI empties the house of its miserable belongings, Daniel sarcastically warns the reader to be alert to the scene "so that you may record in clarity one of the Great Moments of the American Left. The American Left is in this great moment artfully reduced to the shabby conspiracies of a couple named Paul and Rochelle Isaacson" (*BD*, p. 125). The extent of their real power and contribution to the left probably is best summarized by a *New York Times* reporter, who tells Daniel that they "'had to have been into some goddam thing. They *acted* guilty. They were little neighborhood commies probably with some kind of third-rate operation that wasn't of use to anyone except maybe it made them feel important. Maybe what they were doing was worth five years. Maybe'" (*BD*, p. 230).

Daniel's understanding of the complexity of his parents' relationship to the old left influences his perception of the people and program on the new left. When his sister proposes to use a trust fund that had been established on their behalf to advance a "New Left" cultural revolution, Daniel seems uncertain. Later in the book he thinks, "THEY'RE STILL FUCKING US. . . . The Isaacsons are nothing to the New Left" (*BD*, p. 169). Moreover, as a product of the more conventional moralism of the old left, Daniel feels basically uncomfortable with certain new left character types who live a kind of self-centered existence. The superiority such people express over the previous generation of Isaacson radicals further alienates Daniel from them. They render an easy view of the failures of the past that are part of Daniel's own personal history. Thus, after receiving a beating on the historic 1967 Washington march on the Pentagon, he assures his wife that the wounds are not major. He says, "'It looks worse than it is. There was nothing to it. It is a lot easier to be a revolutionary nowadays than it used to be'" (*BD*, p. 274).

In their attitude toward his parents, many of those Daniel encounters on the new left simply share the so-called dominant culture's disdain for his parents. In a sense, the Isaacsons were born guilty. They are guilty of being losers, guilty of being poor Jews, guilty of not being quite smart enough or powerful enough to escape or transcend the limitations of their environment, guilty of being used and of using others. At the same time, their attitude in death gives them a moral strength that elevates them above their enemies both on the right and the left. For Daniel, they achieve a quality of martyrdom and sacrifice that rises above their political and personal causes and failures. Daniel says, "But they stuck to it, didn't they, Daniel? When the call came they answered. They offered up those genitals, didn't they, Dandan? Yes, they did. There were moments when I thought he would crack, I had my doubts about him. But I knew she would take it finally, to the last volt, in absolute selfishness, in unbelievably rigid fury" (*BD*, 43). In order for Daniel to find a meaning and significance for their death, he must go beyond its political context. He puts their death, as we shall see, in a Jewish framework. As a Jew, he finds a structure through ritual to express and contain his grief, his mourning, his sense of inadequacy, and his guilt as an heir to the pain and burdens of the past.

Throughout the novel, Daniel thinks of his parents as representatives of a lower-middle-class Jewish subculture of radicalism. Their backgrounds, values, life-style, behavior, thought, language, tastes, and opinions epitomize the particular world view of the Jewish left in New York that developed early in the century, reached its peak during the depression and the war years, and quickly declined during the late 1940s and early 1950s. As Stanley Kauffmann says, "The novel faces up squarely and intelligently to the Jewishness of its subject."[20] Jewish identity provides an important frame of reference to help Daniel comprehend his history and the tragedy of his family. The symbol for Daniel of his Jewish past as both a burden and dynamic heritage can be found in his grandmother, Rochelle's mother. She stands for him as an exuberant and eccentric life force. She appears early in the novel as the neighborhood's crazy woman whose story is told in part through the Bintel Brief, or "Bundles of Letters" section of the *Jewish Daily Forward*, which served as both an outlet for expression and a rare source of comfort and advice to thousands of immigrants. The strengths, dedication, deprivation, and psychological trauma in the immigrant generation are evoked in her character. Daniel conjures up a vision of her during which she reminds him that "'this placing of the burden on the children is a family tradition. But only your crazy grandma had the grace to make a ritual of it'" (*BD*, p. 83). During this ghostly visit, she reminds Daniel that he inherited from her the "'shimmering fullness of stored life which always marks the victim. What we have, too much life in each of us, is what the world hates most. We offend. We stink with life. Our hearts make love to the world not gently. We are brutal with life and our brutality is called suffering. We scream into our pillows when we come'" (*BD*, p. 82).

However, the Jewish experience in America as presented in this novel includes more than insights into Jewish radicalism and portrayals of the immigrant generation. The novel deals with the meaning of America to the Jews, and one of the novel's deepest ironies concerns the significance to Daniel's family and people of the idea of America. Nothing represents the hold of the American Way more dramatically than Paul Isaacson's belief, almost until his last breath, in the principles, ideals, and purposes of the American system. He demonstrates the power of the American idea to displace dissent by directing it into a framework of the ideology's own terms. Isaacson typifies Sacvan Bercovitch's thesis that the rhetorical structure of the myth and ideology of America integrates opposition into a consensus of belief in the very ideals and values that comprise the American Way. Thus, Isaacson internalizes the ideology of America even while fighting it. The depth of his bitterness about America makes him a target of its legal system. As a Communist, he oppugns the validity of the American idea. Nevertheless, he believes in America. "It's screwy," Daniel says as he describes how his father's generation of Communists could both challenge and believe so desperately in America. He says, "Lots of them were like that. They were Stalinists and every instance of Capitalist America fucking up drove them wild. My country! Why aren't you what you claim to be? If they were put on trial, they didn't say *Of course, what else could we expect*, they said *You are making a mockery of American justice*! And it was more than strategy, it was more than Lenin's advice to use the reactionary apparatus to defend yourself, it was passion" (*BD*, p. 51). In other words, in terms of the New Covenant, even Paul cannot dissociate himself from the rhetoric of the jeremiad in his radical politics. His Americanism helps to drive him toward a foreign ideology in order to achieve those things he believes to be most American. Daniel remembers his father "eating [his] heart out" while listening to Radio Town Meeting of the Air because the program so perfectly exemplified the failure of American democracy to live up to itself. "He used to turn that on at home," Daniel says. "It would make him furious" (*BD*, p. 50). Daniel insists that "the implication of all the things he used to flagellate himself was that American democracy wasn't democratic enough. He continued to be astonished, insulted, outraged, that it wasn't purer, freer, finer, more ideal" (*BD*, p. 51). In a sense, Paul's belief in America follows the pattern of the family's drive toward self-destruction. It could be argued that his undiminished belief in those American ideals that his more "patriotic" and "American" persecutors defame and corrupt leads to his electrocution as a traitor and spy. In the Death House at Sing Sing he says to his children, who a moment before had hysterically insisted upon being searched by a guard before the visit, "'You cannot put innocent people to death in this country. It can't be done'" (*BD*, p. 265).

Daniel's life as an Isaacson represents only one phase of his life and one aspect of the Jewish experience in America. It gives him roots in the radical and immigrant-based subculture of the Jewish left. That phase culminates for Daniel when his mother says that her execution should serve as a bar mitzvah, or day of initiation into manhood, for him. At the time of her execution, she says, "'Let my son be bar mitzvahed today. Let our death be his bar mitzvah'" (*BD*, p. 314). Considering the significance of the bar mitzvah in Jewish life, as well as Daniel's general helplessness at the time, the words amount to a curse on his head. They are an act against the living that helps propel her son into a life of anguish. The mother's words also conclude what had been a period of devastation for the children, including the arrest of the father, the steady isolation of the family, the horrible failure of the mother to return home one day after saying good-bye to them because she also has been arrested, the sense of abandonment that leaves the children with almost no emotional support and love, the loneliness of living with an inept and grotesque aunt, and the nightmare of a public shelter in which Susan screams at night and recedes into old habits like wetting the bed. At one point during this period, Daniel from his own place in the shelter believes that he can hear his sister scream from another part of the building. He soon masterminds their escape, and they return to their old house as though believing that everything can be made normal and safe in the old surroundings. Instead, of course, they find nothing and in turn are found alone in the house by the Isaacson's lawyer, a stream of the girl's urine on the floor.

Following the execution, a new phase begins for the Isaacson children with their adoption by a liberal law professor and his wife. However, since the novel defies traditional chronological plot development, we know from the beginning that this new phase marks just a temporary reprieve for the children. Their new parents are ideal in conventional middle-class terms. They can give the children a new life, but they cannot rewrite the history the children already have had. Nevertheless, in terms of the Jewishness of the novel and its success in rendering the meaning of the story of the Jews in America, the new parents, Robert and Lise Lewin, are vitally important. While Paul Isaacson believes devoutly in the aspect of the American idea that relates to social justice and equality, Robert Lewin adheres with comparable vigor to another view of the American idea. Together, for Daniel, they move his book closer toward presenting a total view of the relationship between the Jews and America. Daniel directly addresses the question of Lewin's significance as a bond between Judaism and Americanism in a comment about a letter he receives from him. Daniel writes, "It is interesting to note, aside from everything else, the operating pressure of fatherhood in Robert Lewin's letter. He wants to stabilize me with responsibility. That is a true blue american puritan idea. In that idea is the fusion of the Jew and America, both of them heirs of the ancient seafarers: you ride the sea best with lead in your keel. My lawyer father is no accident, and it is no accident that he loves American Law, an institution that constantly fails and that he constantly loves, like a bad child who someday in his love will not fail, stabilized with responsibility" (*BD*, p. 171).

The marriage between the Jews and America that Lewin represents is further developed through the character of Jacob Ascher, the defense counsel for the Isaacsons and the law partner of Lewin's father. Ascher served as the children's only real friend and companion throughout the period of the trial. Daniel writes, "Ascher was a pillar of the Bronx bar. He was not brilliant, but his law was sound, and his honor as a man, as a religious man, was unquestionable. He was an honest lawyer, and was dogged for his clients. I picture him on Yom Kippur standing in the pew with his homburg on his head, and a tallis around his shoulders. Ascher could wear a homburg and a tallis at the same time" (*BD*, p. 132). The symbols of the tallis, or Jewish prayer shawl, and the homburg combine to form one symbol of the union between the American Way and the Jewish Way in thought and life-style. Daniel writes, "Ascher was not a political man, you could imagine him voting for anyone he found morally recognizable, no matter what the party. If anything, he was conservative. He perceived in the law a codification of the religious sense of life. He was said to have worked for years on a still unfinished book demonstrating the contributions of the Old Testament to American law" (*BD*, p. 133).

The prominence of Ascher and Lewin in the novel emphasizes the point that *The Book of Daniel*, like its biblical model, is the story of the Jews in a foreign land. However, through them Doctorow is also able to dramatize the marriage between American and Jewish life and thought. In a sense, the novel suggests that the Jews have become the modern archetypal Americans. They are almost super Americans. Accordingly, the Isaacsons' saga in the history of America becomes literally a Jewish story of America. Isaacson himself talks of the Jewishness of the event during his trial. However, from his point of view they all have become slaves bowing before the enemy. He writes to Rochelle, "My darling have you noticed how many of the characters in this capitalist drama are Jewish? The defendants, the defense lawyer, the prosecution, the major prosecution witness, the judge. We are putting on this little passion play for our Christian masters. In the concentration camps the Nazis made guards of certain Jews and gave them whips. In Jim Crow Harlem the worst cops are Negro" (*BD*,

p. 213). His hatred is particularly directed toward the Jewish judge named Hirsch and the Chief U.S. Attorney General, Howard "Red" Feuerman. "Feuerman," he writes, "in his freckles and flaming red hair, this graduate of St. John's, the arch assimilationist who represses the fact that he could never get a job with the telephone company—Feuerman is so full of self-hatred HE IS DETERMINED to purge us. Imperialism has many guises, and each is a measure of its desperation" (*BD*, p. 213). As told in this part of the novel through Paul's perspective, his judgment upon these two lawyers seems just. He thinks, "Hirsch has heard more cases brought by the government in the field of subversive activities than anyone else. He is Jewish. He wears a striped, ivy league tie, the knot of which can be seen under his judicial robe" (*BD*, p. 201). It is commonly believed, he reports, that the judge hopes his role in the trial will earn him a place on the Supreme Court. The insensitivity and vulgarity of Hirsch and Feuerman do not diminish the moral authority of either Ascher or Lewin. Nor do they weaken the Isaacsons' passion for justice. However, they do round out the Jewishness of the story in a way that avoids sentimentality. *The Book of Daniel* does not turn all Jews into American heroes, but it does dramatize the significance of their role in American culture.

To adequately tell this story of the marriage between two cultures required Doctorow to unite in one form history, literature, and moral prophecy while he wove into a single web stories of initiation, crime and punishment, self-destruction, courage, and moral triumph. In a sense, the whole story turns the Jews into a prophetic tribe of Daniels casting multiple perspectives on the totality of the American experience. The result is an ingenious reconstitution of the myth of regeneration in America. Daniel is ultimately rescued and saved. Moreover, he gives himself three choices of how to dramatize his regeneration. The first two endings deal with Daniel's ability to confront and transcend his past and express a form of reconciliation. In the first suggested ending, he returns to the old house in the Bronx that was the scene of his youth. As he observes a family of strangers in the house, Daniel seems able to leave, finally, that part of his life. The second ending proposes two funerals. In the first funeral, both he and Susan bury their parents. In the second, Daniel and his new parents bury his sister. In this scene, which recalls the command of his grandmother to remember the dead, Daniel initiates one of the most important rituals in the Jewish religion, a Mourner's Kaddish, or prayer for the dead.

The moment reveals Daniel's sense of himself as a Jew as well as his ability to use Judaism as a way to confront his experience. It thereby becomes an act of integration of his Jewish and American selves as part of a reconciliation between his sense of the past and his hope for the future. At his sister's grave, he dismisses "the company rabbi" (*BD*, p. 317) but calls together the other Jews at the cemetery—the kind of souls who make their living as Jews by praying for a fee for other Jews—and they say Kaddish. Daniel suddenly becomes part of this community of mourners, and, as they pray, he finds himself forcing them to continue. Throughout the entire novel Daniel has had to be a rock. However, in this graveside scene he turns into a human. He writes, "The funeral director waits impatiently beside his shiny hearse. But I encourage the prayermakers, and when one is through I tell him *again*, this time for my mother and father. Isaacson. Pinchas. Rachele. Susele. For all of them. I hold my wife's hand. And I think I am going to be able to cry" (*BD*, p. 318).

Both endings suggest freedom for Daniel, but the third ending discusses the subject of freedom itself. In this ending, Daniel is in the library at work on *The Book of Daniel* and trying to conceive of an ending for it. Suddenly a man interrupts Daniel's work to order him to leave because the students are closing the library as part of their protest against the university. The intruder shouts, "'Close the book, man, what's the matter with you, don't you know you're liberated?'"(*BD*, p. 318). Daniel feels compelled to smile at this announcement of his new freedom by a stranger. "It has not been unexpected," he writes (*BD*, p. 318).

Daniel is free. Not because of the student rebellion but because of his ability to complete his book, he achieves a form of liberation. He has freed himself from the task of the book. He has written a book of freedom—a lesson in freedom—because through it he gives everything of himself to fulfill his obligations to his parents and his sister, to his present, and to his hopes for the future. He liberates his life by humanizing it through the exertion of his moral and historic consciousness. Not just an animal or a victim, he overcomes his mother's cry and achieves his own form of bar mitzvah by initiating himself into the realm of those willing to accept moral responsibility for themselves. It is as though Daniel has been striving to achieve a degree in humanity and finally receives it. He writes, "DANIEL'S BOOK: A Life Submitted in Partial Fulfillment of the Requirements for the Doctoral Degree . . ." (*BD*, p. 318). The final words in the book are in italics and come from the biblical Book of Daniel (12:1–4, 9). They say that Daniel has done all that he can for his own deliverance and for the deliverance of his people: *"and there shall be a time of trouble such as never was since there was a nation . . . and at that time the people shall be delivered, everyone that shall be found written in the book. . . . But thou , O Daniel, shut up the words, and seal the book, even to the time of the end. . . . Go thy way Daniel: for the words are closed up and sealed till the time of the end"* (*BD*, p. 319).

In *The Book of Daniel* and in his subsequent novel *Ragtime*, Doctorow achieves a level of literature that fits Warner Berthoff's category of the mythic. Berthoff writes, "That work of fiction, in brief, has most authority which most abundantly opens itself to the modality of the mythic. But to be a mythmaker, to move toward myth, is not simply to invent new fictions, including exploratory or ironic reconstructions of famous individual myths. It is rather to compose by way of continuously refreshing the substance of what people characteristically say in each other's presence up and down the whole range, or some great part of it, of purposeful human utterance."[21] Both novels are attempts to relate fiction to myth in Berthoff's sense of transforming the language and thought of an era into an art form that reflects and touches all aspects of culture. Doctorow again endeavors in *Loon Lake* to develop and modernize "famous individual myths" for the purpose of capturing the essence of American culture.

In *Loon Lake*, Doctorow elaborates upon the mythic, historical, and cultural significance of a fictional geographic landmark in a way that attempts to re-create and modernize the relationship between the landscape and the American imagination. He invents a geographic region to demonstrate how such a space becomes a region of the mind. The physical space functions as a means of cultural self-identification only to be corrupted by the culture itself, which fails to live up to the meaning it implanted into its own geography. As a fictional reenactment of this process, the novel attempts to get to the heart of the American spirit. In a Nietzschean manner we get history as a symbol. Moreover, Doctorow inhabits this region of the mind with characters and images that are themselves products of the American mythic and literary imagination. Parallels and interesting connections between *Loon Lake* and such works as *Walden*, *The Great Gatsby*, and *U.S.A.* abound.

Thus, in *Walden* the loons become symbolic of both Thoreau's and the pond's independence. He writes, "I am no more lonely than the loon in the pond that laughs so loud, or than Walden Pond itself. What company has that lonely lake, I pray?"[22] In another part of his narrative, Thoreau describes in detail his attempts to chase down a loon who keeps hitting the surface from flight and disappearing under the water, only to emerge again at an unexpected place in the lake. The loon seems to mock Thoreau's attempts to understand him. He sends forth loud "demoniac laughter" that taunts Thoreau with its suggestion that the loon possesses some unique knowledge. Thoreau writes, "While he was thinking one thing in his brain, I was endeavoring to divine his thought in mine. It was a pretty game, played on the smooth surface of the pond, a man against a loon." The loon's ability to thrive on all three realms of the lake—above the water, on the surface, and below—demonstrates the bird's possession of special gifts. Thoreau writes, "How surprised must the fishes be to see this ungainly visitor from another sphere speeding his way amid their schools!"[23] Thoreau also notes "that loons have been caught in the New York lakes eighty feet beneath the surface, with hooks set for trout."[24] It is at such a lake situated in the Adirondacks in New York that Doctorow picks up the mystery of the loon.

As in *Walden*, the history of the meaning to mankind of Loon Lake goes back to the time of the Indians, and the story of the lake symbolizes the continuing profanation of the purity of the natural environment by society. In the novel, a poet named Warren Penfield functions as the consciousness who describes the meaning of the lake. Naturally, his book is called *Loon Lake* so that the physical landmark merges with the poetic and intellectual construct. Penfield writes, "All due respect to the Indians of Loon Lake / the Adirondack nations, with all due respect. / What a clear cold life it must have been."[25] Penfield the poet sees the loons as symbolic of an eternal process of death and rebirth. The image of the loons connects the past of the Indians with the present. "The loons they heard were the loons we hear today," Penfield writes (*LL*, p. 54). The representation of the lake in the poem as the embodiment of the natural and spiritual purity of America contrasts with the current uses of the lake. Following the invasion of the Adirondacks by artists and painters who helped invent "the wilderness as luxury" business (*LL*, p. 46), the lake became the property of a wealthy industrialist named F. W. Bennett. Under Bennett, the wilderness of Loon Lake changes into a beautiful mountain camp where leading celebrities as well as the corrupt and the criminal are entertained. As though to dramatize the change, a loon appears from nowhere while gangsters speedboat along the lake's surface. The loon catches in midair a cigarette that the wind had "whipped out" of the mouth of one of the gangsters. "The crazy bird" seems almost trained to do it, as though they are now part of the entertainment for the corrupt company at the camp (*LL*, p. 47).

The novel's best example, however, of the change to the new America of industrial exploitation and waste can be found in a character named Joe who functions as the most significant consciousness in the novel. Born Joseph Korzeniowski, he is called Joe Paterson after his native city. Primarily through Joe's consciousness, we get compact, intense, and personal visions of experience that remind one of the "Camera Eye" sections of Dos Passos's *U.S.A.* A wanderer and loner, Joe also seems modeled after several Dos Passos types, especially Joe Williams, who represents in *U.S.A.* the consciousness of the common-man victim. Thus, in style and substance, Doctorow recognizes and consciously elaborates upon the mythic constructs in much of modern American literature. Joe Paterson's story, however, seems most related to that of F. Scott Fitzgerald's Gatsby. The pattern of Joe's development and metamorphosis follows the one established by Gatsby, and the cultural implications that Gatsby's story embodies are duplicated by Joe. Gatsby, of course, was born Jay Gatz and through the intervention of a wealthy benefactor achieves a new life. For Gatsby, the sponsor fulfills the role of both God and father. This help enables Gatsby to create a new identity for himself based on his understanding of what success and power mean in America. Fitzgerald writes, "The truth was that Jay Gatsby of West Egg, Long Island, sprang from his Platonic conception of himself. He was a son of God—a phrase which, if it means anything, means just that—and he must be about His Father's business, the service of a vast, vulgar, and meretricious beauty. So he invented just the sort of Jay Gatsby that a seventeen-year-old boy would be likely to invent, and to this conception he was faithful to the end."[26] Similarly, Joe Paterson in *Loon Lake* achieves a new identity through the intervention of the industrialist Bennett who sees himself in certain ways as a mythic or God-like figure. Bennett adopts Joe. Joe in turn develops into the corporate, social, and political image of his new father. In a summary of his career at the end of the novel, Doctorow provides Joe with all the ac-

coutrements of modern-day corporate and social success. His titles, orga-
nizations, positions, achievements, and memberships represent the things
that Doctorow obviously detests about contemporary America. Joe's success, therefore, constitutes a political and moral failure. Along with all his
achievements, including duty as "Deputy Assistant Director of the C.I.A."
and an ambassadorship, Joe can call himself "Master of Loon Lake." The
last title on the list indicates the ultimate betrayal in terms of the novel's
values.

In *Loon Lake*, Doctorow continues to maintain a radical perspective on
American culture. Imbued with the literary and mythic sensibility of an
earlier radical generation, he still attacks corporate bureaucracy and capitalistic exploitation. However, like Daniel Isaacson, he embodies a new
radical consciousness that reflects contemporary concerns and realities.
For example, in his description of Disneyland in *The Book of Daniel* (*BD*,
pp. 301–9), Doctorow discusses the power that enables mass culture and
the entertainment media to turn our great narratives into palliatives for
complacency and conformity and to undermine the existential challenge of
literature. As a writer, he wants to repossess the culture's natural resources
of myth and narrative in order to restore the culture and to reaffirm the
values of individual freedom and responsibility. Similarly, Doctorow uses
psychology to develop a new radical perspective that can offer possible
insights unavailable to traditional radical politics. Thus, early in the novel,
he describes the sexual relations between Daniel and his wife, Phyllis, in a
way that combines physical and political terms. The description implies
that in a modern radical ideology the psychological roots of oppression
may be as important as the economic. Portraying Phyllis as a "sex martyr"
and Daniel as a "tormentor" who makes her suffer "yet another penetra-
tion," Doctorow plays with the idea of the sexual origins of political
power as Daniel "explores the small geography of those distant island
ranges, that geology of gland formation, Stalinites and Trotskyites, the
Stalinites growing down from the top, the Trotskyites up from the bottom" (*BD*, p. 16).

The different elements that form Doctorow's political and literary vision can be discerned from the figures he quotes at the beginning of
The Book of Daniel. The quotations are from the Prophet Daniel, Walt
Whitman, and Allen Ginsberg. All three indicate Doctorow's attraction to
prophets who become aliens in their own lands partly because they often

speak for the values and ideals of the very cultures that ostracize them and resist their messages. They are vital and distinct landmarks in Doctorow's moral and cultural consciousness and represent major aspects of his thought and his literary and political program—Jewish, American, and radical. Although important differences separate Daniel, Whitman, and Ginsberg, they are also related elements of one moral vision. They are like the various selves that comprise the one mythic American Self for both Whitman and Emerson. Their examples encourage Doctorow to continue his effort to meld together the literary, historic, and mythic to express the meaning of America. Taken together, the figures of Daniel, Whitman, and Ginsberg dramatize how well Doctorow propels the thrust of the New Covenant. As a Jewish writer and thinker, he contributes to the development of the American idea by being at once both the most conservative and the most radical of Americans. He is the most conservative because of his concern for preserving those institutions and values of democracy that constitute the American idea. At the same time, he is the most radical because he extends and modernizes the ideology and meaning of America to make it relevant to contemporary American life, thought, and needs. Like Daniel, he brings together the social visions of both the Isaacsons and Lewins into one unified whole. Thus, because of his purposes as a writer and thinker and his philosophy of the American idea Doctorow demonstrates that he holds a position of leadership in the New Covenant tradition in America.

Chapter 10

Postscript
Toward a New Consensus

I t has been more than a century since the beginning of the great wave of Jewish immigration from Eastern Europe to the United States. During this period, a special relationship has matured between Jewish writers and thinkers and American culture that I have been describing as the New Covenant. The tradition involves the fascination of many Jewish writers with the idea of America as a unique experience in human history. For those in the New Covenant, this fascination manifests itself in their linguistic leadership in developing rhetorical and narrative structures for expressing the American idea. The ideology of the American Way with its fulfillment of the promise of freedom and emancipation for Jews provides the historic foundation for the New Covenant that goes back at least to the beginning of the Republic. In terms of the development of the ideology and its application to modern American political life, the New Covenant became an important force during the early decades of this century through the efforts of such people as Oscar Straus, Louis Brandeis, and Louis Marshall. Their work to unite the Jewish Way and the American Way helped to establish a framework through which Jews could form an important part of the liberal consensus that dominated American politics for at least several decades after the New Deal. Concomitant with this upsurge in Jewish political authority during the middle decades of the century, the broader literary and cultural manifestations of the New Covenant achieved what has been called a "breakthrough" in the post-World War II period. As discussed earlier, Malin and Stark's concept of "breakthrough" implies an identification between Jewish and American cultures as well as a harmony between Jewish and American voices.

However, the New Covenant tradition does not imply a conflict-free paradigm of the relationship between the Jews and America. Nor does it support what Ellen Willis brilliantly condemns as "the myth of the powerful Jew." Most of the writers in the New Covenant tradition would agree with Willis's belief in the pervasive anti-Semitism of much of American leadership and culture and of the vulnerability of the Jews within American society as a whole. She argues, in fact, that as both a source and a result of anti-Semitism the false impression of excessive Jewish power actually serves as an important weapon against the Jews. The anti-Semitic reaction to the myth helps to assure that the Jews will fail "the real test of power," which concerns "whether Jews can protect specifically Jewish interests when they diverge from—or conflict with—the interests of non-Jews." She sees the myth as part of the overall psychology of anti-Semitism. She writes, "Jews are simultaneously perceived as insiders and outsiders, capitalists and communists, upholders of high ethical and intellectual standards and shrewd purveyors of poisonous subversive ideas. The common theme of these disparate perceptions is that Jews have enormous power, whether to defend established authority or to undermine it. It is this double-edged myth of Jewish power that has made Jews such a useful all-purpose scapegoat for social discontent."[1] These concerns about anti-Semitism and the ambiguity of the place of the Jew in American society permeate the works of those in the New Covenant tradition. However, they respond to these issues in accordance with their perception of the American idea of values, institutions, and traditions that safeguard against the dangers of anti-Semitism. As an ideology in competition with the world's other "isms," the American Way still maintains its promise. They continue to see and criticize America in terms of the American idea.

Willis's insight into the position of the Jews in American society puts the New Covenant tradition in a new light that emphasizes some interesting ironies and paradoxes. Even though the New Covenant reveals continuities between American and Jewish cultures, one of its most vigorous aspects derives from the tradition of the jeremiad which guarantees the existence of conflict and dissent. The moral authority of the jeremiad not only gives the New Covenant power but also constitutes a source of danger. The New Covenant, which seems to make Jewish writers and thinkers so American, also feeds into what Willis considers to be one of the most important reasons behind anti-Semitism. She writes, "I think anti-Semitism is bound up with people's anger not only at class oppression but at the whole structure of patriarchal civilization—at the authoritarian family and state, at a morality that exalts the mind, denigrates the body, and represses sexuality. It's no coincidence that a Jew, Sigmund Freud, was first to observe that 'civilized' self-denial generates an enormous reservoir of unconscious rage."[2] Willis argues, with George Steiner, that Jews embody patriarchy and the subsequent excesses of the overactive cultural superego. The argument constitutes a psychological explanation for the historic ability of ruling elites to exploit anti-Semitism for their own political purposes. Willis says, "The advantage to ruling classes of keeping Jews around as surrogate authority figures, outside agitators, and enemies of the people is obvious."[3] In other words, the Jews suffer a double victimization from both the power structure and the repressed and resentful majority. In this way, the continued support by Jewish writers in the New Covenant tradition of the moral rhetoric of the jeremiad can serve as a double-edged sword. In helping to perpetuate the moral vision of America, Jewish writers invite the kind of situation Willis both dreads and, perhaps, anticipates. When they assume the role of New Jeremiahs, the writers and thinkers in the New Covenant achieve the kind of authority that invites criticism and attack.

Willis also dramatizes an important question concerning the status of the tradition of the New Covenant in contemporary American political life. She developed this argument originally in the *Village Voice* as a response to an earlier article that was part of the growing controversy surrounding the resignation in August 1979 of the United States ambassador to the United Nations, Andrew Young. The controversy exacerbated the ongoing crisis in the relations between Jews and blacks, which in this case related both to Young's interest in establishing connections with the Palestine Liberation Organization and to the growing sympathy among blacks for the Arab cause in general. A brief but excruciatingly intense debate in the *Nation* between Leonard Kriegel and James Baldwin indicates the kinds of wounds the Young affair inflicted and reopened within both the Jewish and the black communities.[4] Moreover, the Young affair weakened the already ulcerous condition of the old liberal consensus in which the Jews and the blacks had so closely worked together as partners.

The reasons behind the deterioration in recent years of the relationship between Jews and liberalism have been delineated by Lawrence Fuchs, the author of a major study in the mid-fifties of Jewish political behavior and attitudes.[5] About twenty years after the appearance of that study, Fuchs writes that "the litmus test issues of liberalism which have become so familiar these past twenty-five years" grew so much more complicated in the seventies that Jewish attitudes were harder to gauge.[6] In comments that anticipate a special issue of *Commentary* (January 1980) entitled "Liberalism and the Jews," Fuchs notes the change since 1953 in Jewish attitudes toward the "standard issues." He says, "This [change occurred] before the landmark decisions of the Warren Court, the domestic legislative triumphs of the Johnson administration, and the packing of the United Nations with petty dictatorships. It was before the sexual revolution, the increased divorce rate, massive juvenile crime, family disorganization and other symptoms of social malaise unpredicted by any but evangelical preachers in 1953. It was before the Women's Movement and its issues, the Viet Nam War, or Angola."[7] Fuchs believes Jews contributed to the confusion of these developments through "the liberal triumphs of the 1950s and 1960s in which American Jews played such a disproportionate role" in advancing civil and voting rights, housing, and education.[8] Compounding the complexity of the times are activities in the international scene involving Israel, the Third World, and the Soviet Union. The new atmosphere created by these changes, he says, complicates issues that once presented no problem to Jews such as:

> protection of the rights of the accused versus protection against street crime; affirmative action to compensate members of some groups for past discrimination against those groups versus protection against quotas which discriminate against members of other groups; support for the United Nations versus protection of those who aspire for freedom against totalitarian and dictatorial regimes which are capable of producing automatic majorities in the United Nations General Assembly; increased business regulations versus protection for honest, job-creating entrepreneurs against the encroachment of irrational regulation; support for labor unions versus protection of working people against the abuse of power by authoritarian labor leaders; the integration of schools versus protecting the influence which parents should have in educating their children, including the choice of schools for them to attend; support for welfare programs against the defense of working middle-class taxpayers

who are demoralized and who are threatened by the bankruptcy of cities and towns; and the reduction of military expenditures versus the protection of those aspiring to be free here and abroad from Soviet military pressure.[9]

Fuchs's statement makes up a comprehensive concatenation of complex events and issues of great significance for the meaning of liberalism in America and for the relationship of Jews to the American ideological consensus. If a number of Jews are disavowing some of the old liberal issues and at least some of the traditional allies that once shaped their political identity and marked their contribution to the American ideology, then questions become apparent about the political life of Jews in America. Based on his own analysis of issues and events, Fuchs predicts that Jews, at least partly through force of habit, will retain "visceral attachments" to previous liberal positions but in the long run will become "more pluralistic" and "increasingly divided" as to how to apply traditional Jewish values like *Zedakah* (charity) to political issues.[10]

The political debate in the late 1970s and the early 1980s among Jewish intellectuals, at least as usually presented in the pages of *Commentary* and *Dissent*, justified Fuchs's expectations of division. Norman Podhoretz, the editor of *Commentary*, has been the major force in that magazine's campaign to challenge radical and liberal positions through the establishment of a centrist, or neoconservative, philosophy of politics and culture. An acerbic style and a penchant for placing himself in the forefront of the movement to discredit the left made him the target of his former political allies' outrage. Nevertheless, the almost violent reaction to Podhoretz indicates his importance as at least a representative of aspects of current political thought. As Willis says, "Anyone so hated by people who insist he doesn't matter must be hitting a nerve."[11] Willis believes that because Podhoretz and his radical and liberal Jewish opponents have such similar backgrounds and styles, his arguments have a special impact upon Jewish intellectuals. While this reasoning may explain some of the emotion behind the attacks against Podhoretz, it also should be noted that he has the courage to risk unpopularity and to invoke much wrath for the way he excoriates the left. The problem, however, is that although he may be right about the need to challenge Soviet expansionism and to modify radical ideologies, his writings often do not offer a social vision upon which to build. Insensitivity in the neoconservative movement to women, minorities, and the poor and a lack of interest in the wishes of people for both disarmament and an idealistic foreign policy undermine the movement. Podhoretz and other neoconservatives often appear more obsessed with fighting old wars with former radical allies than with helping to proffer a vision of the future that is consistent with the kind of leadership Jewish thinkers have rendered throughout much of this century.

Some Jews claim that Podhoretz and other *Commentary* contributors are betraying an important Jewish tradition. For example, Bernard Avishai argues in *Dissent* that as the editor of *Commentary* Podhoretz now removes that influential and important journal of the American Jewish Committee from the mainstream of Jewish life and thought. Avishai maintains that before Podhoretz's neoconservative phase the magazine had been perhaps the leading outlet for the country's most important and talented Jewish writers and thinkers. It not only published the established writers but also nurtured newer and younger Jewish talent. The magazine, for Avishai, now stands as a sign of weakness and a source of embarrassment. He writes:

> A good number of American Jews, in fact, have been deeply demoralized by *Commentary*'s obscuring of the actual political traditions we've had in America since 1881. Our élan has not been in our "interests" but in our roots: the sweatshops, the unions, the *Forwards*, the New Deal, the anti-fascist leagues, the civil rights movement; and in figures as different as Emma Goldman, Abe Cahan, Aaron Copeland, and Justice Brandeis. Their ideals are not made and unmade by income brackets, but have been the stuff of our families' dinner conversations long before we could all speak English. Such ideals entail heroes, sensibilities, moral taste, the civil religion to which we try to make converts by insisting on a sense of history.[12]

The Jewish tradition of political freedom and democracy to which Avishai refers becomes a source of being for Jews in America. It achieves this status, however, not as a political orthodoxy of belief and sentiment but as an openness to new ideas and experience. Thus, if history provides any clues to our present situation, the rancor and passion of the current debate about the future direction of American political life could be signs of health and new life rather than of permanent separation and debilitation. Just as Cahan, Brandeis, and Hillman in their day helped in the regeneration of the American Way, so also in our time can we discern the makings of a similar thrust toward new life in the works of contemporary Jewish writers and intellectuals. The current debate may represent the efflorescence of fresh insights that will help provide the structure for a watershed of the American idea in our age. Ensconced within the bitter differences of the participants in this cultural dialogue are elements of a new consensus. Even while vowing to take into the streets his battle against the threat of the "Right Menace" to destroy important social welfare programs, Irving Howe recognizes how the new conservatism emerges out of real economic, social, and cultural problems. He also acknowledges that some aspects of conservatism can provide important lessons to the left. He writes, "People like myself, democratic socialists or socialist liberals, have learned something from traditional conservative thought—perhaps more accurately, from the ideas of the great tradition of liberalism that have been stressed by more reflective conservatives in recent years." Howe presents a long list of lessons such as those involving the fear of "excessive concentration of power in any human agency, be it the state or the corporation, trade union bureaucracies or political parties"; "the dynamic of politics that is to be found, say, in *The Federalist Papers*"; the understanding that "bureaucracy creates problems almost certain to survive the life-span of capitalism or any other social system"; the recognition that "a limited market might help to lubricate the social relationships that would arise in a democratic socialist society based on decentralized and largely autonomous units of production and distribution." Howe states that "above all else, we value democracy as a good in itself, indeed, *the supreme good of political life*, not reducible to any particular system of 'relations of production.'" Howe also notes how in recent years conservatives and socialists have come together at times in their response to cultural issues.[13] Thus, Howe's political program takes into account previously unrecognized conservative elements.

Similarly, at the other end of the political spectrum, Podhoretz has proclaimed the emergence of the "New American Majority" and has oppugned attempts to revitalize the Coalition for a Democratic Majority, but he also has envisioned "that the Democrats will try to move back to the Center" under the leadership of such senators as Daniel Patrick Moynihan and Henry Jackson.[14] Meanwhile, Norman Mailer, in his continuing battle to sustain and revolutionize the American idea, presents perhaps the most dramatic attempt at a new synthesis with his left conservatism. Thus, although support for the liberalism of the 1960s and 1970s certainly has faded, elements for a new consensus exist. They indicate that we may be going through one of those periods of adjustment and rebalancing that characterize the viability and flexibility of the American idea. Jewish writers and thinkers will need to draw upon their own history in America as builders and critics of the American Way in order to contribute to the formation of such a new consensus.

At the same time, the nature of any new political consensus including Jewish participation will reflect unpredictable future events. Developments in America and the Mideast will not only directly influence political alignments and power, but they will also help determine how American Jews will act and see themselves. Unfortunately, American Jews are caught in an unenviable situation. Profound shifts are occurring in the political, ideological, and economic aspects of American life at the very time that the situation in Israel and the Mideast remains unstable. The conservative swing to the right, as dramatized geographically by the emergence of an important power base in the Sunbelt, has encountered an economy that defies conventional analysis, understanding, and action. Jews continue to search for their place in this changing domestic scene while wondering about the nature of their relationship to Israel, which is also in transition. Fears about the diminution of Jewish influence in America often seem justified by political events, diplomatic actions, and shifts in public attitudes. Equally significant is the developing division between some American Jews and important, perhaps dominant, forces in Israel. Steadily brewing as a reaction to the leadership in Israel of Menachim Begin, the split erupted following the invasion by Israel into Lebanon and the catastrophic Beirut massacre in 1982. Historically, as we have seen, Jews have felt a deep consistency between their commitment to the principles of the American idea and their loyalty to Jewish life and interests. In the tradition of Brandeis, many Jews maintain that Jewish values and experiences reenforce their American identity. However, the tragedy in Beirut brought to the surface the simmering belief for some Jews of a possible variance between their values and traditions as Jewish Americans and the direction of Israeli politics and culture. When placed in the context of the vicious anti-Semitism and anti-Zionism of many peoples and countries, the undiminished and unrelenting hostility of Israel's Arab enemies, and the signs of a reemerging anti-Semitism in America, the crisis and dilemma for Jews in America seems enormous.

Nevertheless, Jews such as Irving Howe, Daniel Bell, Nathan Glazer, and Seymour Martin Lipset find themselves having to distinguish between a democratic, compassionate Israel and the militant nationalism of some of its leaders, just as they often feel compelled to criticize America for failing to maintain its principles and history. As Howe writes in the *New York Times*, "We are experiencing a conflict between the values of democratic conciliation and the goal of imperial domination, between the visions personified by Chaim Weitzmann's liberal Zionism and Vladimir Jabotinsky's ultra-nationalist Zionism. We are in the midst of a struggle over the character of Jewish life, both in Israel and the Diaspora."[15] Howe's argument concerning the division of Jewish opinion and values between the "we" of liberalism and the nationalistic other repeats the moral pattern and rhetorical structure of the jeremiad. Ultimately, changes in Israel and events in the Mideast may induce some Jews to reaffirm the belief in America as a new Zion with a message for the world.

Ever since Moses Seixas's words in 1790 came back to him in the form of George Washington's amazing Newport declaration of Jewish liberties, rights, and emancipation, Jews have felt a special commitment and relationship to the American idea. For generations, Jewish immigrants have thought of the American idea as a unique environment of institutions and values that could nurture and sustain Jewish life and welfare. It provided a shelter for both individuality and even radical dissent. Thus, the maintenance and perpetuation of that environment developed into a basic strategy for the freedom and success of the Jews. This relationship with what remains the relatively young American experiment in democracy and freedom constitutes a momentous event in the long history of the Jews. The sundering of the bond between the Jews and the American idea would be an equally momentous event, certainly for the Jews but also for the American experience. Such a development would at least imply a cataclysmic change in the meaning of America and would suggest an upheaval for Jews in terms of their options for freedom and life.

A famous statement by Delmore Schwartz, the tortured Jewish poet, dramatizes the intensity with which Jewish intellectuals and writers in the New Covenant tradition have come to view the importance of America. Schwartz said:

But since the Second World War and the beginning of the atomic age, the consciousness of the creative writer, however detached, has been confronted with the spectre of the totalitarian state, the growing poverty and helplessness of Western Europe, and the threat of an inconceivably destructive war which may annihilate civilization and mankind itself. Clearly when the future of civilization is no longer assured, a criticism of American life in terms of a contrast between avowed ideals and present actuality cannot be a primary preoccupation and a source of inspiration. For America, not Europe, is now the sanctuary of culture; civilization's very existence depends upon America, upon the actuality of American life, and not the ideals of the American Dream. To criticize the actuality upon which all hope depends thus becomes a criticism of hope itself.[16]

Of course, Schwartz's description of America's importance to the world amounts to his own appeal to the American Dream and the American idea. Moreover, the quote from Schwartz serves to dramatize the dilemma of the American Jew today. Acquiescence to the temptation to avoid criticizing America out of fear of weakening her in effect would amount to a desertion of, in Mailer's words, "the mysteries of America buried in these liberties to dissent" (*AN*, p. 114). Such a failure of nerve would undermine the whole meaning of the American idea and the historic relationship of the Jewish intellectual and writer to American culture. At the same time, a failure to recognize the importance of the American idea and American survival to the Jews and to human history as a whole would be equally disastrous and irresponsible. Given the complex political and cultural changes since Schwartz's lecture on poetry in 1958, how we deal with this dilemma today depends to a considerable extent upon the wisdom and strength of those who inherit the mantle of our prophets and judges. Future generations may find in the absence of such leadership a reason for how it came to be that Ronald Reagan once stood as the new voice of the American Way, calling his conservative flock back to the city on the hill, while the rest of us believers wandered aimlessly on the desert below.

Notes

CHAPTER 1

1. There are, of course, many other ways to relate the story of the Jews in America. For valuable one-volume histories of the Jews in America that include extensive bibliographies see Dimont, *The Jews in America*; Feldstein, *The Land That I Show You*; and Handlin, *Adventure in Freedom*. For an economic history of the Jews in America see Gross, ed., *Economic History of the Jews*, and the "Special Bicentennial Issue: American Jewish Business Enterprise," *American Jewish Historical Quarterly* 66 (September 1976). For an analysis of the current political situation of the Jews see "Special Bicentennial Issue: Jews and American Liberalism: Studies in Political Behavior," *American Jewish Historical Quarterly* 66 (December 1976). For an outstanding survey of themes and subjects dealing with the Jewish American experience see Rosen, ed., *Jewish Life in America*. Important studies of the Jewish immigrant experience and the relationship between Jewish and American culture include Rischin, *The Promised City*, and Howe, *World of Our Fathers*. For important studies of the sociology of the Jewish experience see Glazer, *American Judaism*, and Sklare, *America's Jews*. Blau, *Judaism in America*, concentrates on the history of Jewish religious thought in America. A valuable reference work for the history of Jews in America can be found in Fishman, ed., *The Jews of the United States*.

2. Liebman, *Jews and the Left*, pp. 27, 33–34. In "The Ties That Bind," Liebman says, "Although a significant proportion, probably more than a majority of the Left, was Jewish in the later 1920's, 1930's, 1940's, or 1950's, the vast majority of Jews were not in the left. The left throughout the post-World War I United States was numerically small in number" (p. 308).

3. See Konvitz, *Judaism and the American Idea*; Schechner, "Jewish Writers," p. 193.

4. Podhoretz, *Breaking Ranks*, pp. 349–50. On the *Partisan Review* and the Jews see Kazin, *New York Jew*, p. 65.

5. Kaplan, *O My America!*, p. 11.

6. Mailer, *The Armies of the Night*, pp. 170, 171.

7. Slavin was compared to Goodman, Kazin, and others in reviews of the book. See Bell, "A Remarkable First Novel," pp. 73–75, and Kotker, "New Found Land," pp. 440–41.

8. See Sollors, "Literature and Ethnicity," pp. 649–53.

9. Kaplan, *O My America!*, p. 286.

10. Mailer, "Modes and Mutations," *Commentary*, March 1966, p. 37; reprinted in Mailer, *Cannibals and Christians*, pp. 95–103.

11. See Howe, *World of Our Fathers*,

p. 123; Alvarez, "Flushed with Ideas,"
p. 22; Neusner, *Stranger at Home*, p. 15.

12. See Barthes, *Mythologies*, p. 112.

13. Bercovitch, "The Rites of Assent,"
p. 6.

14. White, *Metahistory*, pp. 31, 30, xi,
426.

15. Ibid., p. x.

16. Malin and Stark, eds., *Breakthrough*,
p. 1.

17. See Miller, "Errand into the Wilderness."

18. Bercovitch, *The American Jeremiad*,
p. xi.

19. Ibid., p. 176.

20. Winthrop, "A Model of Christian
Charity," p. 93.

21. Guttmann, *The Jewish Writer in
America*, p. 16. For an exhaustive study of
how Jews were portrayed in American literature see Harap, *The Image of the Jew in
American Literature*.

22. See Smith, *Virgin Land*; Slotkin,
Regeneration through Violence; Cawelti, *Adventure, Mystery, and Romance*; Marx, *The
Machine in the Garden*; Trachtenberg,
Brooklyn Bridge; Lewis, *The American
Adam*; Fiedler, *Love and Death in the
American Novel*, rev. ed.; Ward, *Andrew
Jackson*; Kolodny, *The Lay of the Land*;
Fryer, *The Faces of Eve*; Douglas, *The Feminization of American Culture*; Kasson, *Civilizing the Machine*; and Wright, *Six Guns
and Society*.

23. Antin, *The Promised Land*, pp. 197,
364.

24. Mailer, *The Armies of the Night*,
p. 288.

25. Bercovitch, *The American Jeremiad*,
p. 191.

26. See Gold, *Jews without Money*, and

Folsom, ed., *Michael Gold*.

27. Slotkin, *Regeneration through Violence*, pp. 3, 4.

28. Ibid., pp. 12, 13.

29. Bercovitch, *The American Jeremiad*,
p. 201.

30. See Vanderbilt, *The Achievement of
William Dean Howells*, pp. 96–143, and
Kirk and Kirk, "Abraham Cahan and William Dean Howells," pp. 27–57.

31. See Baumgarten, *City Scriptures*; see
also Fine, *The City, The Immigrant, and
American Fiction, 1880–1920*.

32. Fiedler, "Genesis," p. 28. For the first
part see Fiedler, "The Breakthrough," pp.
15–35.

33. McCarthy, *Ideas and the Novel*,
p. 121.

34. Sherman, *The Invention of the Jew*.
See also Schulz, *Radical Sophistication*.

35. Weinstein, "The Creative Imagination in Fiction and History," p. 268.

36. Way, "Formal Experiment and Social
Discontent," p. 263.

37. Krassner, "An Impolite Interview
with Joseph Heller," *Realist*, pp. 18–31;
reprinted in Scotto, ed., *Catch-22*, p. 458.

38. Bellow, "The Thinking Man's Waste
Land," p. 20.

39. See Wisse's discussion of Bellow in
her chapter, "The Schlemiel as Liberal Humanist," in *The Schlemiel as Modern Hero*,
pp. 92–107.

40. Loris, "*Mr. Sammler's Planet*,"
p. 217; see also Malin, "Seven Images,"
p. 168.

41. Bellow, *The Dean's December*, p. 123.

42. Bellow, "I Took Myself as I Was . . .,"
p. 3. See also Hook, "Morris Cohen—Fifty
Years Later," p. 435.

CHAPTER 2

1. Bercovitch, *The American Jeremiad*, p. 181.

2. Hapgood, *The Spirit of the Ghetto*, p. 37.

3. Adams, *The Education of Henry Adams*, p. 238.

4. Baltzell, *The Protestant Establishment*, pp. 92, 93.

5. Quoted in Aaron, "Some Reflections on Communism and the Jewish Writer," p. 269, nn. 17, 21.

6. Turner, "The Significance of the Frontier in American History," pp. 61, 62.

7. Kazin, *A Walker in the City*, p. 60.

8. Ravage, *An American in the Making*, pp. 196, 234, 264, 263.

9. Cahan, *The Rise of David Levinsky*, pp. 325, 327.

10. Malamud, *A New Life*, p. 20 (hereafter cited in the text as *NL*).

11. Fiedler, "Malamud's Travesty Western," p. 218.

12. Malamud, *The Tenants*, p. 206.

13. Bercovitch, *The American Jeremiad*, p. 11.

14. Higham, *Send These to Me*, p. 230.

15. See Steinfels, *The Neoconservatives*.

16. Sowell, *Ethnic America*, pp. 98–99.

CHAPTER 3

1. Baron, "The Emancipation Movement and American Jewry," p. 20.

2. For recent studies of Jews in America that emphasize the significance and obduracy of anti-Semitism see Dobkowski, *The Tarnished Dream*, and Belth, *A Promise to Keep*. See also Higham, *Send These to Me*, which has become a classic study of American anti-Semitism.

3. For a discussion of the meaning of emancipation in American Jewish history see Baron, "The Emancipation Movement in American Jewry," pp. 80–105. In "America Is Different," Halpern says, "What is characteristic of American Jewry, and what makes it different from all these together, is that it began its real history as a post-Emancipation Jewry. Emancipation was never an issue among American Jews: they never argued the problems it presented in America, nor did they ever develop rival ideologies about it and build their institutions with reference to them" (p. 70).

4. Konvitz, "Equality and the Jewish Experience," pp. 47, 52.

5. See Williams, *Marxism and Literature*, pp. 55–71, and Halpern, "'Myth and Ideology' in Modern Usage," pp. 129–49.

6. Arieli, *Individualism and Nationalism in American Ideology*, p. 21.

7. Ibid., p. 19.

8. Schappes, ed., *A Documentary History of the Jews in the United States, 1654–1875*, p. 79.

9. Ibid., p. 80.

10. Fuchs, "Introduction," in "Special Bicentennial Issue: Jews and American Liberalism: Studies in Political Behavior," p. 183.

11. Morris, "The Role of the Jews in the American Revolution in Historical Perspective," p. 25.

12. Quoted in Karp, ed., *Golden Door to America*, pp. 44, 45.

13. For population statistics see Fishman, ed., *The Jews of the United States*, pp. 12, 17–18, 29, 33–34, 36, 284.

14. Konvitz, "Equality and the Jewish

Experience," p. 31. Konvitz also exonerates Grant from any serious charges of anti-Semitism that the General Order incident suggests (p. 30).

15. Birmingham, *"Our Crowd,"* p. 126.

16. Higham, "Ideological Anti-Semitism in the Gilded Age," pp. 130–31.

17. See Cohen, *A Dual Heritage*.

18. Straus, *The Origin of Republican Form of Government in the United States of America*, p. 117.

19. Ibid., p. 131.

20. Ibid.

21. Ibid., pp. 139–40.

22. Straus, "America and the Spirit of American Judaism," pp. 291–92.

23. Cohen, *A Dual Heritage*, pp. x, 296.

24. Straus, "Our Commercial Age," p. 191.

25. Straus, "Cardinal Farley," p. 353.

26. Cohen, *A Dual Heritage*, p. 299.

27. De Haas, *Louis D. Brandeis*, pp. 40, 41.

28. Gal, *Brandeis of Boston*, p. 80.

29. Urofsky, *A Mind of One Piece*, p. 3.

30. Gal, *Brandeis of Boston*, p. 81.

31. Ibid., p. 83.

32. Brandeis, "A Call to the Educated Jew," p. 64.

33. Brandeis, "True Americanism," p. 5.

34. See De Haas, *Louis D. Brandeis*, p. 42.

35. Brandeis, *Business—A Profession*, p. 344.

36. Beard, Foreword to *The Social and Economic Views of Mr. Justice Brandeis*, p. xx.

37. See Gal, *Brandeis of Boston*, p. 109.

38. Ibid., p. 119.

39. Brandeis, "Life Insurance," pp. 158–59.

40. Both quotes are from Poole, "Brandeis," pp. lii, li–lii.

41. Brandeis, "The Road to Social Efficiency," pp. 58–59.

42. Brandeis, "The New Haven—An Unregulated Monopoly," pp. 297, 299.

43. Brandeis, "The Incorporation of Trades Unions," p. 88.

44. See Brandeis, "The Employer and Trades Unions," p. 16.

45. Brandeis, "Absolutism in Industry," p. 382.

46. Gal, *Brandeis of Boston*, p. 126.

47. De Haas, *Louis D. Brandeis*, p. 151.

48. Brandeis, "The Jewish People Should Be Preserved," p. 44.

49. Brandeis, "Palestine Has Developed Jewish Character," p. 145.

50. Brandeis, "A Call to the Educated Jew," p. 67.

51. Brandeis, "The Jewish Problem, How to Solve It," p. 32.

52. Brandeis, "A Call to the Educated Jew," pp. 60–61.

53. Brandeis, "True Americanism," p. 10.

54. See Gal, *Brandeis of Boston*, pp. 150–53.

55. Brandeis, "The Fruits of Zionism," p. 49.

56. Brandeis, "Sympathy for the Zionist Movement," p. 36.

57. Brandeis, "Dreams May Be Made into Realities," p. 72.

58. Brandeis, "A Call to the Educated Jew," p. 63.

59. Brandeis, "The Jewish Problem, How to Solve It," p. 27.

60. Gal, *Brandeis of Boston*, pp. 165, 189.

61. Cohen, *Not Free to Desist*, p. 165.

62. Ibid., p. 560.

63. Marshall, *Louis Marshall*, 1:113, 391, 400.

64. Rosenstock, *Louis Marshall, Defender of Jewish Rights*, p. 282.

65. Rischin, "From Gompers to Hillman," p. 201.

66. Quoted in Josephson, *Sidney Hillman*, p. 45.

67. Ibid., p. 80.

68. Ibid., pp. 66–67.

69. Ibid., p. 251; Rischin, "From Gompers to Hillman," p. 199.

70. Budish and Soule, *The New Unionism in the Clothing Industry*, p. 57.

71. Soule, *Sidney Hillman*, p. 157.

72. Rischin, "From Gompers to Hillman," pp. 199–200.

73. See Josephson, *Sidney Hillman*, p. 374.

74. Ibid., p. 618.

CHAPTER 4

1. Heine, "The Rabbi of Bacherach," p. 68.

2. Baron, "Ghetto and Emancipation," p. 61.

3. Baron, "The Emancipation Movement and American Jewry," pp. 82, 105.

4. Kazin, *New York Jew*, p. 292.

5. See Howe, ed. *Twenty-Five Years of Dissent*.

6. Harap, *The Image of the Jew in American Literature*, p. 487.

7. Cahan, *The Education of Abraham Cahan*, p. 158 (hereafter cited in the text as *EAC*).

8. Sanders, *The Downtown Jews*, p. 157.

9. Chametzky, *From the Ghetto*, p. vii.

10. Sanders, *The Downtown Jews*, p. 154.

11. Ibid., pp. 147–49.

12. Ibid., p. 347, details the differences between the articles and the book.

13. Quoted in Halpern, "America Is Different," p. 71.

14. Fitzgerald, *The Great Gatsby*, p. 182.

15. Cahan, *The Rise of David Levinsky*, p. 61 (hereafter cited in the text as *RDL*).

16. See Cawelti, *Apostles of the Self-Made Man*, and Rischin, ed., *The American Gospel*

of Success.

17. Sklar, Introduction to *The Plastic Age*, 1917–1930, p. 17.

18. See Rischin, eds., *The American Gospel of Success*, pp. 10–20.

19. Howe, *World of Our Fathers*, p. 138.

20. Higham, "Abraham Cahan," pp. 90, 91.

21. Chametzky, *From the Ghetto*, p. 143.

22. See Rosenfeld, "David Levinsky," p. 280; Engel, "The Discrepancies of the Modern," pp. 68–91.

23. Engel, "The Discrepancies of the Modern," pp. 83, 82.

24. Dinnerstein, *The Mermaid and the Minotaur*, pp. 121, 122.

25. Ibid., p. 123.

26. Ibid., p. 130.

27. Ibid., p. 133.

28. McLuhan, *The Mechanical Bride*, p. 99.

29. See ibid., pp. 117, 128.

30. Ibid., p. 144.

31. Rosenfeld, "David Levinsky," p. 273.

32. Engel, "The Discrepancies of the Modern," pp. 89–90.

CHAPTER 5

1. See Wirth, *The Ghetto*.

2. See Fishman, ed., *The Jews of the United States*, p. 33.

3. Rose, Introduction to *The Ghetto and*

Beyond, p. 4.

4. Lawrence, *Studies in Classic American Literature*, p. 13.

5. See Kazin, "The Most Neglected

Books of the Past Twenty-five Years,"
p. 478; Howe, "Life Never Let Up," pp. 1,
60–61; Fiedler, "Henry Roth's Neglected
Masterpiece," pp. 102–7; Rideout, "'O
Workers' Revolution . . . the True Messiah,'" pp. 157–75, and *The Radical Novel
in the United States, 1900–1954*, pp. 186–
90; Allen, "Two Neglected American Novelists," pp. 77–84.

6. Fiedler, "Henry Roth's Neglected
Masterpiece," p. 106.

7. Epstein, "Auto-Obituary," pp. 38, 39.

8. Freedman, "A Conversation with
Henry Roth," pp. 155, 152.

9. Lyons, "Interview with Henry Roth,
March 1977," p. 54.

10. Ibid., p. 53.

11. See Lyons, *Henry Roth*, pp. 117–23,
160–62.

12. See Brown, *Life Against Death*, pp.
206, 202.

13. Ibid., pp. 210, 211.

14. Ibid., p. 215.

15. Allen, Afterword to *Call It Sleep*,
p. 443, and Fiedler, *Love and Death in the
American Novel*, p. 487.

16. Roth, *Call It Sleep*, p. 160 (hereafter
cited in the text as *CS*).

17. Brown, *Life Against Death*, pp. 232,
287, 297–98.

18. Ibid., p. 307.

CHAPTER 6

1. Yezierska, "The Miracle," p. 17 (hereafter cited in the text as *OC*).

2. See Podhoretz, *Making It*, and Epstein, *Ambition*.

3. Cawelti, *Apostles of the Self-Made Man*,
p. 5. Cawelti identifies the other strands of
success as the "conservative traditon of the
middle-class Protestant ethic" and a second
largely economic tradition emphasizing
"the individual's getting ahead" (pp. 4, 5).

4. Ibid., p. 12.

5. Kessler-Harris, Introduction to *Bread*

Givers, p. ix.

6. Yezierska, *Bread Givers*, pp. 65, 138
(hereafter cited in the text as *BG*).

7. See Lasch, *Haven in a Heartless World*,
p. 178.

8. See Mitchell, *Psychoanalysis and Femi-
nism*; Janeway, "Who Is Sylvia? On the
Loss of Sexual Paradigms," pp. 4–20; and
Strouse, ed., *Women and Analysis*.

9. Guttmann, *The Jewish Writer in
America*, p. 33; Chametzky, "Yezierska,"
pp. 753–54.

CHAPTER 7

1. Roth, "Writing American Fiction," in
Reading Myself and Others, p. 120 (hereafter cited in the text as *RM*).

2. Pinsker, *The Comedy That "Hoits*,"
p. 103.

3. Roth, *The Ghost Writer*, pp. 11–12,
12.

4. For a discussion of Jewish "exception-
alism," alienation, and modern American

national character, see Bluestein, *"Portnoy's
Complaint*," pp. 66–76.

5. Roth, *My Life as a Man*, p. 61 (hereafter cited in the text as *MLM*).

6. See Trilling, "On the Teaching of
Modern Literature," pp. 3–30.

7. See Graff, *Literature Against Itself*.

8. Roth, *Zuckerman Unbound*, p. 10.

9. See Malin, "Looking at Roth's Kafka,"

pp. 273–75.

10. Roth, *The Professor of Desire*, p. 183 (hereafter cited in the text as *PD*).

11. Roth, *The Breast*, p. 72.

12. See Howe, "Philip Roth Reconsidered," pp. 69–77, and Podhoretz, "Laureate of the New Class," pp. 4–7.

13. Rodgers, *Philip Roth*, p. 89.

CHAPTER 8

1. See White, *Metahistory*, pp. ix–xi, x, 1–42.

2. Mailer, *Of a Fire on the Moon*, pp. 382, 10.

3. Spencer, "Mr. Mailer's American Dreams," p. 143.

4. Wagenheim, "Square's Progress," p. 63.

5. Mailer, Preface to *Advertisements for Myself*, p. v (hereafter cited in the text as *AM*).

6. Adams, *Existential Battles*, p. 3.

7. Poirier, *Norman Mailer*, p. 121.

8. Adams, *Existential Battles*, p. 121. In *The Law of the Heart*, I discuss Whitman more extensively in terms of the jeremiad (pp. 52–65).

9. Walt Whitman to Ralph Waldo Emerson, August 1856, in Whitman, *Leaves of Grass*, pp. 739–40. I also make reference to this letter in *The Law of the Heart* in an expanded explanation and discussion of Whitman's "sex program" (p. 59).

10. Whitman, "Song of Myself," p. 28.

11. Ibid., p. 51.

12. Mailer, *Marilyn*, pp. 15, 16, 15.

13. Gutman, *Mankind in Barbary*, p. 40.

14. Mailer, *The Armies of the Night*, p. 185 (hereafter cited in the text as *AN*).

15. Mailer, *Miami and the Siege of Chicago*, p. 63.

16. Adams, *Existential Battles*, p. 140.

17. Manso, ed., *Running against the Machine*, pp. 12, 13, 14.

18. Spencer, "Mr. Mailer's American Dreams," p. 143.

19. Whitman, "Democratic Vistas," p. 461.

20. Mailer, "Modes and Mutations," pp. 95–103.

21. Cowan, "The Americanness of Norman Mailer," p. 152.

22. See Trachtenberg, "Mailer on the Steps of the Pentagon," p. 701.

23. See Mailer, *The Presidential Papers*, pp. 187–98; Marcus, "An Interview with Norman Mailer," p. 32.

24. Kaufmann, *Norman Mailer*, pp. 105, 108.

25. Leeds, *The Structured Vision of Norman Mailer*, p. 28.

26. Guttmann, *The Jewish Writer in America*, p. 154.

27. Mailer, *Cannibals and Christians*, p. 77.

28. Hollowell, *Fact and Fiction*, p. 111.

29. Zavarzadeh, *The Mythopoeic Reality*, p. 161.

30. Ibid., p. 56.

31. Ibid., pp. 55, 56.

32. Ibid., p. 158.

33. Doctorow, *The Book of Daniel*, p. 269 (hereafter cited in the text as *BD*).

34. See Kenner, "To Die in Deseret," pp. 230–31; McConnell, review of *The Executioner's Song*, pp. 28–30; Rovit, "True Life Story," pp. 376–78.

35. Mailer, *The Executioner's Song*, p. 384 (hereafter cited in the text as *ES*).

36. Mailer, *Cannibals and Christians*, p. 131.

37. Ibid., p. 132.

38. Mailer, *An American Dream*, p. 251.

39. Spencer, "Mr. Mailer's American Dreams," p. 140.

40. Quoted in Manso, ed., *Running against the Machine*, p. 9.

41. Ibid., p. 15.

42. Ibid., pp. 8–9.

43. See Kakutani, "The Strange Case of the Writer and the Criminal," pp. 1, 36–39.

CHAPTER 9

1. The idea of "metahistory" as used throughout this study relates to an interesting new work on "the political unconscious" that relies heavily for its theoretical basis upon such thinkers as Freud, Lacan, Althusser, and Marx. See Jameson, *The Political Unconscious*.

2. See White, *Metahistory*, p. 334.

3. Nietzsche, *The Use and Abuse of History*, p. 39.

4. See Nietzsche, *The Genealogy of Morals*, p. 209.

5. Nietzsche, *The Birth of Tragedy*, p. 137.

6. Ibid., p. 106.

7. White, *Metahistory*, p. 371.

8. Quoted in Clemons, "Houdini, Meet Ferdinand," p. 76.

9. White, *Metahistory*, p. 372.

10. Henderson, *Versions of the Past*, pp. 283, 270.

11. Doctorow, *Welcome to Hard Times*, p. 214.

12. Ibid., p. 213.

13. Ibid., p. 215.

14. Doctorow's second novel, *Big as Life*, also distinguishes him from an apocalyptic vision of history and demonstrates his interest in popular myth. *Big as Life* is written in the mode of science fiction and concerns the chaotic reaction of New York to the appearance of two monsters in New York harbor. Although events in this novel approach the same kind of catastrophe that

befalls Hard Times, the conclusion reaffirms Doctorow's humanistic vision as the characters after near bedlam pull themselves together in anticipation of a new beginning.

15. See Kauffmann, "Wrestling Society for a Soul," pp. 25–27; Charyn, "The Book of Daniel," p. 6; Bell, "Writers and Writing," pp. 17–18; Richmond, "To the End of the Night," pp. 627–29.

16. Foley, "From *U.S.A.* to *Ragtime*," p. 95.

17. Kriegel, "The Stuff of Fictional History," p. 632; Seelye, "Doctorow's Dissertation," pp. 22–23, 22.

18. Doctorow, *The Book of Daniel*, p. 193 (hereafter cited in the text as *BD*).

19. See Zins, "Daniel's 'Teacher' in Doctorow's *The Book of Daniel*," item 16. See also a comparison between *The Book of Daniel* and *All the King's Men* in Hamner, "The Burden of the Past," pp. 55–61, and Stark, "Alienation and Analysis in Doctorow's *The Book of Daniel*," pp. 101–10.

20. Kauffmann, "Wrestling Society for a Soul," p. 25.

21. Berthoff, "Fiction, History, Myth," p. 54.

22. Thoreau, *Walden*, p. 92.

23. Ibid., pp. 157, 156.

24. Ibid., p. 156.

25. Doctorow, *Loon Lake*, p. 54 (hereafter cited in the text as *LL*).

26. Fitzgerald, *The Great Gatsby*, p. 99.

CHAPTER 10

1. Willis, "The Myth of the Powerful Jew," pp. 243, 231, 235.

2. Ibid., p. 236.

3. Ibid., p. 235; see also Steiner, *In Bluebeard's Castle*, pp. 33–47.

4. See Baldwin, "Open Letter to the Born Again," pp. 263–64, and Kriegel, "James Baldwin—A Reply," pp. 324–25.

5. See Fuchs, *The Political Behavior of American Jews*.

6. Fuchs, "Introduction," in "Special Bicentennial Issue: Jews and American Liberalism: Studies in Political Behavior," p. 187.

7. Ibid., p. 188.

8. Ibid.

9. Ibid., pp. 188–89.

10. Ibid., p. 189.

11. Willis, "My Podhoretz Problem—and His," p. 245.

12. Avishai, "Breaking Faith," p. 254.

13. Howe, "The Right Menace," p. 33.

14. Podhoretz, "The New American Majority," p. 27; *New York Times*, 23 May 1983, p. 8.

15. Howe, "Warm Friends of Israel," p. 29.

16. Quoted in Atlas, *Delmore Schwartz, American Poet*, p. 323, from Schwartz, "The Present State of Modern Poetry," pp. 27–28, reprinted in *Selected Essays of Delmore Schwartz*, p. 46.

Bibliography

Aaron, Daniel. "Some Reflections on Communism and the Jewish Writer." In *The Ghetto and Beyond: Essays on Jewish Life in America*, edited by Peter I. Rose. New York: Random House, 1969.

Adams, Henry. *The Education of Henry Adams*. 1918. Reprint. Boston: Houghton Mifflin Co., 1961.

Adams, Laura. *Existential Battles: The Growth of Norman Mailer*. Athens, Ohio: Ohio University Press, 1976.

Allen, Walter. Afterword to *Call It Sleep* by Henry Roth. New York: Avon Books, 1964.
_____. "Two Neglected American Novelists." *London Magazine* 2 (May 1962).

Alvarez, A. "Flushed with Ideas." Review of *Levitation: Five Fictions* by Cynthia Ozick and *Waking* by Eva Figes. *New York Review of Books*, 13 May 1982.

Antin, Mary. *The Promised Land*. 1912. Reprint. Boston: Houghton Mifflin Sentry Edition, 1969.

Arieli, Yehoshua. *Individualism and Nationalism in American Ideology*. Baltimore: Penguin Books, 1966.

Atlas, James. *Delmore Schwartz: The Life of an American Poet*. New York: Avon Books, 1978.

Avishai, Bernard. "Breaking Faith: *Commentary* and the American Jews." *Dissent* 28 (Spring 1981).

Baldwin, James. "Open Letter to the Born Again." *Nation*, 29 September 1979.

Baltzell, E. Digby. *The Protestant Establishment: Aristocracy and Caste in America*. New York: Vintage Books, 1964.

Baron, Salo W. "The Emancipation Movement and American Jewry." In *Steeled by Adversity: Essays and Addresses on American Jewish Life*, edited by Jeannette Meisel Baron. Philadelphia: Jewish Publication Society of America, 1971.
_____. "Ghetto and Emancipation." In *The Menorah Treasury: Harvest of Half a Century*, edited by Leo W. Schwarz. Philadelphia: Jewish Publication Society of America, 1972.

Barthes, Roland. *Mythologies*. Translated by Annette Lavers. New York: Hill and Wang, 1957.

Baumgarten, Murray. *City Scriptures: Modern Jewish Writing*. Cambridge, Mass.: Harvard University Press, 1982.

Beard, Charles A. Foreword to *The Social and Economic Views of Mr. Justice Brandeis*, edited by Alfred Lief. New York: Vanguard, 1930.

Bell, Pearl K. "A Remarkable First Novel." *Commentary*, April 1980.
_____. "Writers and Writing: Guilt on Trial." *New Leader*, 28 June 1971.

Bellow, Saul. *The Dean's December*. New York: Harper and Row, 1982.

————. "I Took Myself as I Was. . . ." *ADL Bulletin*, December 1976.

————. "The Thinking Man's Waste Land." *Saturday Review*, 3 April 1965.

Belth, Nathan C. *A Promise to Keep: A Narrative of the American Encounter with Anti-Semitism*. New York: Times Books, 1979.

Bercovitch, Sacvan. *The American Jeremiad*. Madison, Wis.: University of Wisconsin Press, 1978.

————. "The Rites of Assent: Rhetoric, Ritual, and the Ideology of American Consensus." In *The American Self: Myth, Ideology, and Popular Culture*, edited by Sam B. Girgus. Albuquerque, N.M.: University of New Mexico Press, 1981.

Berthoff, Warner. "Fiction, History, Myth: Notes towards the Discrimination of Narrative Forms." In *Fiction and Events: Essays in Criticism and Literary History*, edited by Warner Berthoff. New York: E. P. Dutton, 1971.

Birmingham, Stephen. *"Our Crowd": The Great Jewish Families of New York*. New York: Dell Books, 1967.

Blau, Joseph L. *Judaism in America: From Curiosity to Faith*. Chicago: University of Chicago Press, 1976.

Bluestein, Gene. *"Portnoy's Complaint*: The Jew as American." *Canadian Review of American Studies* 7 (Spring 1976).

Brandeis, Louis D. "Absolutism in Industry." In *The Social and Economic Views of Mr. Justice Brandeis*, edited by Alfred Lief. New York: Vanguard, 1930.

————. *Business—A Profession*. Boston: Small, Maynard and Co., 1925.

————. "A Call to the Educated Jew." In *Brandeis on Zionism: A Collection of Addresses and Statements by Louis D. Brandeis*, edited by Solomon Goldmark. Westport, Conn.: Hyperion Press, 1942.

————. "Dreams May Be Made into Realities." In *Brandeis on Zionism: A Collection of Addresses and Statements by Louis D. Brandeis*, edited by Solomon Goldmark. Westport, Conn.: Hyperion Press, 1942.

————. "The Employer and Trades Unions." In *Business—A Profession*. Boston: Small, Maynard and Co., 1925.

————. "The Fruits of Zionism." In *Brandeis on Zionism: A Collection of Addresses and Statements by Louis D. Brandeis*, edited by Solomon Goldmark. Westport, Conn.: Hyperion Press, 1942.

————. "The Incorporation of Trades Unions." In *Business—A Profession*. Boston: Small, Maynard and Co., 1925.

————. "The Jewish People Should Be Preserved." In *Brandeis on Zionism: A Collection of Addresses and Statements by Louis D. Brandeis*, edited by Solomon Goldmark. Westport, Conn.: Hyperion Press, 1942.

————. "The Jewish Problem, How to Solve It." In *Brandeis on Zionism: A Collection of Addresses and Statements by Louis D. Brandeis*, edited by Solomon Goldmark. Westport, Conn.: Hyperion Press, 1942.

————. "Life Insurance: The Abuses and the Remedies." In *Business—A Profession*. Boston: Small, Maynard and Co., 1925.

————. "The New Haven—An Unregulated Monopoly." In *Business—A Profession*. Boston:

Small, Maynard and Co., 1925.

———. "Palestine Has Developed Jewish Character." In *Brandeis on Zionism: A Collection of Addresses and Statements by Louis D. Brandeis*, edited by Solomon Goldmark. Westport, Conn.: Hyperion Press, 1942.

———. "The Road to Social Efficiency." In *Business—A Profession*. Boston: Small, Maynard and Co., 1925.

———. "Sympathy for the Zionist Movement." In *Brandeis on Zionism: A Collection of Addresses and Statements by Louis D. Brandeis*, edited by Solomon Goldmark. Westport, Conn.: Hyperion Press, 1942.

———. "True Americanism." In *Brandeis on Zionism: A Collection of Addresses and Statements by Louis D. Brandeis*, edited by Solomon Goldmark. Westport, Conn.: Hyperion Press, 1942.

Brown, Norman O. *Life Against Death: The Psychoanalytical Meaning of History*. New York: Vintage Books, 1959.

Budish, J. M., and Soule, George. *The New Unionism in the Clothing Industry*. New York: Harcourt, Brace and Howe, 1920.

Cahan, Abraham. *The Education of Abraham Cahan*. Translated by Leon Stein, Abraham P. Conan, and Lynn Davison. Philadelphia: Jewish Publication Society of America, 1969.

———. *The Rise of David Levinsky*. 1917. Reprint. New York: Harper Colophon, 1969.

Cawelti, John G. *Adventure, Mystery, and Romance: Formula Stories as Art and Popular Culture*. Chicago: University of Chicago Press, 1976.

———. *Apostles of the Self-Made Man: Changing Concepts of Success in America*. Chicago: University of Chicago Press, 1965.

Chametzky, Jules. *From the Ghetto: The Fiction of Abraham Cahan*. Amherst, Mass.: University of Massachusetts Press, 1977.

———. "Yezierska." In *Notable American Women: A Biographical Dictionary*. Cambridge, Mass.: Harvard University Press, Belknap Press, 1980.

Charyn, Jerome. "The Book of Daniel." *New York Times Book Review*, 4 July 1971.

Clemons, Walter. "Houdini, Meet Ferdinand." Review of *Ragtime* by E. L. Doctorow. *Newsweek*, 14 July 1975.

Cohen, Naomi W. *A Dual Heritage: The Public Career of Oscar Straus*. Philadelphia: Jewish Publication Society of America, 1969.

———. *Not Free to Desist: A History of the American Jewish Committee, 1906–1966*. Philadelphia: Jewish Publication Society of America, 1972.

Cowan, Michael. "The Americanness of Norman Mailer." In *Norman Mailer: A Collection of Critical Essays*, edited by Leo Braudy. Englewood Cliffs, N.J.: Prentice-Hall, 1972.

De Haas, Jacob. *Louis D. Brandeis: A Biographical Sketch*. New York: Bloch, 1929.

Dimont, Max I. *The Jews in America: The Roots, History, and Destiny of American Jews*. New York: Simon and Schuster, 1978.

Dinnerstein, Dorothy. *The Mermaid and the Minotaur: Sexual Arrangements and Human Malaise*. New York: Harper Colophon, 1977.

Dobkowski, Michael N. *The Tarnished Dream: The Basis of American Anti-Semitism*. Westport, Conn.: Greenwood Press, 1979.

Doctorow, E. L. *Big as Life*. New York: Simon and Schuster, 1966.
———. *The Book of Daniel*. 1971. Reprint. New York: Bantam Books, 1977.
———. *Loon Lake*. New York: Random House, 1980.
———. *Welcome to Hard Times*. 1960. Reprint. New York: Bantam Books, 1977.
Douglas, Ann. *The Feminization of American Culture*. New York: Avon Books, 1978.
Engel, David. "The Discrepancies of the Modern: Reevaluating Abraham Cahan's *The Rise of David Levinsky*." *Modern Jewish Studies Annual* 3 (1979).
Epstein, Gary. "Auto-Obituary: The Death of the Artist in Henry Roth's *Call It Sleep*." In "A Special Issue: Henry Roth's *Call It Sleep*: 1934–1979." *Studies in American Jewish Literature* 5 (Spring 1979).
Epstein, Joseph. *Ambition: The Secret Passion*. New York: E. P. Dutton and Co., 1981.
Feldstein, Stanley. *The Land That I Show You: Three Centuries of Jewish Life in America*. New York: Doubleday and Co., Anchor Books, 1978.
Fiedler, Leslie A. "The Breakthrough: The American Jewish Novelist and the Fictional Image of the Jew." *Midstream* 4 (Winter 1958).
———. "Genesis: The American-Jewish Novel through the Twenties." *Midstream* 4 (Summer 1958).
———. "Henry Roth's Neglected Masterpiece." *Commentary*, August 1960.
———. *Love and Death in the American Novel*. Rev. ed. New York: Delta Books, 1966.
———. "Malamud's Travesty Western." *Novel* 10 (Spring 1977).
Fine, David M. *The City, the Immigrant, and American Fiction, 1880–1920*. Metuchen, N.J.: Scarecrow Press, 1977.
Fishman, Priscilla, ed. *The Jews of the United States*. New York: New York Times Book Co., Quadrangle Books, 1973.
Fitzgerald, F. Scott. *The Great Gatsby*. 1925. Reprint. New York: Charles Scribner's Sons, 1953.
Foley, Barbara. "From *U.S.A.* to *Ragtime*: Notes on the Forms of Historical Consciousness in Modern Fiction." *American Literature* 50 (March 1978).
Folsom, Michael, ed. *Michael Gold: A Literary Anthology*. New York: International, 1972.
Freedman, William. "A Conversation with Henry Roth." *Literary Review* 19 (Winter 1975).
Fryer, Judith. *The Faces of Eve: Women in the Nineteenth-Century American Novel*. New York: Oxford University Press, 1976.
Fuchs, Lawrence H. "Introduction." In "Special Bicentennial Issue: Jews and American Liberalism: Studies in Political Behavior." *American Jewish Historical Quarterly* 66 (December 1976).
———. *The Political Behavior of American Jews*. Glencoe, Ill.: Free Press, 1956.
Gal, Allon. *Brandeis of Boston*. Cambridge, Mass.: Harvard University Press, 1980.
Girgus, Sam B., ed. *The American Self: Myth, Ideology, and Popular Culture*. Albuquerque, N.M.: University of New Mexico Press, 1981.
———. *The Law of the Heart: Individualism and the Modern Self in American Literature*. Austin: University of Texas Press, 1979.
Glazer, Nathan. *American Judaism*. 2d ed. Chicago: University of Chicago Press, 1972.
Gold, Michael. *Jews without Money*. 1930. Reprint. New York: Avon Books, 1972.
Graff, Gerald. *Literature Against Itself: Literary Ideas in Modern Society*. Chicago: University of Chicago Press, 1979.

Gross, Nacham, ed. *Economic History of the Jews*. New York: Schocken Books, 1975.

Gutman, Stanley T. *Mankind in Barbary: The Individual and Society in the Novels of Norman Mailer*. Hanover, N.H.: University Press of New England, 1975.

Guttmann, Allen. *The Jewish Writer in America: Assimilation and the Crisis of Identity*. New York: Oxford University Press, 1971.

Halpern, Ben. "America Is Different." In *The Jew in American Society*, edited by Marshall Sklare. New York: Behrman House, 1974.

————. "'Myth and Ideology' in Modern Usage." *History and Theory* 1 (1961).

Hamner, Eugenie L. "The Burden of the Past: Doctorow's *The Book of Daniel*." *Research Studies* 49 (March 1981).

Handlin, Oscar. *Adventure in Freedom: Three Hundred Years of Jewish Life in America*. 1954. Reprint. Port Washington, N.Y.: Kennikat Press, 1971.

Hapgood, Hutchins. *The Spirit of the Ghetto: Studies of the Jewish Quarter of New York*. 1902. Reprint. New York: Schocken Books, 1976.

Harap, Louis. *The Image of the Jew in American Literature: From Early Republic to Mass Immigration*. Philadelphia: Jewish Publication Society of America, 1974.

Heine, Heinrich. "The Rabbi of Bacherach." In *Great Jewish Short Stories*, edited by Saul Bellow. New York: Dell Books, 1963.

Henderson, Harry B., III. *Versions of the Past: The Historical Imagination in American Fiction*. New York: Oxford University Press, 1974.

Higham, John. "Abraham Cahan." In *Send These to Me: Jews and Other Immigrants in Urban America*. New York: Atheneum, 1975.

————. "Ideological Anti-Semitism in the Gilded Age." In *Send These to Me: Jews and Other Immigrants in Urban America*. New York: Atheneum, 1975.

————. *Send These to Me: Jews and Other Immigrants in Urban America*. New York: Atheneum, 1975.

Hollowell, John. *Fact and Fiction: The New Journalism and the Nonfiction Novel*. Chapel Hill: University of North Carolina Press, 1977.

Hook, Sidney. "Morris Cohen—Fifty Years Later." *American Scholar* 45 (Summer 1976).

Howe, Irving. "Life Never Let Up." *New York Times Book Review*, 25 October 1964.

————. "Philip Roth Reconsidered." *Commentary*, December 1972.

————. "The Right Menace." In *The Threat of Conservatism*. Dissent Pamphlets I. New York: Foundation for the Study of Independent Social Ideas, n.d.

————. "Warm Friends of Israel, Open Critics of Begin-Sharon." *New York Times*, 23 September 1982.

————. *World of Our Fathers*. New York: Harcourt Brace Jovanovich, 1976.

————, ed. *Twenty-Five Years of Dissent: An American Tradition*. New York: Methuen, 1979.

Jameson, Fredric. *The Political Unconscious: Narrative as a Socially Symbolic Act*. Ithaca, N.Y.: Cornell University Press, 1981.

Janeway, Elizabeth. "Who Is Sylvia? On the Loss of Sexual Paradigms." In *Women: Sex and Sexuality*, edited by Catharine R. Stimpson and Ethel Specter Person. Chicago: University of Chicago Press, 1980.

Josephson, Matthew. *Sidney Hillman: Statesman of American Labor*. Garden City, N.Y.: Doubleday and Co., 1962.

Jruegek, Keibard. "The Stuff of Fictional History." *Commonweal*, 19 December 1975.

Kakutani, Michiko. "The Strange Case of the Writer and the Criminal." *New York Times Book Review*, 20 September 1981.

Kaplan, Johanna. *O My America!*. New York: Harper and Row, 1980.

Karp, Abraham J., ed. *Golden Door to America: The Jewish Immigrant Experience*. New York: Penguin Books, 1977.

Kasson, John. *Civilizing the Machine: Technology and Republican Values in America, 1776–1900*. New York: Penguin Books, 1977.

Kauffmann, Stanley. "Wrestling Society for a Soul." *New Republic*, 5 June 1971.

Kaufmann, Donald L. *Norman Mailer: The Countdown (The First Twenty Years)*. Carbondale: Southern Illinois University Press, 1969.

Kazin, Alfred. "The Most Neglected Books of the Past Twenty-five Years." *American Scholar* 25 (Autumn 1956).

――――. *New York Jew*. 1978. Reprint. New York: Vintage Books, 1979.

――――. *A Walker in the City*. New York: Harcourt, Brace and World, 1951.

Kenner, Hugh. "To Die in Deseret." *National Review*, 22 February 1980.

Kessler-Harris, Alice. Introduction to *Bread Givers* by Anzia Yezierska. 1925. Reprint. New York: Persea, 1975.

Kirk, Rudolf, and Kirk, Clara M. "Abraham Cahan and William Dean Howells: The Story of a Friendship." *American Jewish Historical Quarterly* 52 (1962).

Kolodny, Annette. *The Lay of the Land: Metaphor as Experience and History in American Life and Letters*. Chapel Hill: University of North Carolina Press, 1975.

Konvitz, Milton R. "Equality and the Jewish Experience." In *Jewish Life in America: Historical Perspectives*, edited by Gladys Rosen. New York: KTAV Publishing, 1978.

――――. *Judaism and the American Idea*. Ithaca, N.Y.: Cornell University Press, 1978.

Kotker, Norman. "New Found Land." *Nation*, 12 April 1980.

Krassner, Joseph. "An Impolite Interview with Joseph Heller." *Realist*, November 1962. Reprinted in Joseph Heller, *Catch-22: A Critical Edition*, edited by Robert M. Scotto. New York: Delta Books, 1973.

Kriegel, Leonard. "James Baldwin—A Reply." *Nation*, 13 October 1979.

――――. "The Stuff of Fictional History." *Commonweal*, 19 December 1975.

Lasch, Christopher. *Haven in a Heartless World: The Family Besieged*. New York: Basic Books, Harper Colophon, 1979.

Lawrence, D. H. *Studies in Classic American Literature*. 1923. Reprint. New York: Doubleday and Co., Anchor Books, 1951.

Leeds, Barry H. *The Structured Vision of Norman Mailer*. New York: New York University Press, 1969.

Lewis, Anthony. "The End of a Policy." *New York Times*, 20 September 1982.

Lewis, R. W. B. *The American Adam: Innocence, Tragedy, and Tradition in the Nineteenth Century*. Chicago: University of Chicago Press, 1955.

Liebman, Arthur. *Jews and the Left*. New York: John Wiley, 1979.

――――. "The Ties That Bind: The Jewish Support for the Left in the United States." In "Special Bicentennial Issue: Jews and American Liberalism: Studies in Political Behavior." *American Jewish Historical Quarterly* 66 (December 1976).

Loris, Michelle Carbone. "*Mr. Sammler's Planet*: The Terms of the Covenant." *Renascence* 30 (Summer 1978).

Lyons, Bonnie. *Henry Roth: The Man and His Work*. New York: Cooper Square Publishers, 1976.

———. "Interview with Henry Roth, March 1977." In "A Special Issue: Henry Roth's *Call It Sleep*: 1934–1979." *Studies in American Jewish Literature* 5 (Spring 1979).

McCarthy, Mary. *Ideas and the Novel*. New York: Harcourt Brace Jovanovich, 1980.

McConnell, Frank. Review of *The Executioner's Song*. *New Republic*, 27 October 1979.

McLuhan, Marshall. *The Mechanical Bride: Folklore of Industrial Man*. Boston: Beacon Press, 1951.

Mailer, Norman. *An American Dream*. 1965. Reprint. New York: Dell Books, 1976.

———. *The Armies of the Night: History as a Novel, the Novel as History*. New York: New American Library, 1968.

———. *Cannibals and Christians*. New York: Delta Books, 1966.

———. *The Executioner's Song*. Boston: Little, Brown and Co., 1979.

———. *Marilyn*. New York: Grosset and Dunlap, 1973.

———. *Miami and the Siege of Chicago: An Informal History of the Republican and Democratic Conventions of 1968*. New York: Signet Books, 1968.

———. "Modes and Mutations: Quick Comments on the Modern American Novel." *Commentary*, March 1966. Reprinted in *Cannibals and Christians*. New York: Delta Books, 1966.

———. *Of a Fire on the Moon*. 1970. Reprint. New York: Signet Books, 1971.

———. Preface to *Advertisements for Myself*. 1959. Reprint. New York: Perigree, 1981.

———. *The Presidential Papers*. New York: Bantam Books, 1964.

Malamud, Bernard. *A New Life*. New York: Dell Books, 1963.

———. *The Tenants*. New York: Pocket Books, 1972.

Malin, Irving. "Looking at Roth's Kafka; Or Some Hints about Comedy." *Studies in Short Fiction* 14 (Summer 1977).

———. "Seven Images." In *Saul Bellow and His Critics*, edited by Irving Malin. New York: New York University Press, 1967.

Malin, Irving, and Stark, Irwin, eds. *Breakthrough: A Treasury of Contemporary American-Jewish Literature*. New York: McGraw-Hill, 1964.

Manso, Peter, ed. *Running against the Machine: The Mailer-Breslin Campaign*. Garden City, N.Y.: Doubleday and Co., 1969.

Marcus, Steven. "An Interview with Norman Mailer." In *Norman Mailer: A Collection of Critical Essays*, edited by Leo Braudy. Englewood Cliffs, N.J.: Prentice-Hall, 1972.

Marshall, Louis. *Louis Marshall, Champion of Liberty: Selected Papers and Addresses*, edited by Charles Reznikoff. 2 vols. Philadelphia: Jewish Publication Society of America, 1957.

Marx, Leo. *The Machine in the Garden: Technology and the Pastoral Ideal in America*. New York: Oxford University Press, 1964.

Miller, Perry. "Errand into the Wilderness." In *Errand into the Wilderness*. Cambridge, Mass.: Harvard University Press, 1956.

Mitchell, Juliet. *Psychoanalysis and Feminism*. New York: Vintage Books, 1975.

Morris, Richard B. "The Role of the Jews in the American Revolution in Historical Perspective." In *Jewish Life in America: Historical Perspectives*, edited by Gladys Rosen. New York: KTAV Publishing, 1978.

Neusner, Jacob. *Stranger at Home: "The Holocaust," Zionism, and American Judaism*. Chicago: University of Chicago Press, 1981.

Nietzsche, Friedrich. *The Birth of Tragedy*. 1872. Reprinted in *The Birth of Tragedy and the Genealogy of Morals*. New York: Doubleday and Co., Anchor Books, 1956.

————. *The Genealogy of Morals*. 1887. Reprinted in *The Birth of Tragedy and the Genealogy of Morals*. New York: Doubleday and Co., Anchor Books, 1956.

————. *The Use and Abuse of History*. 1874. Reprint. Indianapolis: Bobbs-Merrill, 1957.

Pinsker, Sanford. *The Comedy That "Hoits": An Essay on the Fiction of Philip Roth*. Columbia: University of Missouri Press, 1975.

Podhoretz, Norman. *Breaking Ranks: A Political Memoir*. New York: Harper and Row, 1979.

————. "Laureate of the New Class." *Commentary*, December 1972.

————. *Making It*. 1967. Reprint. New York: Harper Colophon, 1980.

————. "The New American Majority." *Commentary*, January 1981.

Poirier, Richard. *Norman Mailer*. New York: Viking Press, 1972.

Poole, Ernest. "Brandeis." Foreword to *Business—A Profession* by Louis D. Brandeis. Boston: Small, Maynard and Co., 1925.

Ravage, M. E. *An American in the Making: The Life Story of an Immigrant*. New York: Harper and Brothers, 1917.

Richmond, Jane. "To the End of the Night." *Partisan Review* 39 (Fall 1972).

Rideout, Walter B. "'O Workers' Revolution . . . the True Messiah': The Jew as Author and Subject in the American Jewish Novel." *American Jewish Archives* 11 (October 1959).

————. *The Radical Novel in the United States, 1900–1954*. New York: Hill and Wang, 1966.

Rischin, Moses. "From Gompers to Hillman: Labor Goes Middle Class." *Antioch Review* 13 (June 1953).

————. *The Promised City: New York's Jews, 1870–1914*. Cambridge, Mass.: Harvard University Press, 1977.

————, ed. *The American Gospel of Success: Individualism and Beyond*. New York: Quadrangle Books, 1965.

Rodgers, Bernard F., Jr. *Philip Roth*. Boston: Twayne Publishers, 1978.

Rose, Peter I. Introduction to *The Ghetto and Beyond: Essays on Jewish Life in America*, edited by Peter I. Rose. New York: Random House, 1969.

Rosen, Gladys, ed. *Jewish Life in America: Historical Perspectives*. New York: KTAV Publishing, 1978.

Rosenfeld, Isaac. "David Levinsky: The Jew as American Millionaire." In *An Age of Enormity*, edited by Theodore Solotaroff. Cleveland: World Publishing Co., 1962.

Rosenstock, Morton. *Louis Marshall, Defender of Jewish Rights*. Detroit: Wayne State University Press, 1965.

Roth, Philip. *The Breast*. New York: Holt, Rinehart and Winston, 1972.

————. *The Ghost Writer*. New York: Farrar, Straus and Giroux, 1979.

————. *My Life as a Man*. New York: Holt, Rinehart and Winston, 1974.

————. *The Professor of Desire*. New York: Farrar, Straus and Giroux, 1977.

————. "Writing American Fiction." In *Reading Myself and Others*. New York: Farrar, Straus and Giroux, 1975.

————. *Zuckerman Unbound*. New York: Farrar, Straus and Giroux, 1981.

Rovit, Earl. "True Life Story." *Nation*, 20 October 1979.

Sanders, Ronald. *The Downtown Jews: Portraits of an Immigrant Generation*. New York: New American Library, 1976.

Schappes, Morris U., ed. *A Documentary History of the Jews in the United States, 1654–1875*. 3d ed. New York: Schocken Books, 1976.

Schechner, Mark. "Jewish Writers." In *Harvard Guide to Contemporary American Writing*, edited by Daniel Hoffman. Cambridge, Mass.: Harvard University Press, Belknap Press, 1979.

Schulz, Max F. *Radical Sophistication: Studies in Contemporary Jewish/American Novelists*. Athens, Ohio: Ohio University Press, 1969.

Schwartz, Delmore. "The Present State of Modern Poetry." In *American Poetry at Mid-Century*. Washington, D.C.: Library of Congress, 1958. Reprinted in *Selected Essays of Delmore Schwartz*, edited by Donald Dike and David H. Zucken. Chicago: University of Chicago Press, 1970.

Scotto, Robert M., ed. *Catch-22: A Critical Edition*. New York: Delta Books, 1973.

Seelye, John. "Doctorow's Dissertation." *New Republic*, 10 April 1976.

Sherman, Bernard. *The Invention of the Jew: Jewish-American Education Novels, 1916–1964*. New York: Thomas Yoseloff, 1969.

Sklar, Robert. Introduction to *The Plastic Age, 1917–1930*, edited by Robert Sklar. New York: George Braziller, 1970.

Sklare, Marshall. *America's Jews*. New York: Random House, 1971.

Slotkin, Richard. *Regeneration through Violence: The Mythology of the American Frontier, 1600–1860*. Middletown, Conn.: Wesleyan University Press, 1973.

Smith, Henry Nash. *Virgin Land: The American West as Symbol and Myth*. Cambridge, Mass.: Harvard University Press, 1950.

Sollors, Werner, "Literature and Ethnicity." In *Harvard Encyclopedia of American Ethnic Groups*, edited by Stephan Thernstrom. Cambridge, Mass.: Harvard University Press, 1980.

Soule, George. *Sidney Hillman: Labor Statesman*. New York: Macmillan Co., 1939.

Sowell, Thomas. *Ethnic America: A History*. New York: Basic Books, 1981.

"Special Bicentennial Issue: American Jewish Business Enterprise." *American Jewish Historical Quarterly* 66 (September 1976).

"Special Bicentennial Issue: Jews and American Liberalism: Studies in Political Behavior." *American Jewish Historical Quarterly* 66 (December 1976).

Spencer, Benjamin T. "Mr. Mailer's American Dreams." In *Prospects II*, edited by Jack Salzman. New York: Burt Franklin and Co., 1976.

Stark, John. "Alienation and Analysis in Doctorow's *The Book of Daniel*." *Critique: Studies in Modern Fiction* 16, no. 3 (1975).

Steiner, George. *In Bluebeard's Castle: Some Notes towards the Redefinition of Culture*. New Haven: Yale University Press, 1971.

Steinfels, Peter. *The Neoconservatives: The Men Who Are Changing American Politics*. New York: Simon and Schuster, 1979.

Straus, Oscar S. "America and the Spirit of American Judaism." In *The American Spirit*. 1913. Reprint. Freeport, N.Y.: Books for Libraries Press, 1968.

———. "Cardinal Farley." In *The American Spirit*. 1913. Reprint. Freeport, N.Y.: Books for Libraries Press, 1968.

———. *The Origin of Republican Form of Government in the United States of America*. 2d ed. 1885. Reprint. New York: G. P. Putnam's Sons, 1926.

———. "Our Commercial Age." In *The American Spirit*. 1913. Reprint. Freeport, N.Y.: Books for Libraries Press, 1968.

Strouse, Jean, ed. *Women and Analysis*. New York: Dell Books, 1975.

Thoreau, Henry David. *Walden*. 1854. Reprinted in *Walden and Civil Disobedience*. New York: W. W. Norton and Co., 1966.

Trachtenberg, Alan. *Brooklyn Bridge: Fact and Symbol*. New York: Oxford University Press, 1965.

———. "Mailer on the Steps of the Pentagon." *Nation*, 27 May 1968.

Trilling, Lionel. "On the Teaching of Modern Literature." In *Beyond Culture: Essays on Literature and Learning*. New York: Viking Press, 1965.

Turner, Frederick Jackson. "The Significance of the Frontier in American History." In *Frontier and Section: Selected Essays of Frederick Jackson Turner*, edited by Ray Allen Billington. Englewood Cliffs, N.J.: Prentice-Hall, 1961.

Urofsky, Melvin I. *A Mind of One Piece: Brandeis and American Reform*. New York: Charles Scribner's Sons, 1971.

Vanderbilt, Kermit. *The Achievement of William Dean Howells: A Reinterpretation*. Princeton: Princeton University Press, 1968.

Wagenheim, Allan J. "Square's Progress: *An American Dream*." *Critique: Studies in Modern Fiction* 10 (1967).

Ward, John William. *Andrew Jackson: Symbol for an Age*. New York: Oxford University Press, 1955.

Way, Brian. "Formal Experiment and Social Discontent: Joseph Heller's *Catch-22*." *Journal of American Studies* 2 (1968).

Weinstein, Mark A. "The Creative Imagination in Fiction and History." *Genre* 9 (Fall 1976).

White, Hayden. *Metahistory: The Historical Imagination in Nineteenth-Century Europe*. Baltimore: Johns Hopkins University Press, 1973.

Whitman, Walt. "Democratic Vistas." In *Complete Poetry and Selected Prose*, edited by James E. Miller, Jr. Boston: Houghton Mifflin Co., 1959.

———. *Leaves of Grass*, edited by Sculley Bradley and Harold W. Blodgett. New York: W. W. Norton and Co., 1973.

———. "Song of Myself." In *Complete Poetry and Selected Prose*, edited by James E. Miller, Jr. Boston: Houghton Mifflin Co., 1959.

Williams, Raymond. *Marxism and Literature*. New York: Oxford University Press, 1977.

Willis, Ellen. "My Podhoretz Problem—and His." In *Beginning to See the Light: Pieces of a Decade*. New York: Alfred A. Knopf, 1981.

_____. "The Myth of the Powerful Jew." In *Beginning to See the Light: Pieces of a Decade.* New York: Alfred A. Knopf, 1981.

Winthrop, John. "A Model of Christian Charity." In *Puritan Political Ideas, 1558–1794,* edited by Edmund S. Morgan. Indianapolis: Bobbs-Merrill, 1965.

Wirth, Louis. *The Ghetto.* 1928. Reprint. Chicago: University of Chicago Press, 1956.

Wisse, Ruth R. "The Schlemiel as Liberal Humanist." In *The Schlemiel as Modern Hero.* Chicago: University of Chicago Press, 1971.

Wright, Will. *Six Guns and Society: A Structural Study of the Western.* Berkeley: University of California Press, 1975.

Yezierska, Anzia. *Bread Givers.* 1925. Reprint. New York: Persea Books, 1975.

_____. "The Miracle." In *The Open Cage: An Anzia Yezierska Collection,* edited by Alice Kessler-Harris. New York: Persea Books, 1979.

Zavarzadeh, Mas'ud. *The Mythopoeic Reality: The Postwar American Nonfiction Novel.* Urbana: University of Illinois Press, 1976.

Zins, Daniel L. "Daniel's Teacher in Doctorow's *The Book of Daniel.*" *Notes on Modern American Literature* 2 (Spring 1979).

Index